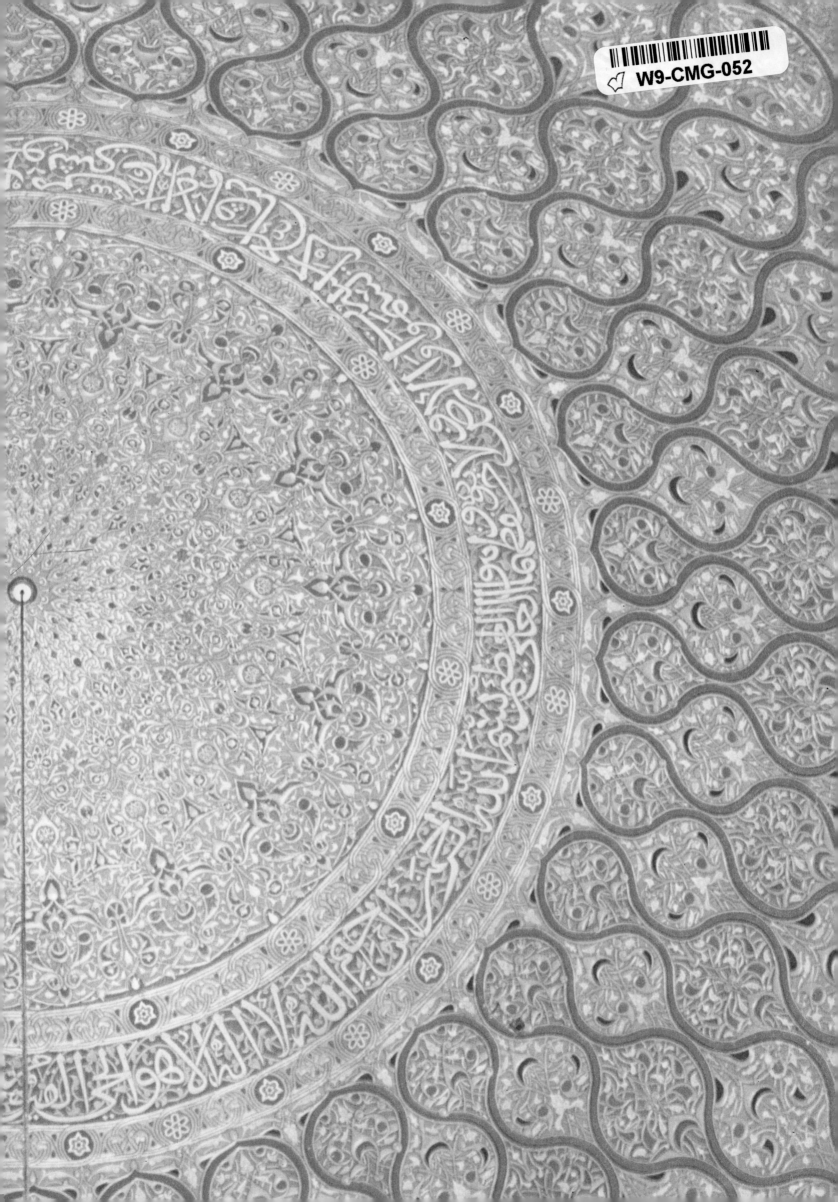

Featuring the photography of
William Curwen and Nick Meers
Designed by Philip Clucas
Edited by David Gibbon
Produced by Ted Smart

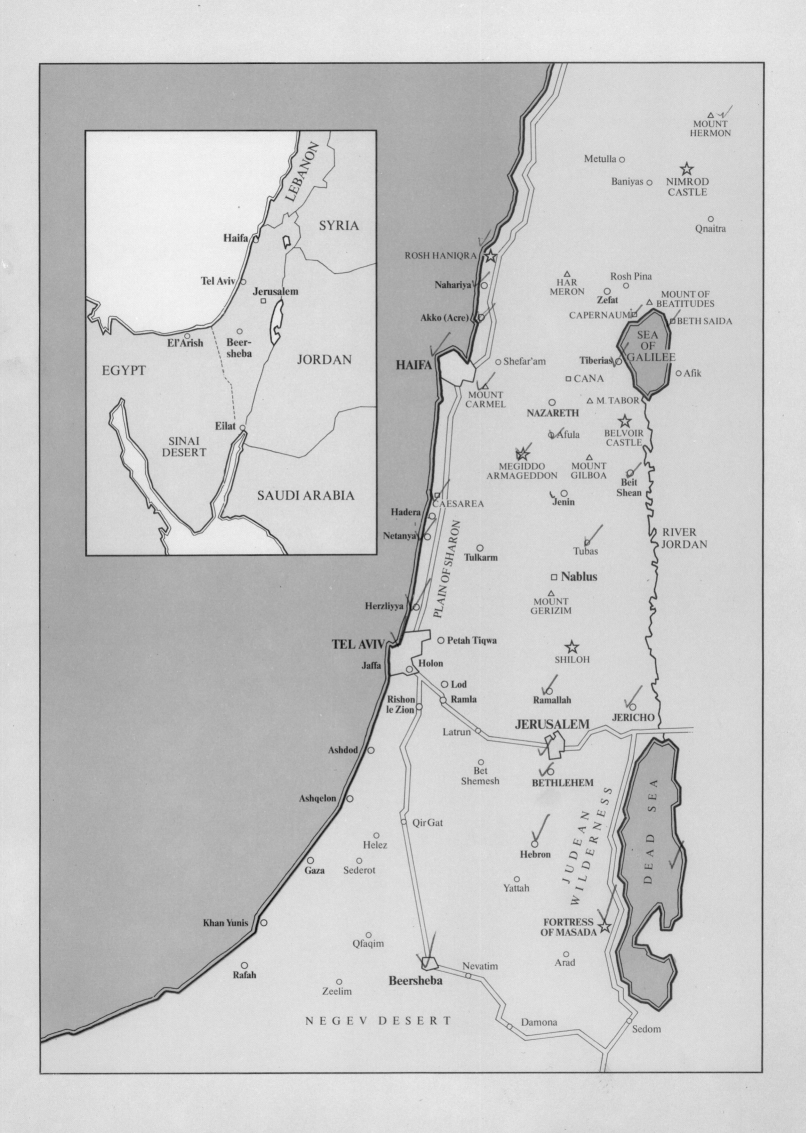

ISRAEL
THE PROMISED LAND

Text by
Bill Harris

Foreword by
the Honorable Jacob K. Javits

MAYFLOWER BOOKS · NEW YORK CITY

Foreword

For years Israel has captivated not only tourists, but artists, writers and photographers. For it is a land of paradoxes – apparent to all, but the special delight of the artistic imagination. It is a land of "milk and honey" and barren, forbidding deserts. It is a land with an ancient, deep-rooted history and a modern, technologically advanced society. It is a land dotted with historic monuments to enlightenment, peace and freedom, and with the debris of war. It is a land of shrines and temples, both humble and spectacular, of three major world religions. It is a land whose people are symbolized by the sabra – tough on the outside, soft on the inside. It is a land where the religious and secular, Arab and Jew, modern and traditional co-exist. These contrasts give the land – and its people – a special quality, unique in the world.

The richness and accomplishments of Israeli society are all the more remarkable because Israel is only 32 years old and its citizens number only three million. An extra dimension has been added because, as a center for the "gathering of the exiles," Israel has opened its arms and attracted immigrants from every corner of the world, united by their Jewish heritage and their desire to live again as one people in their own state. Each has brought his own culture and customs, all of which somehow meld in a dazzling display of light and shadow. Out of a small, inhospitable piece of land and out of a multinational, incredibly varied group of immigrants has been created a highly developed society with a common sense of purpose. Out of a language, Hebrew, that few spoke for more than two thousand years, Israel has developed one that is vital and modern – the vehicle for literary accomplishments recognized throughout the world. And out of a dream that Jews have dreamed for two millenia, Israel has flourished as a new reality.

As the meeting point for the three major world religions, Israel is imbued with the holy spirit found in no other land. The steady stream of pilgrims of all faiths who come to Israel to pay homage to their holy places gives special meaning to the phrase "Holy Land."

In my frequent visits to Israel, I have never left the country without a renewed sense of profound admiration and respect – quite apart from religious or ethnic ties. Few who have been to Israel can fail to be moved by the sense of purpose, the pioneer spirit, the intense commitments that Israelis feel toward their country and toward the new life they feel privileged to be building. Despite the difficulties and dangers under which most Israelis live, one senses a willingness to sacrifice and to give increasingly for the good of their new society. The results are evident with each visit to the country – a new town sprung from the earth like a garden, a lush field in the midst of a desert, a new highway.

Israel is a constant fulfillment of a once impossible dream.

Jacob K. Javits, U.S.S.
New York
1980

II

What's a nice, middle-aged man like Bob Shapiro of Kenosha, Wisconsin, doing in a place like Netanya on the Mediterranean coast of Israel? He's running a hi-fi store, and doing very nicely, thank you. But if you had met him 40 years ago and told him that one day he'd leave the American Midwest to go to the Middle East to sell sound systems made in Japan, you'd have been laughed out of Kenosha.

Unlike many who came to Israel at the beginning, Bob didn't arrive with stars in his eyes and a dream in his heart. His dream was to go back to Wisconsin and settle down with a good wife, a nice little business and some children he could be proud of. But after he mustered out of the U.S. Navy at the end of World War II, he realized there was still a bit of unfinished business to take care of.

All over Europe, the pitiful survivors of Hitler's death camps were enduring conditions grim even for them, to find some means of getting to Palestine, the Promised Land.

It was their only hope for picking up the pieces of their ruined lives and they needed help desperately. They found it in men like Bob Shapiro who knew that even though peace had come it was still necessary to put their lives on the line to make sure that freedom had come with it.

Before the war, the British Government, which controlled Palestine, had issued a White Paper limiting immigration to 75,000 persons. By the end of the war, the quota had long since been exhausted, but tens of thousands were going across Europe on foot toward the Mediterranean ports where they hoped to find ships that would take them across to Haifa and a new home.

People like Bob Shapiro reasoned to themselves that these wanderers had suffered enough. So many had died, so few had survived, it was immoral not to help them. There was no choice, he thought, and so rather than going home to accept the thanks of a grateful nation, Bob made his way to Marseille to see what he could do to help establish a new nation.

Together with other ex-GI's who shared his enthusiasm, he was able to convert a war surplus hulk into what passed for a passenger ship big enough to carry 1500 refugees to Palestine. Twice they were able to elude British patrols to land their cargo under cover of darkness, but on the third trip they never got past the entrance to Haifa harbor.

They tried fighting back, but it was hopeless. They were herded aboard a prison ship and sent to one of the

internment camps that had been set up on Cyprus for "displaced people" like these. In a matter of weeks, Bob was able to escape and slip into Palestine aboard a prison ship on its way back for fresh cargo. As he tells the story today, he just "happened to have" some dynamite with him, and before the ship could be loaded, it mysteriously exploded, causing no end of confusion and buying valuable time for more refugees trying to slip past the British net.

Bob went back to America after that, but he didn't abandon the cause. It took him to Newport News, Virginia, where several British corvettes were being de-commissioned. With the help of some friends who were as daring as he was, they were able to smuggle one of the ships out of the harbor loaded with guns and ammunition. It would become their gift to the Israeli Navy. They were able to sail the ship all the way to Israel, which by then had become the world's newest democracy, and this time, they all agreed, it made a lot of sense for them to stay there.

And what happened to his dream? He found a good wife in the person of a concentration camp survivor he himself had delivered to the Promised Land three years before. His daughter, an army veteran, teaches in the academy of music at Tel Aviv University. Her son is a pilot in the Israeli Air Force. Business is good. Netanya, the town he lives in, boasts some of the best beaches on the Mediterranean. He misses what he calls "pioneering," but he never for a moment regrets having left Kenosha.

Though he became an official resident in 1948, Bob is a relative newcomer compared to some Israelis. The dream of Palestine as a recreated Jewish nation goes back to the 1880's when Jews in Central Europe began to admit for the first time that there was no way for them to rise above the ghettoes that had been created for them. They knew that their only hope was to create their own state.

Ideas like that had already caught fire in the American and French Revolutions, and equality and freedom had suddenly become something more than just words.

. . . Go in and possess the land which the Lord sware unto your fathers.

– Deuteronomy 1:8

By 1880, small groups of Jews began trickling into Palestine and within 20 years had established 17 farming villages with names like Petah Tikvah, "Gateway of Hope," and Rishon-le-Zion, "First in Zion." The societies that produced the settlements were known in Europe as Hovevei Zion, "Lovers of

The sun rises in splendor *previous page* over the hills of the Judean wilderness as it has since the dawn of history. Sun-baked hills *left* from Mizpeh Shalem near the Dead Sea.

Zion." But they called themselves BILU, from the Hebrew initials of the Biblical quotation: "Oh House of Jacob, Come ye and let us go."

They were poor people, but some of the early settlers had a rich friend, Baron Edmond de Rothschild. The Baron had expressed interest in setting up colonies in Palestine and at first the interest was translated into a rumor among the Jewish people of Yemen that he had bought big blocks of land near Jerusalem and was planning to give it away to any Jews willing to go there to claim it. Two hundred responded and learned a bitter lesson about rumors. Not only was there no free land, but there were no jobs, either. It didn't stop the tide, though, and during the next four years, about 500 Jews moved from Yemen to become charity cases in Palestine.

At the same time, the Czar was making life difficult for Jews in Russia and the BILU movement began attracting new enthusiasts. Not many were able to respond and take the long, expensive trip. Those who did found the Promised Land a little less than promising.

The Turks who controlled Palestine hardly welcomed them with open arms. The religious Jews who had been born there turned their backs on the newcomers. The Arabs simply didn't understand them and didn't want to be bothered. They had come "home," but couldn't help wondering if it had been worth the trip. The climate was nothing like Russia at all. The terrain was as alien to them as the craters of the moon. Many contracted malaria. Almost all of them suffered in ways they had not even imagined back in Europe.

Baron Rothschild kept them going with massive doses of money. Although the Zionist Movement was beginning to take hold in Europe, the Baron wasn't part of it. He was less concerned with establishing a Jewish nation than with colonizing a country he thought could be fruitful and ultimately profitable. He knew it would be a wonderful place to establish vineyards and a wine industry. He saw Palestine as an opportunity for Jews to become farmers. He encouraged them to take advantage of the huge reservoir of cheap labor the Arabs provided. The people he helped almost never thought of themselves as the foundation of a new nation any more than did the French in Algeria.

The farmers and the idealistic young students who had come from Russia as *Biluim* didn't see eye-to-eye at all. The students had grown up in Europe's feudal system and didn't want any part of it. They wanted to be farmers, but not colonials. They had vague plans for establishing communities where everyone would work and share equally in the profits. A fine idea, said the established farmers, but don't ask *us* to go along with it. They didn't fit into Rothschild's plans, either, and so

they were doomed to become part of the labor pool that had helped make the big plantations profitable. But there was a catch: The Arab laborers were willing and able to work for less. Eventually some immigrants drifted back to Europe. Though defeated, their dream was still very much alive and their enthusiasm for it spread to Jewish communities everywhere. The Zionist movement was growing. Hope was spreading through the Jewish world. And if the First Aliyah, as the first wave of immigration was called, was less than successful, there was a great deal to be learned from it about what *not* to do.

The idea of Zionism was hardly new at the end of the 19th century. One of the basic elements of the Jewish religion has always been a belief in eventual return to Zion. Traditional prayers, even grace after meals, contain strong hopes for the rebuilding of Jerusalem. The most holy of all Jewish holy days, Yom Kippur, ends with the recitation of the Kaddish by the cantor, and a long note sounded on the ram's horn. At the sound, the entire congregation shouts in unison, *Leshanah Habaah Birushalayim,* "Next year in Jerusalem." It has more meaning today than ever, but the dream was kept alive in exile for nearly 2,000 years.

Life wasn't easy for Jews during those years of exile, and outright hatred against them reared its head during the great crusades in the Middle Ages when Christian adventurers set out to free the Holy Land from the Infidel. It didn't matter to them that the Jews had been hankering to do that since the days the ancestors of the crusaders were still living in caves. Along the way they became obsessed with the idea that Jews were responsible for the death of Jesus Christ and that they themselves were responsible for avenging that death by killing as many "Christ killers" as they could find. They missed the irony of the fact that their religion holds the death of Christ as the cornerstone of their redemption.

By the middle of the 19th century, the hatred had reached a fever pitch. In 1871, after losing a war against Prussia, the leaders of the French Army began spreading rumors that they could easily have won the war if the Jews had not stabbed them in the back by accepting money from the Prussians to keep France in a weakened state. It didn't occur to anyone in France that German philosophers had already begun comparing the "superior Aryan race" to the "inferior Jewish race."

In spite of the beliefs of the French high command, a young Jew named Alfred Dreyfus managed to become a member of the General Staff. They caught up with him at the end of 1894. He was accused of having sold military secrets to the Germans and brought to trial. He didn't have a chance. He was found guilty and sentenced to imprisonment on Devil's Island. At the end of the trial, he was ceremoniously stripped of his rank and marched past the officers of the French Army who shouted "down with the Jews!"

A Paris newspaper called the affair yet another chapter in the history of the Jews.

They were right, but for the wrong reasons. Another newspaper was represented at the Dreyfus trial, the *Neue Freie Presse* of Vienna. It was represented by a 34-year-old man named Theodor Herzl who had been sent to Paris to "furnish the paper with everything of interest" to be found there.

The Dreyfus Affair was more than just interesting.

Herzl had written plays and short stories, and seemed headed for a brilliant literary career. But on that winter day in 1894, his career was sidetracked by shouts of "Jew! Judas! Traitor!"

"Most of us had believed that the solution to the Jewish question was to be patiently waited for as part of the general development of mankind," he wrote. "But when a people which in every other respect is so progressive and so highly civilized can take such a turn, what are we to expect from other peoples, which have not even attained the level which France attained a hundred years ago?"

After that, Herzl became single-minded about founding a nation "where we can live at last as free men on our own soil and where we can die peacefully in our own fatherland." It made perfect sense. "For surely God would not have kept us alive for so long if there were not assigned to us a specific role in the history of mankind."

Herzl didn't know it, but his ideas weren't exactly new. Back in 1862, anti-Semitism had spread to the Mid-east for the first time when seven Jewish leaders were arrested on charges of ritual murder of Christians. Their torture shocked the Jewish world and moved Moses Hess, a German, to write in *Rome and Jerusalem* that ". . . The German objects less to a Jew's peculiar beliefs than to his peculiar nose." The only answer, he argued, was true emancipation of the Jews in their own homeland.

Twenty years later, pogroms in Russia moved Leo Pinsker to write that to have a life of his own, the Jew desperately needed a home of his own.

Neither Hess nor Pinsker were specific about where the homeland should be, and Russian and Romanian Jews were running to places like South Africa and South America, the United States and even France. Many found their way to Palestine, to be sure, but they never dreamed what was coming.

It took Herzl to show them the way.

The difference was that Herzl understood politics. He knew writing books and pamphlets wasn't enough.

He knew that he had to get straight to the masses as well as the wealthier Jews who had traditionally been the go-betweens with the Establishment in most European countries. Saying that even the most well-intentioned of individuals were still individuals, Herzl issued a call for a Zionist Congress to create a forum ". . . for which each member may be made to account for what he does or fails to do in Jewry."

The Congress was held at Basel, Switzerland, in August, 1897. In his opening remarks, Herzl told the assembly:

"We are here to lay the foundation stone of the house which is to shelter the Jewish nation. . . . Zionism is the return of the Jews to Judaism even before their return to the Jewish land. We seek to awaken the Jewish people everywhere to self-help . . . to create a permanent organ which the Jewish people has lacked until now."

The program officially adopted by the Congress called for the creation of a secure, legally recognized Jewish State. It agreed to promote settlement by agricultural and industrial workers with Jewish backgrounds. It established local and international organizations in as many countries as possible to organize the whole Jewish people.

Any Jew over the age of 18 was encouraged to join the Zionist Organization. The initiation fee was one shekel, an ancient Hebrew coin. Since no one had an actual shekel, the contribution was made in local currency of the same value. In the United States it was a half dollar.

Every country had a central organization made up of delegates from local groups called Shekel Unions. The Unions were entitled to one delegate for each 1,500 members. In addition to uniting world Jewry, the organizations also worked to raise money to buy land in Palestine.

The First Zionist Congress also produced a flag for the new country. A Cologne businessman had brought a banner with a blue star of Zion in the center of a white field and broad stripes at the top and bottom. Both the color and the design had been inspired by his own prayer shawl, but most of the delegates believed it was the flag of their ancestors.

Though their resolution called for establishing a country in the land of their ancestors, they were divided over whether they should move right in and begin establishing settlements or wait until they could get a legal charter from the Turks who were in control. Herzl was at the forefront of the latter idea and spent the rest of his life trying to get the charter. In the process, he was offered an alternative by the British Government to settle in their East African Protectorate, the place known as Uganda today. Convinced that the charter would never come, he proposed that the sixth Zionist Congress, held in 1903, accept the offer. They deferred their decision, and the idea was finally rejected in 1905 after Herzl had died, probably of exhaustion, at the age of 44.

. . . We are impoverished, but we will return and build the desolate places.

Malachi 1:4

With their rejection of any alternatives, Palestine became the focal point of their activities from that moment on. Jews who had already settled there were doing reasonably well. And only Palestine could provide the emotional pull the Zionist leaders knew was necessary to convince people to settle in the Jewish State rather than following so many others who had chosen to go to America.

An American named Mark Twain took a trip to Palestine in the 1860's, and gave the world an idea of the challenge the Zionists faced. In *The Innocents Abroad* he wrote:

"It truly is monotonous and uninviting, and there is no sufficient reason for describing it as being otherwise."

"Of all the lands there are for dismal scenery, I think Palestine must be the prince. The hills are barren, they are dull of color, they are unpicturesque in shape. The valleys are unsightly deserts fringed with feeble vegetation that has an expression about it of being sorrowful and despondent. The Dead Sea and the Sea of Galilee sleep in the midst of a vast stretch of hill and plain wherein the eye rests upon no pleasant tint, no striking object, no soft picture dreaming in a purple haze or mottled with the shadow of clouds. Every outline is harsh, every feature is distinct, there is no perspective – distance works no enchantment here. It is a hopeless, dreary, heartbroken land.

"Palestine sits in sackcloth and ashes. Over it broods the spell of a curse that has withered its fields and fettered its energies. Where Sodom and Gomorrah reared their domes and towers, that solemn sea now floods the plain, in whose bitter waters no living thing exists – over whose waveless surface the blistering air hangs motionless and dead – about whose borders nothing grows but weeds and scattering tufts of cane, and that treacherous fruit that promises refreshment to parching lips but turns to ashes at the touch.

"Nazareth is forlorn. About that ford of Jordan where the hosts of Israel entered the Promised Land with songs of rejoicing, one finds only a squalid camp of fantastic Bedouins of the desert. Jericho the accursed lies a mouldering ruin today, even as Joshua's miracle left it more than three thousand years ago. Bethlehem and Bethany, in their poverty and their humiliation, have nothing about them now to remind one that they once knew the high honor of the Savior's presence. The hallowed spot where the shepherds watched their flocks by night and where the angels sang peace on earth, good will to men, is untenanted by any living creature and unblessed by any feature that is pleasant to the eye.

"Renowned Jerusalem itself, the stateliest name in history, has lost all its ancient grandeur and is become a pauper village. The riches of Solomon are no longer there to compel the admiration of visiting Oriental queens. The wonderful temple which was the pride and glory of Israel is gone, and the Ottoman crescent is lifted above the spot where, on that most memorable day in the annals of the world, they reared the Holy Cross.

"The noted Sea of Galilee, where Roman fleets once rode at anchor and the disciples of the Savior sailed in their ships, was long ago deserted by the devotees of war and commerce and its borders are a silent wilderness. Capernaum is a shapeless ruin; Magdala is the home of beggared Arabs; Bethsaida and Chorazin have vanished from the earth, and the 'desert places' around them, where thousands of men once listened to the Savior's voice and ate the miraculous bread, sleep in the hush of a solitude that is inhabited only by birds of prey and skulking foxes.

"Palestine is desolate and unlovely . . . Palestine is no more of this work-day world. It is sacred to poetry and tradition. . . . It is dream-land."

Fortunately, there were dreamers in the world who were ready to risk their lives to change all that.

By the end of the 19th century, there were about 3,000 Jews in 21 settlements in Palestine. The Arab population was well over 100,000. But, as the 20th century began, things were beginning to change dramatically.

In Russia, new pogroms were giving new urgency to plans to find a new life. In the first decade of the 20th century, some two million Jews left Russia to escape persecution. But, in spite of the appeals and promises of the Zionist organization, more than three-quarters of them didn't choose to go to Palestine, but went to America instead. The reason was their very Jewishness.

The Orthodox Jews of Eastern Europe were completely opposed to the idea of returning to the Promised Land until the appearance of the Messiah. Their religion taught them "at the end of days" the Messiah would lead all Jews back to Jerusalem. They would wait, they said.

But there were others who couldn't wait, and some

40,000 went to Palestine including two teenagers, David Ben-Gurion, who became Israel's first prime minister and Yitzhak Ben-Zvi, its second president.

A huge number of teenagers arrived in this Second Aliyah and the majority of them were militant, aggressive, even fanatical. To their minds, the Diaspora had been a period of deep shame for Jews and it was time to do something about it. They believed that hard work was a virtue, and they were ready to put their personal lives aside to, as one of their leaders explained it, ". . . create a new Jewish man in the land of Israel to replace the disfigured human being who has been shaped by his misery and alienation from nature."

All Zionists were revolutionaries, of course. But at this point in their history, they were gingerly stepping around the Orthodox objections to their idea as well as Reform rabbinates who felt that nationalism and religion couldn't mix. They were getting strong opposition from other Jewish organizations which felt a "one nation" idea put doubts on their loyalty to the countries they lived in. They were regarded more as dreamers than fighters.

The new young immigrants had a much different temperament. They were rebels within a revolution. They hadn't known each other back in Russia, but they had shared a common experience. Their grandparents had been confined to slums, forbidden to own land or to work on anyone else's. For generations, they had compensated for what they called "the will of God" by turning inward, for depending on "faith" alone. But their kids felt that faith had failed them. They had no patience with fatalism. Most didn't even believe there was a God.

They didn't have much patience with the past and, unlike their parents, didn't believe the future would take care of itself. They had seen their friends and relatives hauled away to prison, tortured and murdered. The only way to stop it was to start fighting back. They had to start thinking about the here and now, forget about the past and work for the future.

Most of them came from middle class backgrounds, most were educated. Their first step was to turn themselves into peasants.

It didn't take them long to get to know each other once they got to Palestine. They met almost every day looking for work on the big plantations, competing with each other for jobs Arab laborers had already gotten. They met at night in the fields and haylofts where they were forced to sleep. They met along the roads where they scavenged for olives or begged for a glass of tea and a crust of black bread. And when they met, they talked. They talked about the ideas of socialism that were sweeping Europe at the time, and they talked about how those ideas could work for

them. Zionism loomed large in their conversations, too. But when they looked around them, it was easy to see that conversation alone would never build a nation.

They found the conversation stimulating, and they found that by sharing what resources they had, life was a little easier for all of them. Those who could get work shared with those who couldn't and it wasn't long before they were tied to each other in groups.

The Zionist Organization had opened an office in Jerusalem by 1908, and had begun to take notice of these bands of young people who were willing, even eager, to move away from the plantations along the coast. Through their Jewish National Fund, they had already been buying land which they leased for settlement. Since the land was to be leased and not sold, it was a perfect opportunity for the newcomers who could barely afford a piece of halvah, let alone a piece of land.

The Zionists were wary of the pioneers and their revolutionary socialist ideas, but it was obvious that they had the qualities it would take to drain the swamps and tame the wilderness. An offer was made to 10 men and two women from the Ukraine to tame a tract of 750 acres in the Jordan Valley. It was accepted almost without discussion.

They arrived in the middle of summer and went to work. When they weren't fighting yellow fever and malaria, they were knee-deep in mud. If they felt it was their destiny to make the desert bloom, their first attempt was wide of the mark. The spot they had been offered was well below sea level and was more accurately swamp than desert. It took them three years to make it fit for human habitation. Then they decided to settle there permanently.

In 1909 they established a community there and called it Degania because of all the cornflowers around it. It was the first kibbutz.

Degania wasn't the answer to some grand plan. After they had cleared the land, some of the groups wanted to turn it over to new immigrants and move on themselves to reclaim new territory. Most thought this place was challenge enough, and they decided to stay. But they had no idea how they should make their community work. The established pattern was to found settlements and run them through administrators appointed by the Zionist Organization. These Galilee pioneers associated that with European feudalism and didn't want any part of it. They had built this place and considered it theirs. Once they convinced Jerusalem they were able to control their own destinies, they were left to prove it on their own.

Their first break with tradition was to do away with "help wanted" signs. What they grew on their farms, they would grow themselves without the hired labor that was the key to success in other communities. They also decided not to concentrate on cash crops, but to grow what they needed themselves. Their community was to be run less as a community and more as a family, with everything from food to clothing shared by everyone. Their cooking was done in a common kitchen with ingredients from a little garden out back. If there was any food left over, it was sold and the proceeds went back to the community, possibly to buy a cow so they could have fresh milk or some more chickens to give them fresh eggs.

They all ate together in a wooden shack, and in the evenings talked together about their common problems. And, of course, there were plenty of problems to talk about. One of the earliest was what to do about children. It didn't seem right to bring children into an environment as hostile as this. On the other hand, without children they would die out like the Shakers in America who disappeared because of their ideas that prohibited sex. It was suggested that maybe they shouldn't get married for several years. That way, their country would have a future and they wouldn't have the burden of children until they were better prepared for them.

Fortunately, love and marriage won the day, and children were a fact of kibbutz life right from the beginning. The first was a boy named Gideon, son of Yosef and Miriam Baratz in Degania. Though he was their child, decisions about him as well as his schooling was the responsibility of the entire settlement. When he grew to be a young man, he wanted to go to Haifa to study mechanics in a technical school. His parents thought it would be a marvelous opportunity, but other members of the kibbutz felt city life would be a bad influence. The rule of the majority was for the boy to stay in Degania, and stay he did, learning what he needed from other members of the community.

The second child born in Degania, by the way, was also a boy. His name was Moshe Dayan.

It was agreed that children belonged to their parents, but responsibility for them belonged to everyone. In the original kibbutz, a young girl was chosen to take care of the babies in a house they built to be a nursery. It operated like a modern day care center and children spent evenings and weekends with their own parents. As the kibbutz movement grew, other groups adopted the same basic idea, but most required that children and parents could only be together during leisure hours, and there weren't many of those.

The children of the kibbutznik were among the first to learn Hebrew as a mother tongue. But their parents weren't first to revive the language. Credit for that belongs to a sickly young 23-year-old who arrived in Jaffa in 1880. His name was Eliezer Ben Yehuda. If his body was wracked by tuberculosis, his brain was on fire with a passionate idea: to make Hebrew a living language again.

The Lord God hath given me the tongue of the learned.
– Isaiah 50:4

Hebrew had begun to die out as a spoken language some 200 years before the Christian calendar begins marking our time. In the years before the Diaspora, many Jews spoke Greek. As they spread out into other parts of the world, they usually learned the local language. Sometimes they adapted it. In Germany in the Middle Ages, they spoke German, but wrote it in Hebraic letters. Later when their children moved into Russia and Romania, they kept on speaking German. Meanwhile, back in Germany, the language was changing but the change never reached the ghetto and before long the German spoken by Jews was a foreign language to native Germans. Just to add to the confusion, they also added Hebrew words here and there. The language they had created is called Yiddish. It wasn't kept alive out of stubbornness, but because as a patois it allowed Jews to talk among themselves about things they didn't want others to know about.

Jews who had migrated to Spain did the same thing, adapting Spanish into a language that became known as Ladino. They, too, used Hebraic characters in their written language. But the original language lived only in the Bible and in prayer books. It was used by scholars, repeated in prayers. But almost no one spoke Hebrew in conversation. If a Jew from Russia happened to meet another Jew from Morocco, they would communicate with each other in Hebrew, but the talk had to be limited to quotations from poetry or Scripture. And that made it tough to find out if a train was going to leave on time.

An American tourist found out not long ago how tough it was when he had an argument with a Jerusalem taxi driver who proposed to charge him double for a ride he had taken the evening before. Searching for the right Hebrew words to protest, all he could say was ". . . why is this day different from all other days?"

It seems strange to tourists to hear the language of the Bible being used by cab drivers and tour guides, housewives and little babies. It seemed like an odd idea to everyone in Jerusalem when Eliezer Ben Yehuda arrived there with his wife. The Jews in Jerusalem in 1880 spoke Ladino. Yiddish or Arabic. They spoke one or the other, but never admitted understanding more than one. And they never, never spoke to each other. The Yiddish-speaking Ashkenazim from Europe would cross to the other side of the street if they happened to notice a Sephardic Jew coming their way. But if they didn't like each other, they did agree on one thing: Hebrew, *lashon kodesh,* is the language of God Himself. It would be a sacrilege to use it to haggle with a shopkeeper.

But Ben Yehuda was a determined man. On the ship that took them across the Mediterranean, he solemnly told his wife that from that moment on, neither of them would speak any language but Hebrew. If that wasn't enough of a jolt, he also announced that he planned to be the father of 12 children, one for each of the 12 tribes of Israel. Furthermore, he said, none of those children would even be exposed to another language.

Deborah Ben Yehuda found some other shocks in store. The apartment they found was in a dingy slum overlooking the Wailing Wall, and the only way to get to the two empty rooms was by climbing a rope ladder. On her first day there, she was icily informed by a neighbor that no respectable Jewish woman would ever be seen without her head covered, lest the sight of hair might arouse lustful thoughts in strange men. And that explained why men in the street had strangely avoided looking in her direction.

Then her husband, a Lithuanian, came home from his job on a weekly newspaper dressed as an Oriental Jew. From his red tarboosh, the traditional fez, to his long green robe he wasn't the same young man who had gone to work that morning. And he was letting his beard grow, too.

Neither of them was Orthodox, but now it was clear there were going to have to be a lot of changes if his unorthodox ideas were going to take root.

By the time their first child was born, he had already attracted a lot of attention, and had recruited a small army of Biluim, who called themselves "The Army of the Defenders of the Language." They put their loyalty on the line by signing a pact that said: "The members residing in the Land of Israel will speak to each other in Hebrew, in society, in meeting places and in the streets and marketplaces, and shall not be ashamed. They will make it a point to teach their sons and daughters and the rest of their household this language.

"The members will watch in the streets and marketplaces over the Hebrew speech, and when they hear adults speaking Russian, French, Yiddish, English, Spanish, Arabic or any other language, they will not spare a remark even to the eldest amongst them, saying:

"'Aren't you ashamed of yourselves!'"

When their first son was born, his name was Ben Zion, "Son of Zion." The first word his mother said to him was "*valdi*" – "my child." She was, as Ben Yehuda proudly pointed out, "the first Hebrew mother in nearly two thousand years . . . the first woman in so long a time to address her child in the Biblical language."

The boy was isolated from the contamination of any language but Hebrew, as were Ben Yehuda's 10 other children (he fell one short of representing the 12 tribes of Israel). One of his sons later wrote that his father made no bones about the fact they had been brought into the world for just one purpose: to help make Hebrew a living language. He even went so far as encouraging them to pick fights with other kids in the street and forcing them to fight back in Hebrew.

Like his affectation of an Oriental costume, Ben Yehuda, preferred the Oriental pronunciation of the Sephardic Jews. It earned him a lot of support in Sephardic circles, needless to say. Then he began to publish a small newspaper with news of special interest to Ashkenazim. Naturally, it was in Hebrew. When he began planning his paper, he first had to invent a Hebrew word to describe it. Their ancestors didn't have newspapers, so people who spoke Hebrew in the 19th century improvised with the word *michtav- et,* which meant, roughly, "a letter of the time." Ben Yehuda wasn't sure that would roll easily off the tongues of streetcorner newsboys so, using the Hebrew for "time" as a root, he invented a whole new word, *itton,* and he was ready to go into the newspaper business.

He was constantly at work on compiling a dictionary of the language, writing notes on little file cards that would someday become as important as the Bible itself to the new nation. But there was a problem there, too. Ancient Hebrew didn't have a word that could be translated "dictionary." So he invented one. He called it *a millah* after the old word for (as you've probably already guessed) "word."

But words he coined weren't just to suit his own needs. Far from it. And sometimes other people took his words for their own needs without checking with him first. When the first symphony orchestra was established in Palestine, its members wanted a good Hebrew word for it, but, as so often happened, there was no word for "orchestra." One of the members had heard a word Ben Yehuda had used that sounded just right. When the others heard it, they agreed that *tizmoret* was perfectly beautiful and an absolutely perfect word to describe their music.

That wasn't what Ben Yehuda had in mind at all. The word, as he let them know in no uncertain terms, meant "melody." And because of its ancient root, it meant a melody sung in a human voice. No, no . . . it would never do for this aggregation of fiddles, flutes and kettledrums!

They had the last word, though. They told him they had already spent a lot of money for posters and programs in which the word was used, and as poor kibbutznik they just couldn't afford to change them. Faced with a choice like that, Ben Yehuda came up with a new word for "melody."

He came up with new words almost every day and, following the idea "learn a word a day, use it every way," he used the new words in his newspaper as often as he could. And to make sure people got the right pronunciation, he pressed his wife and children into service, ordering them to use them as much as possible. It made for some odd conversations, to be sure, but the idea worked.

As often happens, children were quickest to pick up the words. For one thing, it was fun to know words your teacher may never have heard of. For another, the Ben Yehuda youngsters were good talkers. Good fighters, too.

Among adults, it was a mark of fashion to know the latest words. There were others who thought it was all a lot of nonsense, of course. They felt it was fine to go back to the old language, but not to tamper with it. If the prophets didn't have a word for automobile, maybe the Almighty didn't intend for us to ride around in one.

Sometimes the new words fell flat on their face. The forefathers didn't know about tomatoes and so didn't have a word for them. Their romantic descendants had come to call them *agbanti,* which literally means "sensuous love." It was a bit racy for Ben Yehuda, so he changed the word to *badurah,* from an Arabic word. Whenever his wife went to buy one, she had to explain herself every time. No one gave up the old word but her and her family.

Sometimes he couldn't keep up with the waves of immigration. Before he had come up with a word for "oatmeal," Yiddish-speaking children were keeping their lips sealed tight against steaming spoons of gray stuff their mothers called *kvocker.* They knew for sure that was the proper name for it. It said so right on the box: Q-U-A-K-E-R.

In those days of Turkish rule, it was required that the Turkish language must be taught in every school. It wasn't mandatory that it should be the principal language, though, and Ben Yehuda fought hard to make Hebrew the official language of each school with Turkish and any other languages part of the "foreign language" curriculum. By 1903, teachers formed an organization they called a union to push the idea as far as it would go. Two years later, they founded an all-Hebrew school in Jaffa called Herzlia Gymnasia.

Oddly, they had to resort to the Russian word for school. Ben Yehuda had tried to replace the word "gymnasia" with the Hebrew *midrashah,* but that was another word nobody bought.

With World War I looming in the future, the great European powers began getting in line to establish some sort of toe-hold in Palestine that would help them keep in touch with the Ottoman Empire. Schools were the perfect answer. The Russians, lusting after Constantinople herself, built a teachers' college to train the staffs of some 100 secondary schools they were scattering across the Holy Land. The French and the British moved in, too. It was a golden age for education.

It was a great idea for everybody. Jewish parents in Eastern Europe eagerly sent their children to be educated in the Promised Land, and that was good for the local economy. The big governments were happy to have a foot in the door, and the teachers were pleased because the people who ran the schools were thousands of miles away. Things were looking good for the Hebrew language.

But then the Germans came.

They established several elementary schools and didn't seem to mind a bit that Hebrew was taught in them. But when they began building a technical college in Haifa, they announced that courses there had to be taught in "the most cultured of languages." German.

It's easy to imagine Ben Yehuda's reaction to that! But his protests fell on deaf ears. So he took his protest to the teachers, who immediately went on strike. The German schools were all out of business and soon replaced by makeshift affairs where teaching was done only in Hebrew. And to let the Germans know what they thought of "the most cultured of languages", children marched on the German Consulate in Jerusalem where they made a huge bonfire of their German schoolbooks.

The Germans finally gave in and agreed that Hebrew would be used in their new school after it had been open for four years. It opened in 1914. Four years later, Germany had lost another war and the compromise became academic in quite a different meaning of the word than anyone had intended.

The fight, and its outcome, interested more teachers as well as scientists in joining the effort to coin new words to bring the language into the modern world. The new schools formed in the strike were under local control and flourishing. By the time it was officially recognized as the language of Palestine by the League of Nations in 1922, just three months before Eliezer Ben Yehuda died, Hebrew was used in every school in Palestine. More than that, it was the language of the courts, of business, even of the theater. Most important, broadcasters and newspapermen took up the cause. Though it was easier for immigrants from Europe to hang on to their old language, it was clear they needed this even older one if they wanted to be part of the new country.

The Bible gave Ben Yehuda and his followers less than 8,000 basic words to work with. Today the language, with the help of the official Academy of Hebrew Language, which still keeps churning out new words to suit new needs, has grown to well over 50,000 words.

There are no armies of young militants skulking around the marketplaces listening for shameful foreign tongues these days. Older Israelis and newcomers speak them and have no difficulty being understood. Among people born in Israel, Hebrew is the first language, though most are multi-lingual. Even the Arab minority in most cases speaks Hebrew as a second language, even though there are Arabic schools and radio and television broadcasts in Arabic.

Most Israelis speak English, too. It's a required course in elementary schools, and required reading in Israeli universities is often in English. And street signs are usually in both Hebrew and English, a blessing for American tourists who have trouble with Hebrew script.

But Ben Yehuda would be proud. He was once referred to as "the fiercest fanatic in the history of Zionism." He worked 17 and 18 hours a day for 41 years to give the movement its own language as well as a special pride. Thanks to him, the language the whole world regarded as dead is very much alive.

But there is a spirit in man: and the inspiration of the Almighty giveth them understanding.

– Job 32:8

It was virtually a single-handed effort, but there were hundreds who joined the fight right at the beginning and without their help modern Israel would probably be no better off than Babel itself.

One of them was a young boy from a little town called Motol in the Russian province of Minsk who had been sent away to the great city of Pinsk to get an education. Though he was only about 25 miles from home, he was the first from his village to ever go so far away to school. The city wasn't large by most standards, but it was a center of a movement that would later be formalized with the title "Zionism." The movement had a profound effect on the boy, and in later years he would have an even more profound effect on it.

His name was Chaim Weizmann.

Even before he was a teenager, Weizmann distributed folders and leaflets from house to house and collected a few kopeks from as many as could afford them to help support the Choveve Zion movement. And he took great pride in the fact that he never wrote letters to his father in any language except Hebrew. So did his father. The one letter addressed to him in Yiddish was returned to the boy unopened. In 1886, Ben Yehuda's modern touches hadn't reached Pinsk, so young Weizmann couldn't have asked his father for a bicycle in one of those letters. It was probably just as well. Even though he was one of the wealthiest men in Motol, wealth was a matter of degree in this backwater of the Pale of Settlement, the territory set aside by the Czar to keep the Jews out of sight and out of mind. He couldn't afford anything more for his sons than an education.

Once young Chaim graduated from the gymnasium in Pinsk, his father encouraged him to leave Russia to get more education and some experience of life in the West. Fortunately, he was able to get a job teaching Hebrew and Russian in a boarding school in Germany and that provided funds for him to go to a German university.

It didn't take him long to find students who shared his views on the new Zionist movement, and almost any Saturday night they could be found discussing those views well into Sunday morning. They generally met in a small cafe in Berlin where it was easy to get beer and sausages on credit. But the food for thought was the main thing, and what they called "the redemption of our people" was first in their thoughts.

By the time the first Zionist Congress was held, Weizmann had developed a rare understanding of the differences between Eastern and Western thinking and as a result had a slightly different view than Herzl of what had to be done to get world support for Zionist ideals. His idea was to go to the masses to give organization and direction. And he was prepared to do the job himself. He helped organize the Russian delegations to the Congress, and though he wasn't part of it himself, the delegates he inspired had a profound effect on the Westerners.

Herzl himself was impressed. "They possess that inner unity which has disappeared from among the Westerners," he said. ". . . They are not tortured by the idea of assimilation, their essential being is simple and unshattered. . . . They manage to remain erect and genuine. And yet they are ghetto Jews! The only ghetto Jews of our time! Looking on them, we understood where our forefathers got the strength to endure through the bitterest of times."

But in spite of that, the movement in the early days was aimed at educated and influential people. In the opinion of the leadership, the masses in Russia would surely benefit in the end but had little to contribute towards reaching their goals.

Of course, Weizmann didn't agree with that at all. He formed an opposition group of delegates who called themselves the Democratic Faction and went to work to change the attitudes of the Zionist Organization from within. As a teacher in a Swiss university, he moved easily in academic circles. In vacation periods he moved equally easily among the common people back in Russia. Wherever he went, he impressed people with his ideas and soon became one of the Organization's most important leaders. But many of the people he talked with came from the same background and found his concepts easy to grasp.

His big challenge came when he decided to go to England in 1904. He picked England because he felt he had been neglecting his career as a chemist, and felt it was the only place where a Jew would be left alone to live his own life and to be judged on his own accomplishments.

His accomplishments there were incredible.

He moved to Manchester because he respected the university there and because it was a center of the chemical industry. He also wanted to get away from Zionism for a while, and felt this would give him the isolation he needed at that point in his life. He was almost right.

He threw himself into his work and for several months didn't talk to anyone about much more than the English fog and the fascination of hydrocarbons. But as it turned out it wasn't fascinating enough for him. He didn't get involved with British Zionists at first. Their leaders were pushing hard at the idea that the site of a new Jewish state ought to be in Uganda. Weizmann didn't agree with that idea, but he was in no mood to argue about it.

But it was only a matter of time before he was drawn into the discussion as a guest speaker at a Manchester Zionist meeting. Before long he was back in the movement again, and one of its leaders as well.

He was something of a curiosity in England. By now his views against the British Uganda offer were well known, but not many Englishmen could understand why anyone would be against such a generous, well-meaning gesture. Among the mystified was a candidate for Parliament in North Manchester, a young man named Arthur James Balfour.

Balfour invited Weizmann to London to explain his views on why only Palestine could ever be the Jewish state. After a quick explanation, Balfour was still unconvinced. Frustrated, Weizmann said: ". . . suppose I were to offer you Paris instead of London. Would you take it?"

"But, Dr. Weizmann," the candidate answered, "we already have London."

"That may be true," said Weizmann. "But we had Jerusalem when London was just a swamp."

Balfour was impressed. "Are there many Jews who think like you?" he asked.

Weizmann explained that he was convinced he spoke for millions neither of them would ever see who couldn't speak for themselves, and who one day would become a great force in the world.

The candidate was silent for a minute. Then he said: "It is curious. The Jews I meet are quite different from you."

"Mr. Balfour," replied Weizmann, "you meet the wrong kind of Jews."

Although Weizmann had talked to thousands of people of all kinds about Palestine, he didn't go there himself until 1907 when he took a detour on the way home from the eighth Zionist Congress in The Hague.

His first impression on landing at Jaffa was that it was "dolorous . . . one of the most neglected corners of the miserably neglected Turkish Empire."

Most of the 80,000 Jews who lived mainly in cities like Jerusalem and Hebron were what we like to call "senior citizens" today. It had been customary for centuries for European Jews to move to Palestine when they got old so they might die on holy soil. They spent their days reading holy books, supported by families back home or by organizations dedicated to keeping the tradition alive. The Jewish experience in Jerusalem was about the same as an old folks' home at that time. Hardly a base for building a strong new nation.

He didn't find any pioneering spirit among the young *Biluim,* either. By 1907 they had become planters and small businessmen and were content with the status quo. But the picture wasn't completely discouraging. Weizmann found spirit among recent immigrants and hope for the future in the schools that had been established. He was as convinced as ever that the future of this place was squarely in the hands of ordinary people.

He realized what a big job it would be when his enthusiastic guide took him for a walk into the desert near Jaffa. They stopped at a spot where they were ankle-deep in sand and his friend said excitedly, "here we shall create a great Jewish city!" Even a scientist like Weizmann thought that was a pipe dream of major proportions. It was a wilderness! Nothing would ever grow in all that sand! And how would it be possible to convince people it could be a nice place to live?

"I didn't say it would be easy," said the guide. "But these days anything is possible. Sure, communication will be hard at first. But before long the city will be self-supporting. And it will be modern. That will attract people over from Jaffa. We'll have a fine marketplace over there. And over here in the center, a fine gymnasium to attract students from all over the world. Jews everywhere will want their children to be educated in a Jewish school in a Jewish city!"

Then he gave the dream a name.

"We'll call it Tel Aviv," he said. "Hill of spring."

The guide was Arthur Ruppin, the first director of the Zionist Organization's Palestine office, one of the builders of Israel. Weizmann described him as "correct, reserved, cool . . . almost Prussian." But the exterior didn't fool anyone who knew him. He was passionate about one important thing: the ability of his people to build a great nation.

Weizmann visited Jerusalem on his tour, too, of course, but found it depressing. ". . . All the grand places belonged to others," he wrote. "We had not a decent building of our own. All the world had a foothold in Jerusalem except the Jews."

But if he characterized it as a derelict with no dignity, he was quite taken with the beautiful surroundings of the city. He had been harboring a dream of building a great Hebrew University in the Holy Land and he found the perfect spot for it on the top of Mount Scopus. It was the only hill in Jerusalem that didn't have a church or monastery, only a villa belonging to Lady Grey Hill. It was bought by the Zionist Organization in the middle of World War I, as much to the amazement of the Grey Hill family as to the Zionists themselves who had gotten the money from a Russian philanthropist. It gave all England an odd kind of hope that they could win the war when people who seemed to know what they were doing were willing to invest in territory that would surely be confiscated if they didn't.

Weizmann was back in England when war came, working on an assignment that had been given to him by the First Lord of the Admiralty, a young man named Winston Churchill. The scientist had developed a process for producing an acetone/butyl alcohol combination in the laboratory. A small breakthrough, but a step toward making synthetic rubber. Now that war was imminent, Mr. Churchill placed an order for 30,000 tons of acetone, which was also important in making explosives.

Weizmann knew that once he made a ton, the rest would be easy. But that first ton would be tough. Churchill gave him a blank check, and work began, first in a gin factory, then in special factories all over Britain. It gave Weizmann contact with other scientists as well as with industrialists and politicians. It was important work, and when it was finished successfully, Chaim Weizmann was a much more important man than he had ever been before.

Meanwhile, the Turks had sided with the Germans in the war and the Jewish community in Palestine sided against them. Some 900 volunteers were attached to the British Army as a transport battalion called the Zion Mule Corps. It was disbanded after the Gallipoli Campaign, and its veterans went on to form the nucleus of the Jewish Legion, a force of 5,000 men that had been organized in Britain and augmented by the first Judean Regiment, made up of volunteers from the United States and Canada.

It was the first Jewish military unit the world had seen since the fall of Judea.

As a unit, they served under General Allenby and helped chase the Turks out of Palestine, at which time their Promised Land became a part of the British Empire. And with that, the dream only a few dared dream came closer to reality.

During the war, Arthur James Balfour had become Britain's Secretary of State for Foreign Affairs. He had also become a closer friend of Dr. Weizmann, not to mention some of the people Weizmann had called "the right kind of Jews." On November 2, 1917, he wrote a letter to Lord Rothschild that said:

"His majesty's Government view with favor the establishment in Palestine of a National Home for the Jewish People, and will use use their best endeavors to facilitate the achievement of this object, it being clearly understood that nothing shall be done which may prejudice the civil and religious rights of the existing non-Jewish communities in Palestine or the rights and political status enjoyed by Jews in any other country."

For the first time, the Zionist movement had official international recognition and the power to deal with foreign governments. The Turks and Germans followed with declarations of their own allowing free immigration. And the French and Italians also issued statements giving Zionism their official support. In 1920, the Supreme Council of the Allied Powers endorsed the Balfour Declaration and gave a Mandate for Palestine to England. Two years later, the American Congress issued a resolution giving U.S. approval to Palestine as a National Home for the Jewish People.

Veterans of the Zion Mule Corps went back to their farms, but they didn't beat their swords into plowshares. They would see the day they were glad they didn't!

. . . Strength and gladness are in his place.
– I Chronicles 16:27

The young people who were scratching out a living

in the hills of Galilee had been fighting more than just a hostile environment since the very beginning. Bands of Bedouins visited their settlements regularly to see what might be worth taking. It had been a tradition back in Russia for Jews to avoid fighting no matter what the provocation, and the pioneers in Palestine had some of that tradition in their souls. At first they hired other Arabs to protect them, but it didn't take long for them to realize you don't hire a fox to watch over the hen house.

But not all the pioneers were pacifists. Some, who had cut their teeth fighting Cossacks, formed their own guard force, calling themselves *Hashomer,* "the watchmen." For a small fee, they protected any villages that would hire them. A more important price tag on their services was a demand that no Arab laborers could work on land they patrolled. They were good fighters and it didn't take them long to cool Bedouin enthusiasm for raiding farms and villages.

One of the watchmen, David Ben-Gurion, was as good at politics as he was at fighting and by the time the Balfour Declaration was signed, he had become a spokesman for the pioneers already settled in Palestine. And he was passionate about the idea that a Jewish nation depended a lot more on people than on a piece of paper circulating out of London. His response to Balfour's letter was:

". . . It is not in England's power to give Palestine back to us. . . . A country is not given to a people except by its own toil and creativity, by its own efforts in construction and settlement."

The key was people, and before 1923, the Third Wave of immigration brought some 40,000 of them looking for a better life. For the first time, the immigrants knew what to expect thanks to organizations that had sprung up in Eastern Europe. Life wasn't easier for them than it had been for other pioneers, but it didn't hold so many discouraging surprises. Finding work was tough, to be sure. But the British helped by giving out contracts for building roads and other public works. The workers themselves formed "work legions" along the same lines as their kibbutznik cousins. It wasn't long before they banded together into a labor organization they called Histadrut.

They envisioned it as an amalgam of unions open to any worker who agreed not to "exploit" any other worker. They took it on themselves to settle land as well as labor disputes, to set up vocational schools, to help immigrants find jobs and to promote new immigration. The existing political parties, who had been doing some of these things already, but at cross-purposes, agreed to transfer some of their rights and resources to the new organization.

It unified the people behind the idea of organized immigration and settlement with self-sufficiency as their goal. Among the men who unified them was the general secretary of the movement, David Ben-Gurion.

At about the same time, a young American from New Jersey named Eliezer Joffe brought an American idea to Israel: rugged individualism. Like some other Americans, he felt that life on a kibbutz didn't allow for initiative and had a choking effect on family life. He had a better idea. Organizing a group of followers, he went to the Jezreel Valley, where the Jewish National Fund had bought 15,000 acres of swamp land. After they built crude wooden houses, they went to work clearing the swamp. When they were finished, each of them got a loan from the Zionist Organization to set up an independent farm.

Each farm, by mutual agreement, was big enough to feed a family but not so big that a family couldn't run it without hired help. A cooperative was formed to buy supplies and machinery, but what each farmer did with the land assigned to him was his own business as long as he agreed not to try to expand his land holding. As in the kibbutz system, the land itself was owned by the State and the people who lived on it worked to help each other. But the difference was that each person could do anything that made sense to earn a profit and each family was free to do anything with their profits that made sense to them. They called their settlement Nahalal. The system that bound them together was called a moshav. It was a system that quickly became far more popular than the kibbutzim.

The combination of the Balfour Declaration, Histadrut and the moshav made Palestine more attractive to more people. Middle class immigrants began coming in bigger numbers. The Europeans brought new skills as well as some money and a building boom made the old towns look a lot more attractive and the new towns they built made life a lot easier than it had been for centuries. Still not a Garden of Eden, of course, but new industries were being established; Tel Aviv was growing by leaps and bounds and even had its own electric power station. A place that had subsisted for generations by producing wine, soap, wood carving and religious souvenirs had flour mills, cement plants and salt factories. It had a future you could feel in the air.

The Arabs felt it too. There were less than half a million of them in Palestine when the first Jewish pioneers began arriving in the '80s. The number doubled before the end of the 1930's. A lot of them were Bedouin nomads who moved herds of sheep and cattle through the Northern mountains. The majority were fellahin, simple farmers who eked out a meager living on farms belonging to landowners who lived pleasanter lives in the cities. The Palestinian intelligentsia lived in the cities, too, and together with the Muslim clergy and the landowners, they had for generations controlled all the country's wealth.

The European settlements took over some of the old Bedouin grazing land and the more modern farms that were being established made a tough life tougher for the fellahin. To add insult to injury, the landowners had been selling their farms to the Zionists without bothering to tell the fellahin they were out of business.

When the British took over, they made deals like that illegal, and displaced farmers with a few coins in their pockets were able to move into towns where there were jobs enough for everyone at wages that would have amazed the farmers' grandfathers. The landowners got richer as demand for space increased. But they saw the handwriting on the wall and they didn't like it a bit. Under British rule, they were treated like "natives" in any other colony of the Empire. They knew they would never have any influence over the Jewish settlers, and it was obvious they weren't going to stop coming. What was going to happen to their power and authority? They began to use their power to do something about it.

The former government officials and professionals, who had been left out in the cold by the British Mandate led the fight, the landlords kept it going. It was easy enough to do. To the Muslim farmers, their new neighbors led riotous, immoral lives. Women not only worked in the fields, they didn't cover themselves properly at all. And now and then their husbands touched them in public. It was true that Arab peasants were making more money under the new system, but they were forced to work for less than most of the immigrants. And they couldn't get jobs at all on Jewish-owned plantations; that was strictly forbidden.

And still the foreigners kept coming. In the 1930's alone, a quarter of a million, mainly from Poland, and for the first time from Germany, came to put their stamp on the land.

They brought an Eastern European culture with them which combined with the socialism of the settlers already there to create a whole new style of life that gave the National Home a culture all its own. But the government was British.

If the Arabs didn't like being treated as colonial "natives," the Jews hated it. They also weren't too fond of the British idea that Jews and Arabs would eventually be part of the same country, one group speaking Arabic the other Hebrew, but both governed in English. The British themselves began to wonder if it was the right idea when Arabs began rioting against the Jews in 1920. It continued off and on for about a year and then Winston Churchill, Britain's colonial and then Winston Churchill, Britain's Colonial Secre-

tary, decided to do something about it.

He did several things. In a series of White Papers, he changed the terms of the original Balfour Declaration.

The first was quite specific: "The terms of the Balfour Declaration do not contemplate that Palestine as a whole should be converted into a Jewish National Home," it said, "but that such a home should be established in Palestine."

Then he petitioned the League of Nations to change the traditional boundaries of Palestine. The territories that were between the Jordan River and the Arabian Desert would be called Trans-Jordan and declared off-limits to Jewish settlement.

It's an area of some 34,000 square miles, about three times as big as Palestine west of the Jordan. Not many Jews lived there at the time, but a great many leaders had big plans for the territory. But they licked their wounds and held their peace.

Eight years later Arab rioting broke out again. It was time for Britain to issue another White Paper. It reflected an earlier study that seemed to prove that the standard of life of the Arab farmers would be severely cut if as much as one more new settler arrived in Palestine. Of course it ignored the fact that hundreds of fellahin were making more than they ever could have hoped selling vegetables and fish in the marketplace in Tel Aviv, a city that didn't even exist 50 years before.

Reaction was strong all over the world and people were beginning to say that the Jewish National Home was doomed. But its foundations were too solid. Immigration didn't stop. On the contrary, it flourished. Between 1929 and 1935, the Jewish population of Palestine grew from 190,000 to 375,000. And that's just on paper. There were thousands of uncounted illegal immigrants, too, including Arabs from Trans-Jordan and even Egyptians lured by the promise of a better life.

The whole world was beginning to wonder if they'd ever see a better life again by the mid '30s. Hardly a country in the world hadn't been affected by the Great Depression. Japan had taken over Manchuria, Mussolini had invaded Ethiopia, Franco had taken over in Spain and the League of Nations had been brought to its knees.

At the same time, a new name was appearing in world headlines: Adolph Hitler.

One of his staunch allies was the Grand Mufti of Jerusalem, who started a new wave of terrorism in Palestine. He added a new wrinkle by declaring war on his fellow Arabs who refused to join a general strike against the Jews. But the Jews had a new wrinkle of their own. They refused to be goaded into reprisals and the Mufti's campaign fell on its face in just a few months.

But it lasted long enough for the British to move in again for yet another investigation. This time they condemned their own government for not being able to control events in Palestine and declared that their Mandate was simply "unworkable."

After a discussion that lasted almost three years, they issued another in the long series of White Papers. Most people affected by it came to call it a "black paper." It said that all the promises of the Balfour Declaration were now fulfilled and a Jewish National Home was well-established. Therefore, it continued, it's time to stop Jewish immigration. A maximum of 75,000 immigrants would be allowed into Palestine during a five-year period beginning in May, 1939. No land in all but a small part of Palestine could be bought by Jews during the same period.

It was adopted by Parliament, but by a tiny majority, in spite of opposition by some of Britain's greatest leaders, including Winston Churchill who told the House of Commons:

"I should feel personally embarrassed in the most acute manner if I lent myself by silence or inaction to what I regard as an act of repudiation."

It was probably more accurately called an act of appeasement. Within a few months, the policy fell apart and World War II came home to England in spite of Neville Chamberlain's efforts to hold back the tide.

The policy went into effect quickly. Too quickly to slip in refugees from Eastern Europe who wound up going to death camps instead.

. . . There is a noise of war in the camp.

Exodus 32:17

It's one of the most incredible ironies in the history of the Jewish people that at the time they needed a National Home most, its doors were closed. Across the Mediterranean, death was in the air.

Some years after it happened, the world began referring to Hitler's attempt at genocide against the Jews as the Holocaust. It's an English word with a Hebrew root, the word *olah,* which means "to go up." It's the same word that gave us the term *aliyah* for the waves of immigration into Palestine. In this case, the root goes back to ritual sacrifices of ancient times in which the sacrifice was totally consumed by fire to "go up" to God as a wisp of smoke.

Between 1939 and 1945, about 6 million of the 16 million Jews in the world were wiped out in the 19 or so concentration camps that stretched across Europe. It made the survivors, all the Jews in the world, more determined than ever to demand a homeland. More important, it made the rest of the world agree it was a reasonable demand.

In Palestine, the outbreak of World War II was a real dilemma. Very few Jews there had any great love or respect for the British at that point. But they knew the Nazis were bent on their destruction. The Zionist Congress authorized Dr. Weizmann to officially notify the British Government that the Jews "will stand by Great Britain and will fight on the side of the democracies." David Ben-Gurion struck a little closer to the bone by saying "we shall fight the war against Hitler as if there were no White Paper, and we shall fight the White Paper as if there were no war."

But it was the people themselves who spoke most eloquently. Mobilization was completely voluntary. In fact, the British turned down an offer of a Jewish army fighting as a unit. In spite of it, some 130,000 of them volunteered. The authorities accepted a few thousand of them and agreed to let them serve in so-called "Palestinian units." They saw action in France and in Greece, and closer to home at Tobruk and El Alamein. They worked with the underground behind enemy lines in Europe. Some 2,000 of them gave their lives. Yet it wasn't until late in 1944 that the British authorized a special Jewish Brigade at the insistence of people like Winston Churchill, who said: ". . . it seems to be indeed appropriate that a special Jewish unit of that race which suffered indescribable torment from the Nazis should be represented as a distinct formation among the forces gathered for their final overthrow."

In spite of the White Paper, planning for the future never stopped. In 1942, David Ben-Gurion called a special meeting of Zionists in New York calling for unlimited Jewish immigration into Palestine and the establishment of a Jewish Commonwealth. The word "homeland" faded back into history.

He knew the Mandate would end some day and they would have to think about fighting with their Arab neighbors. There was work to be done.

Back in the '20s, a committee had been formed within the Histadrut to coordinate defense among all the communities. It was an underground group, ready for a fight anywhere, any time. It was called Haganah. Haganah was illegal as far as the British were concerned, and at first the Pioneers in the wilderness were content to take matters of defense into their own hands. But the Arab riots in the late '20s established it as a necessity. As an arm of Histadrut, there was a natural resentment against it from among people not connected with the labor movement. Their response was to form a unit of their own, which they called Haganah "B." By the end of the '30s, the differences were resolved, but some 1,500 men and women, still at odds with Histadrut, formed a separate defense organization they called the Irgun.

By 1939, Haganah had grown from a rag-tag militia to a highly-respected fighting force. No Jew in Palestine was too deep in the wilderness not to be able to count on their protection. They did their job so well, the British were able to find loopholes in their own rules to bring the illegal army out of the closet for training and access to more sophisticated weapons.

The British even trained young people for guerrilla fighting at night and they took to it like a duck to water. They learned to move fast and to strike quickly. Most important, they had professional help that ultimately built one of the most impressively professional armies in history. It was no easy accomplishment for the children of people who were passionately pacifist.

The leaders of the Irgun thought Haganah was soft and they deeply resented consorting with the British, whom they felt were the greatest enemy Zionism faced. The leader who felt all that most strongly was Abraham Stern who arrived in Palestine from Poland in 1940 with a small band of followers. The Irgun had already called a truce with Britain for the duration of the war, but Stern had other ideas. He formed an organization he called "Lehi," from the Hebrew words, *Lochamei Herut Israel* meaning "Freedom Fighters of Israel." Most people regarded them as terrorists, especially British newsmen who gave them a more memorable name: "The Stern Gang."

Stern had an odd idea that raises questions about his basic understanding of human nature. He thought the Jews ought to side with Hitler and help him conquer Palestine. Once having freed the territory from the British, according to Stern, the great humanitarian in Berlin would be more than willing to transfer Jews from his concentration camps to a new home in the Middle East.

It should go without saying that he didn't get a lot of support for the idea in Palestine. But he went on doing damage anyway.

He was finally killed by the British in 1942 after a rampage of assassination that included Jews as well as English police officers among its victims. Though most of the members of both the Haganah and the Irgun opposed Stern, even to the point of helping the British track him down, there were many who were impatient with the truce and itching for a fight. One of them was a young man who had known Stern in Poland and had migrated to Palestine in 1942. Many years later he would become Israel's Prime Minister, but within a year of his arrival, Menachem Begin became commander of the Irgun.

He ended the truce with the British, but ordered the 500 men and women who followed him not to kill British soldiers but to destroy buildings and other property instead. Naturally, the British didn't like that much and gave stiff prison sentences to Irgun members they managed to catch. The Jewish establishment didn't like it much either and tried everything from propaganda to pleading to get the Irgun to slow down. To people who had seen the country grow an inch at a time, terrorism was a terrible threat to the future. But to newcomers who had escaped from Europe just one step ahead of the Nazis, the British restrictions that doomed millions by keeping them out of Palestine were as anti-Jewish as anything Hitler was doing. No amount of pleading would get them to stop fighting the British.

The situation came to a head in 1944 when Lehi reared its head again. Two of its agents in Cairo assassinated the British Minister of State for the Middle East, Lord Moyne. It was a black day for the Zionist cause because Lord Moyne was a good friend of Winston Churchill, who quickly withdrew his friendly support of Zionism. It was a bad day for the Irgun, too. Even though they had nothing to do with the assassination, and even denounced it, most people all over the world blamed them for it.

For the first time, the Jews in Palestine and the British authorities were united against a common enemy. A volunteer force within the Haganah was assigned to track down Irgun members. When they found them, they spirited them off to remote kibbutzim for questioning, and when they got the answers they wanted they turned the prisoners loose rather than handing them over to the British. They used the information to find the Irgun leaders, and those were the people they let the authorities haul in. Before long the British had arrested the entire Irgun leadership except for Begin himself and one other, and everyone was congratulating themselves for having eliminated the rebel army without any killing.

The pats on the back were premature.

The anti-Irgun movement fell apart just short of complete victory. People were up in arms over the kidnappings and furious about the fact that Jews were forced to inform on Jews. All those years of persecution in Europe had given Jews a tradition that was stronger than almost any other: never, never inform on anyone.

It made underdogs of Irgun members and it made others eager to join them. But this time they joined the underdogs underground.

Meanwhile, Hitler was being run to the ground, and people all over the world were finding out, many for the first time, about the terrible suffering of the Jews at his hands. Many were being liberated from concentration camps, others came out of hiding. They were wandering aimlessly across the map of Europe with nothing left but life itself. Even hope was gone, and many were convinced that the lucky ones were the ones who had died.

Haganah agents fanned out across Europe to give them hope and a direction. The direction was toward the Mediterranean, hope was on the other side. But, of course, the door was sealed by a piece of White Paper.

Reports of conditions in the Displaced Persons camps made people all over the world with any humanitarian feelings anxious to do something. Many joined the Zionist movement or at least began supporting it for the first time and public opinion cried out to Britain to soften its policy and let these people be saved.

But the British had other fish to fry. Their game was to make the Middle East an important part of the British Empire, and they knew from experience that the Jews in Palestine weren't going to go along with that. They thought they could defuse that problem by uniting the Arabs under their own control. Then they convinced the French it would be a good idea if they moved out of Syria, and settled back to build their empire.

After all those years of dealing with the Palestinian Jews, they apparently hadn't learned a thing.

Haganah agents had smuggled a lot of refugees past the British lines, but it was a tricky business and it seemed every time they found a hole, it was quickly plugged. There was nothing for it, they concluded, but to stop sneaking around and stand up and fight before thousands more died trying to get into Palestine.

War has always made strange bedfellows, and this one was no exception. After years of fighting each other, the Haganah leadership knew that the only way they could accomplish anything was to join forces with the Irgun. It wasn't an easy marriage to negotiate, but in the fall of 1945, they not only joined with the Irgun, but with Lehi, too. They all kept their separate identities, but the Haganah coordinated their efforts under a new organization they called The Hebrew Resistance Movement.

They made their presence known with massive sabotage of the railroad, followed quickly by the destruction of the train station at Lod. Then, while the authorities were still reeling, they attacked the oil refineries at Haifa. When it was all over, almost no lives were lost, but a lot of destruction showed the British they had an unexpected problem on their hands.

As often happens with governments, the British response was to form a commission. They weren't willing to go it alone, though, and invited the United States to join with them in taking a hard look at the refugee problem. While the commission was doing its work, the British also agreed to allow 1,500 refugees into Palestine every month. A small step, to be sure, but at least it was a step in the right direction.

The committee issued its report in less than six months. It recommended that 100,000 should be allowed into Palestine right away. President Harry Truman quickly announced that he agreed with their decision, but the British foreign secretary said his country couldn't possibly allow such a huge mass migration. The place is a hotbed of terrorism, he argued, and the only way the recommendation could be implemented would be for Arabs and Jews to turn in their weapons. Naturally, neither side was ready to even think about doing that and so the door stayed closed.

Jews all over the world were discouraged by it, but the move convinced even the most peace-loving of them that if they were ever going to have a National Home, they were going to have to fight for it.

In the spring of 1946, the fight began when 10 bridges were blown up. The British responded by sending 17,000 soldiers out to find and arrest the Zionist leaders and to disarm as many Haganah members as possible. They found most of the leaders, except David Ben-Gurion, who luckily was out of the country, but they didn't find too many Irgun fighters to disarm. That was their misfortune.

In July, the Irgun struck again by blowing up a wing of the King David Hotel in Jerusalem, which the British had appropriated as their administrative office. The blast killed about 100, including Arabs and Jews who worked there. The blast also severed any ties between Irgun and Haganah once and for all.

It goes without saying that the King David explosion made the British a lot tougher to deal with. They imposed curfews, they staged house-to-house searches for guns and for illegal immigrants, and announced that from that moment on any refugee without an entry certificate would be deported to Cyprus and held in detention pens.

But in spite of tough rules and regulations, the Irgun attracted hundreds of new recruits and new enthusiasm for terror and sabotage.

All over the world, people were trying to find answers to the problem. In London, Jews and Arabs sat down together to figure out how they might live together. They couldn't think of a way. In Paris, members of the Zionist Organization put together a proposal to partition Palestine and make part of it a Jewish State. In Jerusalem, British officials convinced Jewish leaders to denounce the terrorists in return for the release of imprisoned Zionists and the withdrawing of an arrest warrant against David Ben-Gurion. In Washington, President Truman announced that he was foursquare in favor of the Paris proposal for partition.

Britain's days in Palestine were clearly numbered.

By the time the Zionist Organization held its 22nd Congress in 1946, its membership had grown to more than two million, the majority of them Americans. They were in a mood for action by that time, and showed the world they were ready by electing the old fighter David Ben-Gurion as their chairman. And they announced to the world that no matter *what* it took, a Jewish National Home was going to be established.

In Palestine at the same time, Arabs were fighting among themselves, and Jewish terrorists were fighting harder than ever against the British in spite of the threat of flogging and even hanging if they had the misfortune to be caught. They were too determined to be put down, and British determination was beginning to run down.

The Zionist Organization was drumming up support all over the world in spite of the fact that the world was weary of war and found it hard to support the terrorism that appeared to be official policy among the Jews in Palestine. Nowhere in the world was support as strong as it was in the United States. Both Jews and non-Jews alike responded to the call to put pressure on Britain to open the door. Congress had passed declarations making it official. Both Presidents Roosevelt and Truman had pledged support for the establishment of a Jewish commonwealth. The Cold War made the area important to American interests, not only because of Arab oil, but as a base of operations at Russia's back door. The American mood at the end of the war was to pull out of the area and let Britain have the headache. But the Russians had their eye on Turkey and Iran, there was a civil war in Greece and Britain announced she had enough headaches and no longer considered herself a protector of either Greece or Turkey. The United States filled the vacuum with the Truman Doctrine, which made it American policy to guarantee the security of Greece and Turkey and to contain Communist aggression anywhere it appeared. The document brought the Middle East officially into American strategy.

Though Britain seemed to be slowly pulling out of the area, it looked to the Zionists like they'd never leave Palestine. More pressure was needed. Ironically, the final push came directly from the British themselves who had their policy turned against them when a shipload of refugees steamed into Haifa in the summer of 1947.

The ship was an old American merchantman that had begun life under the name *President Garfield*. On that summer day, she had a new name, *Exodus 1947*, and she was crowded with more than 4,500 Displaced Persons. The British Navy intercepted the ship and cabled London for instructions.

Foreign Secretary Ernest Bevin had had enough of the Palestinian problem. He had been accused by Ben-Gurion of establishing a policy of systematic liquidation of the Jewish people, and had countered with a charge that Zionism was nothing more than a carefully-planned Russian Communist plot to get a toe-hold in the Middle East.

His answer to the Navy's cable was to turn the ship around and send it back to Marseilles where it came from. That, he said, would "teach the Jews a lesson." He made an arrangement with the French to accept them, but they had made an agreement with the Haganah not to land anywhere except Palestine. They were finally transferred to other ships and hauled off to the British Zone of West Germany, right back where they started.

. . . All the remnant of Judah . . . shall know whose words shall stand.

– Jeremiah 44:28

The whole world was watching and not many in the world liked what they saw. More important, the British had previously decided to turn the whole problem of Palestine over to the new United Nations Organization and during the weeks *Exodus 1947* was going back and forth across the Mediterranean a special committee was touring the area on a fact-finding mission. It was probably one of the greatest propaganda coups of all time and did more to get more people off the fence on the issue of statehood than a dozen years of terrorism. And to get more people on the right side, novelist Leon Uris told their story in a book that sold more than 5 million copies and was made into a movie seen by millions more.

By the end of August, the UNO Committee submitted a report that called for an end to the British Mandate and a Palestine divided into a Jewish and an Arab state, with the city of Jerusalem under a special trusteeship to safeguard the holy places.

There were differences of opinion among the Committee members about how all that could be accomplished and how long it would take. But it didn't seem to matter much. The Arabs rejected both sides of the opinion. On the other hand, everyone, including the British, agreed that the Mandate wasn't a very good idea and ought to be ended. The Arabs and the Jews agreed on one thing, too: they were going to have a fight on their hands.

But before the war began, they all agreed to talk about it. Though the debate took place in the United Nations, the most intense diplomacy took place in the United States. The American government felt it needed the goodwill of the Arabs as a buffer against

In the arid Negev Desert *these pages and overleaf* are to be found such wonders as King Solomon's Pillars *left* and the umbrella-shaped acacia tree.

33

Russian expansion. Oil under the Arab territory made it even more important. But during the war years, the Zionists had gained a great deal of influence in the United States and there was strong public opinion to establish a Jewish State. Beyond that, there were strong humanitarian considerations, and Harry Truman had been one of the earliest and loudest supporters of letting the Displaced Persons into Palestine. He was a man on a tightrope, but he was also a man who didn't mind making tough decisions. He supported the partition plan, and even the Russians agreed to it.

But like so many things that affected the history of the Jews in Palestine, the plan was just another piece of paper. The British dragged their feet in making it work, even to the point of working against it. The Arabs decided it was time to start fighting and launched a campaign against the Jews that amounted to all-out war. The United Nations debated sending an army to put a stop to the fighting, but couldn't do it

The seemingly-inhospitable desert regions of Israel are a familiar home to many Arab families as well as to their livestock.

from that moment on they were an independent country and that country's name would be Israel.

Another piece of paper? Not very likely this time. Within hours of the Israeli announcement, President Truman announced through his chief United Nations delegate that America would recognize the new country, the third Jewish commonwealth in the history of mankind, the world's newest democracy.

Of course, it's one thing to call yourself a country; being ready to fight for it is quite another. But these people were used to that. They'd already been at war for more than six months. The Arabs had fired the first shot at a Jewish bus back in December and then went on a general strike to gear for more fighting. Sudden death and ambush were a way of life on both sides, but that had been a civil war. Now that they had become a nation, it was clear they would have to go to war with other nations. A lot of them.

The Haganah had been scouring Europe and America for weapons and machinery left over from World War II, but the British blockade had been as effective against guns as it had been against people. If they were going to war they knew they'd better get busy. And if they were going to get weapons, they needed money in huge doses and fast.

He asked for water and she gave him milk; She brought forth butter in a lordly dish.

– Judges 5:25

That massive job fell to a little slip of a woman who had gone to Palestine from Russia by way (of all

without Russian troops, an idea the United States opposed. The United States didn't have the resources to send its own army, and once again the Jews were left to fight for themselves.

In the midst of it all, the British decided to go home.

It was clear that partition wasn't going to work, so President Truman made another decision. Palestine, he said, should come under a special United Nations trusteeship.

What that meant, as far as both Jews and Arabs were concerned, was that it was time to forget about political answers. What really mattered, they said to themselves, was who won the war. The Jews won the first battle.

While the UNO debated, they went on the offensive and managed to take by force of arms just about all the territory the piece of paper had said they ought to have. Then, on May 14, 1948, they told the world that

Two views of the shoreline and coast around
the Dead Sea are shown *right,* the barrenness
of the area providing a complete contrast to the
fields of barley ready for harvest near Afula
overleaf.

The ibex *above* was pictured at the Hai Bar Wildlife
Reserve, north of Eilat.

places!) of Milwaukee, Wisconsin, in 1921. She went
straight to a kibbutz and lived there for several years,
rising to some prominence among her associates as
well as people from neighboring kibbutzim. Years later,
she said it was probably because she and her husband
had brought a phonograph and some records with
them to Palestine, a rare luxury in 1921.

When the Jewish leaders were tossed into prison in
the '40s, she replaced one of them as acting head of the
Political Department of the Jewish Agency in
Jerusalem. The job put her in constant contact with the
British authorities, who, more than likely, found her
tougher to deal with than all the men put together.

Her name, when she arrived in Palestine, was
Golda Meyerson. She became much better known
under the Hebrew name, Golda Meir.

During the early phases of the civil war, she was dis-
patched to the United States by David Ben-Gurion to
raise badly-needed defense funds. Later he described
what she accomplished by saying: ". . . some day it will
be said that there was a Jewish woman who got the
money which made the state possible."

Her audiences must have thought Ben-Gurion had
sent a girl to do a man's job. But when they listened to

her, they knew that "the rock of Israel" understood
perfectly well what he was doing. For Americans, she
explained the Jewish experience in Palestine better
than anyone could have done.

. . . Let the oppressed go free . . . and break every yoke.
– Isaiah 58:6

Once the Jewish National Home had been
established, there were no more restrictions on how
many Jews could go there to live. But by 1948, the
kinds of potential immigrants had changed dramatically. Hitler had done his best to wipe out the
Ashkenazi Jews and of those who had survived, a huge
percentage was trapped behind the Iron Curtain. Some
who had originally migrated to the United States
trickled in, but in the main the new arrivals were
coming for the first time from Muslim countries.

Over the years, the Zionist message didn't reach
many Jews in Middle Eastern countries. Their local
leaders had tried hard to keep cool in the face of Jewish
immigration into Palestine. They had to live among
Arabs and didn't want any suggestion that there was
any link between them and Palestinian Jewry.

But toward the end of 1948 everything changed.
They began arriving from Yemen, from North
Africa, from Turkey and Iraq, some 170,000-strong.
They had sold everything they had and moved on
foot, often under cover of night, hundreds of miles
toward Israel. The early arrivals settled in old Arab
towns, which they converted into cooperatives. But it
wasn't long before there were no Arab towns left, and
still they kept coming.

The answer to the problem was to create a new
form of settlement they called a *ma'abara.* It was
nothing more or less than a city of tents and makeshift
barracks, usually put in a place where there were roads
to be built or where other work could be found. People
lived there rent-free, but had to work for any other
necessities. A modification of the idea, work villages
called *kfar avoda,* were established in areas where help
was needed in establishing farms or reclaiming the
land. As it turned out, the Oriental Jews, particularly
people who had migrated from Yemen, preferred the
rural life.

What brought them in such huge numbers was the
fact that there was a war going on. Once the State of
Israel was proclaimed, its first order of business was to
establish control over the territory the United Nations
had already agreed they should have. Previously the
enemy had been the Mufti of Jerusalem; now it was

A field of unripened barley reaches
toward Mount Tabor *left,* east of Nazareth,
a view from the top of which is
shown *overleaf.*

the Arab League, an organization of five countries who
had marshalled a "Liberation Army."

When they couldn't beat the Israelis on the battlefield, they took out their frustrations on the Jews back
home. The only solution was for those Jews to join
their brothers in the new country.

At first, the war went rather well for the Arab side.
In most parts of Palestine, Jews and Arabs had settled
close to each other. Even Tel Aviv itself was a stones'-
throw from Jaffa, a completely Arab city. Both shared
the same lines of communication with the outside
world. It was the same all over the territory, and it
wasn't hard for the Arabs to isolate villages and to
terrorize travelers.

In the spring of 1948, the Arabs had already isolated
all of the Negev, most of Galilee and Jerusalem, and
planned to cut off the Jezreel Valley and Haifa as well.
But by then, the Haganah had a good plan of its own.
They not only pushed the Arab army back, but
launched a counter-offensive that opened the road to
Jerusalem long enough to move in supplies before the
Arabs could cut it off again.

In the process, Jewish forces took control of dozens
of Arab towns and villages, including Haifa, the
important gateway to the Mediterranean.

Up to that point, they had only claimed what the
United Nations had agreed they should have. Then the
Irgun moved in to attack Jaffa, then Acre. And as the
British moved out, they moved into Jerusalem to
isolate the Arabs there.

That was when the real war began. Five different
Arab armies moved in on them. Fortunately, they were
so different they actually seemed to be working against
each other. Just as fortunately, the Israeli forces were
solidly united against them under David Ben-Gurion,
who had been preparing for this moment for years.
Though the five Arab countries had forty times the
population of Israel, they didn't have the same will.
And lacking that, their combined army was smaller.
They were better-equipped, though, and they hadn't
been fighting a wearying battle for six months.

By the end of the first month of the intensified war,
the Israelis had lost twelve-hundred men. But they
hadn't lost much territory. The Arabs controlled the
Old City of Jerusalem, including Mount Scopus; the
Syrians had captured high ground in the North. At that
point, the UNO general assembly called for a four-

Wildflowers bring color to the countryside of the Galilee
above right, and *center right* are olive trees in the hills near
Awarta, on the West Bank.
A field of mustard *bottom right* stands under a blue sky at
Horshat-Tal in the Golan Heights.

41

Bedouin traders offer their wares, haggle over prices or just pass the time of day at the market at Beersheba *below and left*.

week cease-fire and sent about 100 observers to see what could be done to stop the war.

During the truce period, both sides were asked not to move, train or supply any soldiers. Jewish immigration was allowed to continue into Israel, but none of the new immigrants was to be taught anything about self-defense. At about the same time, Jewish fighting units were organized together into a new Israeli army. The Irgun was allowed to keep its own office in Jerusalem while its members were absorbed into the new organization. Later, that would be recognized as a mistake.

In spite of the truce, the Irgunists arranged to welcome a shipload of trained volunteers who arrived off the coast with a big shipment of guns and ammunition. The Government ordered that the ship should be turned around. The Irgunists ordered that it should move a few miles down the coast toward Tel Aviv. When it tried to land, the army opened fire. Sixteen Irgun members were killed, the ship was run aground and burned, guns and all, to the waterline.

The public was outraged at the idea of Israelis killing their own people, but the incident drove the Irgun leaders into hiding again and gave Ben-Gurion an unopposed solid hold on the army as well as the

45

Archaeology is almost a national pastime in Israel and there are countless, fascinating historic sites. *Above* are old millstones at Capernaum, a wealthy Jewish town in the time of the Romans, and *right and overleaf* are scenes at Armageddon, a name which is, in fact, a corruption of Har Megiddo – the hills of Megiddo – where, according to the New Testament, the last battle of the world will be fought.

government. The Irgun soon formally disbanded and its leaders opted for a more conventional form of protest by forming a new political party, called Herut.

Israel was ready to fight the real enemy when war broke out again in July. Stronger and more united than before, they took the initiative and took big chunks of the lower Galilee, including the important airport at Lydda. Then the UNO asked for another truce. The Arabs were delighted.

On the Israeli side, the truce was less welcome. It's hard to stop fighting when you feel you're winning. But Ben-Gurion used the time to tighten the army's organization and to plan for the time when the truce would be ended.

In the Negev, the Egyptian army was harassing Israeli attempts to supply settlements there, and by September, the Israeli army was ready to do something about it. In their attack, they were able to take Beersheba, but before they could move any further, UNO officials reinstated the truce again.

Within days, the Arab Liberation Army broke the

truce again, this time in the north, and the Israeli counterattack secured all of the upper Galilee. In both cases, the truce was reimposed, but the Israeli army was given the right to establish military bases in the areas they had captured.

Toward the end of the year, the Israelis struck again, this time in an effort to drive the Egyptian army out of the Negev. They managed to drive them out and held them trapped in the Gaza Strip. When they moved into Egyptian Sinai, the British stepped in. The message was clear enough. If the Israelis moved into Egypt they'd have to fight the British army, too. Ben-Gurion pulled back, the British pulled out again, and the Egyptian government asked for peace.

The Israeli War for Independence, as it was called, was over.

At a cost of six thousand dead, including two thousand civilians, Israel added about 2,500 square miles to the 5,600 square miles alloted in the United Nations plan. Trans-Jordan picked up slightly less territory and officially became the state of Jordan. The Israeli territory had been home to some 700,000 Arabs, who were shuffled into Jordan, Syria, Lebanon and the Gaza Strip. Even in their wildest dream, the early pioneers hadn't dared to believe that the Jewish National Home would ever be a place where the Jewish population was in the majority.

In addition to the death figures, the Israelis suffered about 25,000 casualties in the war. The fighting itself touched just about every corner of their country, and in the process involved in one way or another every man, woman and child in Israel. They had been united as a people before, but never like this. It gave them a sense of community and a feeling for the future that few Jews had felt for 2,000 years.

. . . What is thy country? and of what people art thou?
- Jonah 1:8

They had a country of their own and had secured it with their own strength. By the beginning of 1949, they were ready to get on with it.

An old Hebrew maxim had said, "All roads lead to Zion," and by now people from all over the world were traveling those roads. They came from Lapland and China, from India and Java, from Mexico, the United States and Eastern Europe. And for the first time, they were willing to assimilate. For the first time, they had something worth assimilating into.

They are a hodge-podge of nationalities and sects, but they are all children of Israel and their children are

a whole new breed. The older generation is often conservative and tied to the past, but the younger is brash and dynamic with an eye on the future. They call the native-born Israelis *Sabras,* from an Arabic word meaning prickly pear. The early pioneers gave their children the name affectionately. When they first arrived, it was the most common local fruit, but it took a little experience and a lot of patience to enjoy it. The outside is covered with tough spines that irritate you for days if you have the misfortune to bite into one. But the inside is tender and sweet and more than worth the effort.

"Our children are like that," they said. "Tough outside, sweet inside and almost impossible to handle." It's a good description of them even today. They're taller, thinner, more relaxed than their parents, but they feel the same tradition that brought their parents here. This wonderful country is theirs and it pleases them to share it with newcomers who came here to escape persecution. But they're very much aware of an important difference between them. Sabras were born free, and though they're willing to fight to stay that way, persecution is alien to them. Which, of course, is why their parents came here in the first place.

Though native-born Israelis represent the future, and it shows in their faces and their attitudes, the past is very much a part of life in Israel. A tall and deeply-tanned Sabra couple create a strange picture when they meet a Hasidic boy with a pale face and long corkscrew curls, who may be buying sunflower seeds from an immigrant from Eastern Europe who is sitting on the sidewalk cross-legged like an old world tailor.

The old world is passing, though. About half the population of Israel is native-born and most of them are young. The average immigrant is much older. The young Sabras don't identify at all with the recent past of the Diaspora, but regard themselves as descendants of the heroes of ancient Palestine.

One of the most dramatic examples of that is the oath taken by the cadets who graduate each year from the Israeli military academy: "Masada shall not fall again!"

Masada is one of the most spectacular sights in all Israel, a huge, flat-topped mountain rising 1,700 feet above the plain stretching from the shore of the Dead Sea. The top of the mountain is about a half-mile across and has been the site of a fort since the second century. It was a perfect place for one! The only way up was a narrow, winding path; and if an enemy was sure-footed enough to get to the top, he'd have to figure out how to get over the 18-foot wall built around the edge. He'd also have to figure out how to slip past one of the 37 sentries watching from 75-foot limestone towers.

Adjoining Jerusalem's Jaffa Gate is the Citadel *below and right,* also known as David's Tower, which was once the fortress guarding the palace of Herod the Great.

Having done all that, there was another fortress inside, three stories high with 90-foot towers at each corner. It wasn't possible to starve them out, either. The top of the mesa was rich farmland and the fortress was equipped with giant cisterns fed by aqueducts from a nearby waterhole. There were weapons and supplies enough for an army of 10,000. Nobody in his right mind would waste the time trying to bring it down.

Nobody, that is, but the Roman army.

When Jerusalem fell to the Romans in A.D. 70, about 1,000 Jewish patriots, including women and children, escaped to Masada with the Roman Tenth Legion on their heels. The Zealots, as they were called, made it to the mountaintop in time, and the Romans made camp at the base.

The first assault was on the western side where the Roman General, Flavius Silva, ordered his men to build a platform on a projection known as White Cliff. He added another platform to it that got within 150 feet of the top. On top of that, with typical Roman determination, he had his men build a 75-foot-square stone pier which became a base for a 90-foot siege tower equipped with catapults and a battering ram. After all that work, the battering ram didn't make more than a small opening in the wall, and behind it they found a second wall more solid than the first. The space between was filled with loose dirt that got packed in harder when the Roman machines went to work.

But Flavius Silva had a backup plan. The walls were made of wood, so he simply set fire to them and then went back down to the plain to get a good night's sleep.

In the morning, the fortress was still burning and the Romans mounted their final attack. It had taken

them three years to get to this point and they were ready for a good fight. But instead, as Josephus Flavius recorded in his "Wars of the Jews," The Romans ". . . were met with a terrible solitude on every side as well as perfect silence." Two old women and five frightened children who had been hiding in a culvert explained what had happened.

When the walls caught fire, the Zealots were gathered together and reminded of their resolve never to be servants to the Romans nor to anyone else but God. They were asked to burn everything within the fortress except their big supply of food, which would be a testament to the fact they were not starved out, but chose death to slavery. Death was their choice, and ten of them were chosen as executioners. Their job was to kill the 957 survivors, then hold another lottery to kill each other until only one was left to become a suicide.

The act shocked and impressed the Romans who Josephus said ". . . could only wonder at the courage of

their resolution and their immoral concept of death when they went through such an action as that was."

After the Romans went away, almost no one ever went up to the top of the mountain again. Arab camel caravans crossing the desert hugged close to it to take advantage of the shade it provided, but they didn't usually look up. Occasionally young and hardy adventurers climbed up the Snake Path on the eastern side, but when they got to the top, breathless and sweaty, the ruins there didn't mean much to them even though the Masada story was well-known to anyone at all interested in Jewish tradition.

It took an Israeli soldier to show the world what the others had missed.

The Chief of Staff of the Israeli Army during the War of Independence was a 30-year-old archaeologist named Yigael Yadin. Like many Israelis, he was forced to divide his time between his chosen field and the military. Yadin's field was Jewish military history, but

faced with the realities of modern Jewish military affairs in the 1940's, it took him more than ten years to finish the first four years of his education. But his education was important to Israel during the war because as a trained archaeologist he knew more about the Negev than any modern map-maker. More than once he confounded the enemy with knowledge of old roads buried under the sand or ambush points his ancestors had used to turn the tide in their favor.

When the war was over, he attacked Masada.

With the financial help of the *London Observer*, Yadin recruited more than 5,000 volunteers who paid their own expenses to make the trip to Israel from some 28 different countries. They worked for two winters during 1963 and '64 sifting through the debris and clearing 97 per cent of the top of the mountain. Yadin estimated that without the massive army of diggers, most of whom were as passionate about the project as he was, the job would have taken 25 years and probably would have cost too much to take on in the first place.

What they found there is priceless by any standard.

They moved 150,000 cubic yards of dirt, sifting most of it five times, and uncovered enough relics to fill a museum at the Youth Hostel that was built at the base of the mountain. Among them were over 2,000 coins, including the only original silver shekels found in an excavation up until that time.

Inside Herod's private villa, they made a grisly discovery that proved the Masada story was more than just a legend. The skeletons of a man, a woman and a young boy lay intertwined on the floor. The woman's braided hair was still attached to the skull and her sandals were neatly placed not far away. Excavation is still going on, but only about 20 skeletons have been found. Dr. Yadin is sure some of the Zealots must have left notes before dying and is eagerly searching for them.

Meanwhile, they have found arrows and armor, pottery and the remains of food still edible. They've found lamps and jewelry, even a prayer shawl. Some of the buildings have since been restored, and they're easier to get to than they've ever been thanks to a cable car that's been thoughtfully installed. Among the things that make the trip worthwhile are the living

A few miles outside Bethlehem are the so-called Solomon's pools *above left,* considered by most authorities, however, to actually date from the Roman period.

Monuments to the past are to be found everywhere: *left* is an Arad altar in the Israel Museum in Jerusalem, and *overleaf top right* are ancient tombstones on the Mount of Olives.

53

The palm tree carving *above,* and the Star of David *previous page below right* are part of the remains of the synagogue *previous page left* at Capernaum.

quarters that include a Roman bath converted by the Zealots into a *mikve,* the traditional ritual bath.

The palace itself had hot and cold running water and floors covered with mosaics that are easily the oldest remaining in the Holy Land. And not far from it, overlooking the remains of the Roman camp, the oldest synagogue in Israel.

Such knowledge is too wonderful for me . . .
Psalms 139:6

Possibly the most important discovery at Masada was the fragments of scrolls that were buried in the rubble in A.D. 73. They were duplicates of scrolls discovered on the shore of the Dead Sea a few years before by some Arab shepherds who had stumbled into a cave at Khirbet Qumran. The Masada scrolls confirmed their age and probably their authenticity.

Ironically, Dr. Yadin's father, Dr. Elazar Lippe

Sukenik, was the man responsible for the fact that the Dead Sea Scrolls are now one of Israel's great national treasures, housed in the unusual Shrine of the Book at the Israeli Museum in Jerusalem.

Getting them was far from easy.

In 1947, on the same day the UNO decided to partition Palestine, Dr. Sukenik got word that an Armenian black market dealer in the Arab quarter had some interesting old manuscripts for sale. When he found the dealer, he was told he had to go deeper into Arab territory, all the way to Bethlehem, if he wanted to take a look at them. Naturally he did want a look, so he disguised himself as an Arab and hopped on a bus. In Bethlehem he bought three of the Scrolls, wrapped them in newspaper and took a bus back home, fortunately unchallenged.

That night he discovered he had bought documents at least 2,000 years old. One was the Book of Isaiah, easily the oldest Biblical manuscript ever discovered. On the theory that the cave at Qumran must have been used as a store room by a synagogue following the ancient law that holy writing can never be destroyed, he was convinced that there must be more such scrolls where these came from. So Dr. Sukenik did some detective work. It didn't take him long to discover that his theory was right. The Bedouins had sold five more to the Metropolitan of the Syrian Monastery of Saint Mark in Jerusalem.

He managed to borrow them and confirmed they were both authentic and valuable, but his country was at war and he couldn't raise the price the Metropolitan was asking. He died before he could.

In 1954, his son was on a lecture tour in the United States where he happened to pick up a copy of the Wall Street Journal. Someone had told him he'd find something interesting in the classified columns, and he did. It was listed under "miscellaneous:"

"Biblical manuscripts dating back to at least 200 B.C. are for sale. This would be an ideal gift to an educational or religious institution by an individual or group."

The Metropolitan had tried to authenticate and then to sell the Scrolls several times, but most scholars had dismissed them as recent copies that were virtually worthless. His Wall Street Journal ad was a final gesture to recover his original investment.

Yadin knew they were far from worthless and began negotiating to buy them. But the price was stiff: $250,000. It took him more than a month to put the deal together and to find a benefactor in the person of Samuel Gottesman, a paper manufacturer, whose family built the shrine that houses them.

Before running his classified ad in New York, The

The poignant scenes *on these pages* were taken at Judaism's holiest shrine, the Western Wall of Solomon's Temple – often referred to as the Wailing Wall – where pleas and prayers are sometimes pushed into the spaces between the ancient stones *overleaf*.

Metropolitan had announced to the Arab world that he had some old manuscripts he was sure would bring at least a million dollars once he found someone in America rich enough to buy them. It turned hundreds of Arabs into archaeologists overnight. Suddenly it was much more fun to poke around Dead Sea caves than to ambush Israeli buses, and Mohammed the Wolf, the boy who had found the original cache of Scrolls, became something of a local hero.

Finally, in 1952, the search became organized under the control of the Archaeological Museum, who paid the Arabs for their discoveries and set up a program that guaranteed the manuscripts wouldn't be scattered and in the process lost again to the world.

In the years since, about 800 Scrolls including all the books of the Old Testament, except for Esther, have been found. Other writings include commentary on many of the books and a Greek translation by Saint Jerome that long ago became the Douay version of the Bible, the one used by the Roman Catholic Church. They also shed light on the people who wrote them, the Essenes, who thought of themselves as "the children of light" charged with the responsibility of keeping the true faith pure until the Day of Days when all mankind would be judged. They were sure that day was at hand and they would easily be judged purest of all men. In many ways, they were more like the early Christians than the Jews who had preceded them.

They were the direct opposite of the people who died at Masada, who were often referred to as "Dagger Men," and were known to be terrorists. The Essenes were ardent pacifists, and yet there is evidence that in the end they joined the revolt against the Romans and that some of them were among those who gave their lives for freedom at Masada. In any event, both groups are inexorably tied together now and they give us a link not only to the old Jewish civilization, but to the early Christians as well.

The past is everywhere in Israel and archaeology is a national passion. Even among Israelis who aren't religious, the Bible is more than the country's treasure, it's the country's most reliable guidebook. You feel it in all parts of the country, but nowhere like you do in Jerusalem.

I have surely built thee an house to dwell in;
A settled place for thee to abide in forever.

– 1 Kings 8:13

It seems as though Jerusalem must have been here forever. But forever is a long time. Actually it was established as a city by the Canaanites some 5,000 years ago, and though it was their capital for 2,000 of those years, it wasn't much more than a small hill town until King David conquered it in the name of Israel.

The Canaanites were probably the most civilized people on earth up until that time. The Babylonians had developed a written language, but these people developed an alphabet that made it work. Then as now, the location of their city put them in close, often violent contact with powerful neighbors. The Canaanites absorbed the best parts of the civilizations around them and usually added their own improvements.

Their name comes from their word for the color purple. Their main export was a purple dye they extracted from shellfish which all the great kings of the world used to dye their robes as a sign of authority and wealth. Hundreds of years later when the Greeks marched in to see what they could take, they took the Canaanite alphabet and changed the name of their new land to fit their own word for purple . . . *phoenecia.*

But David knew them as Canaanites, and to him they were the enemy. In conquering their city, he set Jerusalem on its course toward becoming the most important city in the world. It became established as the earthly home of the great God Jehovah, the place where ideas of justice and ethics were spelled out. It was the place where the Hebrew nation flowered, where Christianity developed, where Islam saw some of its finest hours.

The Jews were the first people in history to take their God with them wherever they went. Primitive tribes before them worshipped local Gods wherever they were. Sometimes it would be the one who controlled a waterfall or caused earthquakes, but if they moved away from that territory they had to look for a new God to worship just as surely as they had to look for a new waterhole.

As the Jews wandered from place to place, their God wandered with them. When David marched into Jerusalem, their God had come home at last.

They had wandered for hundreds of years with their God. Always at the fringes of the desert, always homeless, they were known everywhere they went as *Habiru,* "outsiders." Their God had given a set of basic rules they should live by to their patriarch, Moses, on Mount Sinai. For generations, those laws went with them everywhere they went and when they arrived in Jerusalem, David had them placed at the top of the highest hill, Zion. It became from that moment on the heart of the nation.

In his lifetime David built a powerful nation and united the tribes of Palestine under his own rule. He also fathered several sons, and naturally as he grew older there was a scramble among them to become his successor. According to legend, he himself chose the son of his favorite wife, Bathsheba. The future king's name was Solomon, and the choice was one of the best things that could have happened to Jerusalem.

Less warlike than his father, Solomon developed trade with other countries and before long many of the people of Jerusalem were quite rich, indeed. They built elaborate houses furnished with riches beyond their fathers' wildest dreams. And while they were doing that, Solomon was at work building the most fabulous temple the world had ever seen.

The Temple itself is long gone, of course. After it was destroyed, a second temple was built, then eventually a third, known as Herod's Temple. David's tabernacle had been a nomad's tent, Solomon's was designed to look like a tent. It was built of stone and cedar wood with the inside divided into two chambers. The smaller of the chambers was called the Holy of Holies and contained the Ark of Jehovah, the larger, called the Holy Place, was the residence of Jehovah on earth.

The site of the First and Second Temples is traditionally believed to be the same rock on which Abraham attempted to sacrifice his son, Isaac. It is also, after Mecca and Medina, one of the Islamic world's most sacred spots. It was from this rock that Mohammed stepped up into Paradise.

When the Romans were in charge, they built a

temple to Jupiter on the rock. In the seventh century, it was replaced by a mosque, which in turn was converted to a Christian church by Crusaders in the 12th century. After the Moslems took over again, it was rebuilt as a mosque which stands there today, showing the splendor of years of embellishment.

The Dome of the Rock, as it's known, is one of Jerusalem's most dazzling buildings. The dome itself is glittering, gold-plated aluminum, complemented by the slightly smaller silver dome of El-Aqsa Mosque next door. The 30-acre site is known in the Islamic world as *Haram es-Sharif,* the Noble Enclosure.

The inside of the dome glistens with intricate, beautiful mosaics and the floors are covered with exquisite oriental rugs. The columns that support the roof originally held up the roofs of Byzantine churches, and no two are exactly alike. Two of them are placed uncomfortably close together, and tradition has it they were set that way to describe the width of the gates of Heaven. If you can fit between them, they say, you'll have no problem getting into heaven itself.

The focal point is the Rock itself, and indeed, if you look closely you may see a footprint there marking the spot where Mohammed had his last contact with the earthly world.

65

Below and below left: the remains of the Roman amphitheater at Beit Shean, the Greek Scythopolis, one of the great cities of the past.

Under the Rock, a grotto called the Well of Souls is the place where it's believed both David and Jesus went to pray. It gets its name from the tale that the dead gather there twice a week to offer their prayers to God.

As one of Islam's Holy places, the Noble Enclosure is off-limits to archaeologists, so it isn't likely that anyone any time soon will find any traces of Solomon's Temple that might be buried under the dust and rubble of centuries.

But all around it there are traces of digging and sifting that has been going on without stop since the late 1960's. And the payoff has been the uncovering of traces of the city through just about every phase of its history, including a fragment of a wall that some experts believe may have been part of the fortification built in Solomon's time.

Real interest in digging down to find the past began in 1838 when an American scholar, Dr. Edward Robinson, made a map of what he concluded to be the roots of the city. Ever since, other scholars have been trying to prove him either right or wrong (mostly he was right), and the work is being systematically carried on today by the Hebrew University and the Department of Antiquities.

One of the early "digs," Charles Warren's efforts to find the base of the walls Herod built around Temple Mount, is still remembered as one of the most difficult,

Below: a partially restored column and
statue at Caesarea, the ancient capital of the
Roman province of Judea.

as well as one of the most productive.

There was so much debris piled around the walls, he was forced to dig shafts well out from them and then when he figured the shafts were deep enough, he cut tunnels to get at the bottom of the wall. When he got there, he found traces of what may well have been one of Jerusalem's Golden Ages of architecture.

After Solomon died and his son Rehoboam became king, ten of the tribes of Israel announced that they had had enough of supporting an expensive court and were tired of working for the glory of the one tribe that didn't have to work at all, Judah. Judah didn't quite have to go it alone. Another tribe, Benjamin, stayed with them and Jerusalem became their capital.

They had their ups and downs over the next several centuries, but mostly the trend was down, and it reached a low point in 586 B.C. when the Babylonians marched in and burned the place down.

Except in the hearts of the Jews, Jerusalem didn't exist for a generation after that. Then the Persians conquered the Babylonians and told the Jews to go ahead and rebuild their Holy City. They were enthusiastic enough, but it took five more generations of them to repair the walls, build a new Temple and get Israel united again.

They had no sooner done it when Alexander the Great swept through. He generally left them alone, but made sure to leave them with a good impression of who was boss. He brought Greek culture with him and some new ideas to Jerusalem. The Jewish and Greek cultures mixed for about 200 years, but nothing the Greeks did ever succeeded in homogenizing them. Quite simply, the Jews believed they were God's people and even though the Greeks seemed to have some good ideas, nothing was as good as that.

Palestine was under control of the Syrian King, himself under control of the Greeks, when things finally came to a head.

Roman legions had been attempting to carve up the Greek empire for themselves and by the time Epiphanes became King of the Syrians . . . and gave himself the name meaning "God manifest" . . . he found his kingdom less grand than it had been in past years. His answer to that was more taxes, basically to fend off the Roman eagle but also to make his country a little more Greek.

He chose Jerusalem as one of the model cities of the movement. Among other things, he took over the Temple and made it into a Greek sanctuary. When the people grumbled, he built a fortress across the road to keep them in line. It was like a bully drawing a line in the dust and challenging others to cross it. When it began to look like someone might, he passed a law that Judaism would be a crime punishable by death.

In response to that, and just as much in protest over the hated "graven images" – statues of the Greek gods and goddesses he erected in Jerusalem, many people simply left town. One of the places they went to was a little town called Modin. Their intention was to keep their religion alive in the wilderness. After all, their ancestors had done it. And if the Temple was destroyed, what of it? The Holy of Holies was what was important, and it didn't really matter where it was.

It mattered to Epiphanes. He sent soldiers to Modin with orders to force the high priest Mattathias to offer incense to the Greek god Zeus. Naturally, Mattathias, who was one of the group called *Hasidim,* "the Godly," refused. When another Jew came forward and lit the incense, the old priest fell on him with a knife and killed him. Then he killed the Greek captain and escaped with his five sons in the confusion.

They went into exile in the wilderness. But not for long.

It didn't take long for others to join them, nor for the Greek troops to find out where they were hiding. Once having found them the Greeks decided to hold off their attack until the Sabbath. They knew that Jews would never fight back on that day and so their fight would be easy. It was.

They killed a great many, who died rather than

break God's law, but they didn't kill the idea that it was
time to start fighting back.

The Hasidim decided that this was no ordinary
fight, but a battle to reclaim God's Temple. It was a war
between Jehovah and Zeus and they would surely be
forgiven for taking part in it, even on the Sabbath.

It was a long war that touched every part of the
country. Everywhere they went, the Hasidim destroyed
Greek temples and sculpture and everywhere they
gathered new recruits.

When Mattathias was killed, his son Judah became
the leader of the movement. He quickly earned the
nickname *Maccabaeus,* "the hammer," as he set out to
cut off Jerusalem and to retake it. By the time he
reached the Holy City, his army had grown to some ten
thousand. They had been fighting for three years at that
point and only the strongest and most devoted had
survived. In their march from the North they had
inspired the people with the idea that Israel could be a
nation again.

The Maccabean army had the city surrounded
when word reached Jerusalem that Epipahes had been
killed in a chariot accident on his way down from
Armenia to put down the Jewish revolt. His viceroy
decided to save his own army for any trouble that
might be forthcoming from the opportunistic Romans
and called a truce with Judas Maccabaeus.

In it, he allowed the Jews to reclaim their Temple
and to move back to Jerusalem where they would be
watched over, but not harassed, by Greek troops. Once
again Temple Mount was the focal point of the Jewish
nation.

When they marched in, they found the place
overgrown with weeds and littered with the charred
remains of parts of their Temple that had been burned.
Most demoralizing of all was the image of Zeus on the
sacred altar. It took them three weeks to clean the place
up. But if it was hard work, it was joyous, and the
greatest joy of all was restoring the purified Temple to
worship. . . . An event remembered each year in the
eight-day celebration of Hanukah.

For the next 90 years the Jews flourished on
Temple Mount while the Greek sympathizers watched
them from the fortress at Acra. The Jews, meanwhile,
were busily building fortresses of their own. Ironically,
after so many of them had fought so hard to free
themselves of Greek influence, their best work in
decorating their buildings and walls freely used Greek
columns and friezes.

And in their commercial life, they were forced to
lean more and more towards Rome. They expanded
their borders and their influence and they quarreled
among themselves over whether the wealthy, foreign-

The River Jordan and the Jordan Valley are pictured *on these pages,* while *overleaf* is shown Nazareth, in the Galilee.

influenced Saducees or the religious Pharisees ought to rule their country. The civil war it created ended when the Romans interfered and Pompey's legions breached the walls in 63 B.C.

It wasn't long before they installed their own rule in Jerusalem and responsibility for it eventually passed to the hands of a man loyal to them, King Herod.

The people didn't like Herod much, but even his worst enemies had to admit that he understood the Jewish people as well as what was going on in the outside world. Jews just shook their heads in disbelief when the Romans made him their king. If Herod wanted to rule them, he'd have to fight for the right, they said.

He spent several years taking control of the countryside, then, when all the Maccabees had fled to Jerusalem he took advantage of their bottled-up situation and took the city. He was smart enough to bribe the Roman soldiers so they wouldn't destroy much of importance, particularly the Temple. Then when the battle was over, he set about rebuilding Jerusalem into something even better than Solomon had created.

The buildings he built, which were in the Roman style except for the important difference that their facades didn't include representations of human figures, would be the pride of the Roman Empire. More important, Jerusalem was once again on the path to becoming one of the world's great cities.

The jewel of his construction binge was to be a replacement of the Temple. The Second Temple, which he had spent so much in bribe money to save, had clearly seen better days by then. And what better way to earn gratitude and respect?

To do it right, he had old records dredged up to get as much detail as he could on what Solomon's Temple had looked like. Then he hired artisans to design him one that was similar, but more opulent. When he made the dramatic announcement that the project was about to begin, he stood back waiting for the cheering to begin and the flowers to be tossed at his feet. But there was no cheering. No flowers, either. "You can't do it," they said. "Only priests are allowed to do sacred work like that and very few of our priests are also stone-masons."

So before he could begin the work, he had to turn the priests into construction workers. It took 10 years to train a thousand of them, and then nearly two more for them (along with 9,000 others who functioned as hod-carriers and did other heavy work) to get the great building finished. But when it was finished, there was a lot of cheering, a lot of flowers and some goodwill (but not much, mind you) for Herod who, after all that

In a restful garden setting, just outside Jerusalem's Damascus Gate, is the Garden Tomb *above,* which has a strong following holding that this, rather than the Holy Sepulcher, is the more likely tomb of Jesus.

trouble must have been having some second thoughts about the business of being king. The building was the most magnificent any of them had ever seen. Of course, some of the older folks said it wasn't as good as the First Temple. But they really didn't know. It had vanished more than 600 years before they were born.

Herod's Temple has not completely vanished even yet. In A.D. 70, during the same bloody war that saw the siege of Masada as well as the beginning of the Diaspora, the Romans virtually destroyed Jerusalem and took great pains to gut the Temple. They even went so far as to plow the ashes into the ground as if in fear that some miracle would cause the Temple to rise again, like the phoenix, from them.

But they didn't, or possibly couldn't, do anything about the massive walls Herod had built around the Temple. It's those walls, towers and gates today's archaeologists find so fascinating.

One of those walls has been a source of fascination and reverence for Jews the world over for generations. All over Jerusalem today there are signs that say simply, "To The Wall." There are plenty of walls in the Old City, but no one is likely to ask "which wall?" The

The Dead Sea Scrolls, discovered in a cave at Qumran *below,* are now housed in the magnificent Shrine of the Book *left and bottom.*

Two of Islam's most important holy places are the El Aqsa Mosque *below* and the "Jewel Box of Islam" – the Dome of the Rock – *previous page and right*.

Jews know it as *Kotel Ha'maaravi*. In English we call it the Western Wall. It's also known as the "Wailing Wall" because it once was the focal point of Jewish pilgrims who went there to see the last visible sign of the greatness of old Jerusalem and to shed tears over the Temple's destruction and the dispersal of their people. Other tourists noticed drops of water on the big old stones and assumed it was from the tears. Actually the dampness is more easily explained as early morning dew caused by the sun on the cold stone, but an explanation like that is no fun at all when you're showing your slides to your neighbors.

But if they didn't wash the stones with their tears, the pilgrims did a good job of keeping the stones polished smooth with loving caresses.

In the early years of the State of Israel, the Wall was off-limits to Jews. It was a time when tears were shed in private, when no little slips of paper offering special prayers for special people were slipped into the chinks in the rock, when it was impossible even to catch a glimpse of the wall from the western side of the city. Then Moshe Dayan led his troops into the Old City in 1967. It had been an Arab quarter until then. Ramshackle buildings had been built right up to the Wall and, worse, the area was a massive tangle of barbed wire laced everywhere with minefields.

Dayan ordered the area cleared. His men were enthusiastic about the project. "Give us two weeks and you won't recognize the place," they said. "I'll give you two days," he said.

They did the job, evicting Arabs and bulldozing houses, digging up the minefields and cutting through the barbed wire. In much less time than they ever dreamed it would take, they cleared a plaza big enough to accommodate thousands replacing a dark old alley only a few would dare venture into. For big festivals like Passover and Succoth crowds as big as 30,000 converge on this outdoor synagogue without too much need for elbowing each other.

On those days prayer is the main attraction with the women on the right-hand side of the Wall, the men on the left. But on an ordinary day, the big plaza has another function, too. It's a place for protest meetings on such subjects as the rights of Soviet Jewry or settlements on the West Bank. It's a place for singing and dancing, a place to look at Israel's future as much as it ever was a place to look at the past glories of the Jewish people.

But there are past glories all around that part of Jerusalem and the diggers are finding more and more of it almost every day.

The Temple Mount in Jerusalem, as built up and filled-in by Herod's builders was probably the biggest such holy place in the ancient world. The walls that enclosed it were built right on bedrock using stones that weigh as much as 100 tons. Which may be one very good reason why the Romans didn't bother to tear them down.

After the '67 war, Israeli workers exposed about 175 feet of the Western Wall that had long been buried. The scholars say there is another 60 feet or more of the original wall going beneath the surface and that only the first few courses above ground were laid in Herod's time. They also found the remains of a monumental stairway leading down into the valley below and the first arch of what was probably a massive bridge crossing the valley to reach the higher ground to the west.

They also cleared away the rubble from the Southern Wall and found much more of the original work, some of it rising as high as 140 feet. The wall includes three gates which were served by a paved street and a broad plaza. The rubble they cleared included pottery, coins and glassware from the first century. They also found evidence of the Roman camp that was built there during the days of occupation.

Temple Mount isn't the only place where Herod left his mark. His palace was in the Upper City not far

Surf-pounded old fortifications at Acre *right,* an important town and seaport since early Biblical times, are contrasted with the solitude of Castle Nimrod *overleaf,* a Crusader castle on Mount Hermon's slopes in the Golan Heights.

from the Jaffa Gate and its solid walls are in some ways more impressive than the ones that enclosed and supported the Temple. Today the Palace walls support the Jerusalem Citadel, which is topped by one of the city's most famous structures, the Tower of David. The tower is supposed to have been built by King David, but the lower portion was built by Herod as one of three massive towers to protect the north side of his palace. The later addition is most likely medieval, but nobody knows for sure who built it.

The Crusaders appropriated the Citadel for themselves and it has generally been used as a fort right up until the day the Jordanian Army gave it back to the Israelis. They, in turn, have turned it into a museum as well as the setting for an impressive sound and light show.

The Jaffa Gate is among the biggest of all the gates leading into the Old City because it was the gate that led to and from Jaffa, Jerusalem's nearest seaport. It had to be wide to accommodate the traffic it attracted, but back in the Gay '90s, the German Kaiser had it enlarged so he and his entourage could make an impressive entrance into the city.

He could have used the Damascus Gate. It's bigger and not far away. It was once the beginning of the road to Damascus, a very important trade route. Even today the old customs seem to still live in the shops and stalls around it and in the marketplace that stretches out from it.

Most of the gates in the two-mile wall were built in the 16th century. There are eight of them. But one, possibly the most beautiful of all, has been closed since before that time. It was closed by Moslems who believed that it was a good way to keep the Jewish Messiah out of Jerusalem.

The closing of the gate to the Messiah was at least an indication to the Jews that the Moslems believed some of the things they had been teaching. They were sure of it when the Moslems established a cemetery inside the gate. It was a sort of insurance in case the Messiah was able to get the gate open. Another of the Jewish teachings is that a priest is forbidden to walk through a cemetery.

Both believe that one day the resurrection of souls will begin near this spot, and that's why one of the oldest Jewish cemeteries in the world is there on the Mount of Olives. It's been there for more than 2,000 years waiting for the Messiah to come. Those small stones on the grave markers date back to an even earlier time when the resting places of the dead were most often in the desert and small stones were the only way to mark them.

Many of the graves in this particular cemetery have

Very little imagination is required to conjure up mental pictures of Crusader knights manning the fortifications of Castle Nimrod *left* and Belvoir *below right,* the best preserved Crusader castle in Israel.

even less to mark them than that. Some years ago, the Jordanians built a road through it and in the process bulldozed the gravestones out of their way. They turned up in "civic improvements" all over Jerusalem. Many of the stones have been recovered and put back, though many have not. But the road has been covered over and peace has come back to the Mount of Olives. It is as it was: one of the most beautiful, inspiring views in the entire world.

It's no wonder they say the Messiah will first appear on earth on this hillside.

There are many in the world who say the Messiah has already been seen on the slopes of the Mount of Olives. According to Christian tradition, this is where Christ ascended into heaven.

There are 12,000 Christians in Jerusalem, representing some 30 different denominations. The Christian religion began here and this is where its dramatic beginnings are commemorated by sacred shrines, churches, chapels and monasteries. As it is to the Jews and to the Moslems, Jerusalem is to the Christians, the most sacred spot on earth.

The biggest Christian body also happens to be the oldest. The Church of Jerusalem, run by the Brotherhood of the Holy Sepulcher, traces its roots back to the second century. It's allied with the Greek Orthodox Church, which is in keeping with the tradition of its founders, who were also Greek-speaking. Like nearly all of the Christians in Israel now, most of its members communicate with each other in Arabic.

One of the churches they run is the fourth century Church of the Holy Sepulcher, site of the 10th to 14th Stations of the Cross. It is possibly the holiest of all the Christian Holy Shrines. It was here that the robe was taken away from Jesus, where He was nailed to the Cross, where He died, where He was buried and then resurrected.

The hill the church was built around is called Golgotha, after the Hebrew word for "skull." The Christian tradition calls it Calvary, from a Latin word with the same meaning. The name doesn't come from the fact that it was a place of death, but rather because in early times it looked more like a skull than a hill. The early Hebrews believed that was a sign to them that Adam's skull was buried under it. That theory has yet to be proved.

There are tombs inside the church, including the empty tomb of Christ and the final resting place of Joseph of Arimathea. There are also elaborate memorials to Christ's final moments and one to St. Helena, who is said to have found the True Cross here after following God's directions to the spot.

The church is shared by a half-dozen different sects, each of which has its own chapels. Only the Protestant religions aren't represented. But first among equals is the Brotherhood, which controls the central portion of the church as well as half the hill. They also control the Church of the Nativity in Bethlehem on the site of the stable where Jesus was born.

As if to make sure the church wouldn't be used as a stable, its sixth-century builders made the door unusually low. There was no way a pilgrim could get through it on horseback or even without bowing his head. Christ's birthplace is in a grotto under the main altar, and the spot is marked by a star set into the floor. An inscription in Latin identifies it as the place where Jesus Christ was born, but there's another inscription not far away marking the place His mother laid him in a manger.

The reason for having two Holy Shrines so close

Crowds throng the Church of the Holy Sepulcher *these pages* during the Greek Orthodox Ceremony of Holy Fire.

together is the vast distance between the Christian sects. The birthplace itself is the property of the Greek Orthodox Church and long ago they decided to make it off-limits to Roman Catholics. They let them burn incense there, but that was as far as they could go. So the Roman Church built a chapel of its own in order to have an altar to use to commemorate the birth of their Savior. It was a compromise worthy of Solomon himself, but it didn't completely settle the question. It wasn't unusual for priests to resort to physical violence to assert their rights of worship.

The peace was finally established when the efficient British Army took charge in Palestine and ordered the clerics to establish a time schedule that gave them all a chance to honor the Prince of Peace without fighting over it. The schedule is still in effect and there hasn't been a good fight in the church in years.

The Brotherhood of the Holy Sepulcher has less of a problem at their Church of the Assumption, which they share with the Armenian Church. Other sects have memorials there, even the Moslems. But they all know their place. This is one of the most unusual churches in the world because it's a full 40 feet underground. Perhaps not so unusual, however, when you consider it was built to contain the tomb of the Virgin Mary who was buried here at the foot of the Mount of Olives by the Apostles.

There are Christian churches everywhere you go in Jerusalem, and Arab mosques. There are synagogues, too, of course, and a tourist hopping from one to the

Her black robes relieved by colorful decoration, an Arab woman is pictured *left* in Beersheba market.

South-west of Bethlehem, the moon rises at sunset behind the mosque on Mount Herodion *below.*

other has to remember a few rules. You never visit a mosque with your shoes on. If you're a man, you shouldn't enter a church with your hat on. On the other hand, women need to cover their heads in Christian churches and there are places they can't go at all in the synagogues. And men must remember never to enter a synagogue without covering their heads. If you should happen to forget any of the rules, there are plenty of people on hand who will remind you.

Though the government of Israel has passed laws respecting the holy places of other religions and the Israeli people generally respect them, many Jews don't mind telling you that the Christians have a Holy City in Rome and the Moslems in Mecca, but Jerusalem is all they have. And the attachment is almost fanatical. Under Jewish law if a man or a woman wants to live in Jerusalem and their spouse refuses to move, it's a legal reason for divorce.

Before the 1967 war, it was a city divided. Most of the places sacred to the Jews were in the Arab Quarter and the only way a Jewish pilgrim got to see them was by looking across from a hilltop or studying an elaborate scale model that had carefully been built.

After the war, the Arab neighborhoods were put under the jurisdiction of the Jerusalem City Government. It didn't take long for Arabs and Jews to mingle, and for each to discover that the others weren't such bad people after all. The Jews found bargains in the Arab markets, the Arabs found it profitable to go into Jewish neighborhoods with things to sell, or simply to find a better job.

The result is a cosmopolitan city that's an odd combination of East and West. In the winding streets of the Old City, the Orient is very much alive and well. People ride on donkeys, small boys offer to guide you around the city for a large price. The shoppers, the soldiers, the monks, the tourists add a bustle that makes New York seem quiet as a church. The atmosphere is from another time and another place, but there's a constant reminder of the present in the form of Border Guards, well-armed and watchful.

The 20th century is outside the center of the city where Israelis are building new neighborhoods and

rebuilding old with a passion not even matched by the efforts of Herod the Great.

Building is going on in the Arab sections, too, but they build in a haphazard fashion, throwing up a house here, a house there. The only real planning seems to be in leaving enough room for aunts, uncles and cousins to move in later. The Jews are much better organized than that.

They concentrate on whole neighborhoods at a time. First they add water and sewage facilities, then electricity. Then they connect the services with clusters of houses. One of the better neighborhoods is Yemin Moshe, not far from Mount Zion, southwest of the Old City. It's a quiet place, almost suburban by American standards, and it's home to artists and writers and

Many and varied are the Christian sects that come together to follow the Way of the Cross in Jerusalem on Good Friday each year, *these pages*.

especially to musicians. People who live there will tell you it's the nicest place in town to bring up kids and that it has quite the finest view of any neighborhood in all Israel. But then, you hear comments like that in most of the communities that surround Jerusalem's Old City.

They have a charming synagogue in Yemin Moshe and the people there support it, but almost no one there considers religion the centerpiece of his life. There are some other parts of town where the story is a whole lot different. In the Northwest corner of the city, Ramot is one of those places.

Ramot has been settled mainly by Hasidim, the most orthodox of the Orthodox Jews. Their big fur hats and severe black coats make them look like they just stepped out of 19th-century Europe. Their houses, on the other hand, look like something out of a nightmare about the 21st century. Like most of the new Jerusalem, they were built quickly over the foundations of bulldozed Arab neighborhoods. They march in even rows of sameness with aluminum and glass-enclosed balconies looking across dirt plazas at more of the same.

But aesthetics aren't too important to these people. Religion is what their life is all about, and they appear outdoors with great regularity taking part in demonstrations calculated to bring the rest of Israeli society into line with the old laws. Their most often-repeated demonstration is to line up at the roadside on the Sabbath to throw rocks at passing cars to wake the drivers up to the fact that this is the day no one is supposed to work and that includes driving automobiles. No one has bothered to ask any of them why driving a car is work but bending down to pick up heavy stones and pitching them into the street is not.

Though communities like Remot don't add a whole lot to the view, the view from them is still terrific. But it seems like only a matter of time before some of those views are going to be blocked by high-rise urban sprawl. There are some who will say it's already happened, but there are others who will point out that most of the new buildings are low structures and many of them add touches of color to relieve the eye from the monotony of the stones of the Old City, which are always the same color as the earth beneath them.

But no one calls the Old City colorless. And everyone agrees it will never lose its character. It will never lose the grafitti that dates back to Roman times, nor the Arab marketplaces they call souks. Its streets will probably always be as much home to bearded beggars, turbaned Arabs and Hasidim in long black coats as it is to the super-energetic Sabras who bustle through them as though they owned the place. Its streets will always welcome immigrants from Russia, from Yemen, from Ethiopia. They will provide a place to stroll and watch beautiful women from Morocco or from Sweden, from South America or from South Africa. There's a variety of different kinds of people in Jerusalem that gives it a beauty all its own. It's as much a worldly city as any of the world's capitals, but there's something about Jerusalem that's different from all of them; different from all the other cities of Israel, for that matter. Call it heavenly if you will. Others have been doing just that for centuries.

Some trust in chariots . . .

– Psalms 20:7

There's a bus station not far from the Jaffa Gate that is the end of the line for buses from just about everywhere in Israel. In fact, it's been said that you can tell where the changing boundaries of the country are

at any given moment by taking a look at where the buses will take you. Wherever they take you, getting there is more than half the fun when you take an Israeli bus.

The bus line, Egged, is one of the country's great institutions. It would be a great institution in any country.

Egged is a giant in a small country. With more than 6,500 vehicles, it's one of the biggest bus companies anywhere in the world. It seems sometimes to have more owners than any giant on the New York Stock Exchange, and that's not just because they take such an active interest in the company. They are the company.

When a young man or woman gets a job with Egged,

they work for several years for a small salary and for a chance to apply for membership in the company. Membership allows them to become an owner of the cooperative by buying shares. Shares may only be owned by employees of the company and the employees hold elections every two years to replace the management from within the ranks. It's very likely that an ordinary bus driver or mechanic could wake up some morning as managing director of one of the biggest transportation giants in the world.

Back some 50 years ago, when the cooperative was first formed, one share in the company was equivalent to the price of a new bus. But in those days buses were smaller, and so was the price of one. Today the cost of a share of Egged is more likely to be equal to a quarter

interest in a bus, which is why there are more owners than vehicles today. The cost is high as well, and so not every employee is a member of the cooperative. But as a casual rider, you'd never know whether the driver of your bus owns it or not. They all act like they do.

The Egged bus drivers are a special breed, not at all like the people who move people around in other places. Usually they're very highly-educated and almost all of them speak several languages fluently. They're a lot like old-fashioned cab drivers, well equipped to talk on just about any subject, sometimes even when you don't feel like talking. But nobody ever doesn't feel like talking when they're a passenger on an Egged bus. Everybody has an opinion and this is one of the places they get it off their chest.

Take, for instance, the time an elderly woman held everyone up for a moment while she painfully made her way aboard the bus. Realizing no one was too pleased, she explained that her legs were stiff and she couldn't bend them as easily as she once did. One of the passengers said heat was the only thing to help that. He had picked up a similar affliction when he was in the army, he said, and that's how he relieves his misery. "No, no," said a woman in the back of the bus. "Heat is the worst thing you can do. It dries out the juices in your joints." The best thing, she concluded, was to add more juice to your system and orange juice was the best kind. It gives you vitamin C.

"And it's good for Israel's economy," added the bus driver, blowing his horn at a passing donkey.

Another woman, who had been on the edge of her seat waiting for a chance to add her opinion, finally added it by saying, "A chiropracter you should see. Then you'll have no more pain."

"I know just the man!" shouted another. "Go and see Dr. Bagelmacher. He's wonderful. Not too expensive and his office is just up the hill there."

"I go to him myself," said a younger woman. "Such hands that man has! He just touches you and the pain goes away!"

"That's against the Holy Law," shouted a young rabbinical student leaping to his feet. "You must never go to such a person no matter how much pain you feel!"

But no one seemed to be listening to him. The doctor's patients were swapping stories among themselves.

"He comes from a long line of bagel-makers in Europe. He was one himself before he came here. That's where he got so much strength in his hands," said one.

A soft and peaceful glow fills
the beautiful Church of All Nations
at Gethsemane *right*.

"What he has in his hands is skill," said the other. "A regular gift from God! It's a blessing to have him here!"

The conversation could easily have gone on for hours more. But while they were talking, the bus came to an abrupt stop. There are Egged signs everywhere you go in Israel to mark the places where the buses are supposed to stop, but there wasn't one in this place. There wasn't even a town. The nearest town was in sight down the road, near enough to walk to, which is what everyone on the bus knew they were going to have to do.

The Egged is like that.

To the average Israeli, the National Bus Company is a convenience that makes the country smaller. To a tourist in Israel it's an ideal way to get close to the people. Most foreigners who have experienced it find their fellow-travelers more than willing to talk about themselves, but much less than willing to open a conversation.

The atmosphere in the buses takes a bit of getting used to. They're usually packed with people who often smell a little in the heat of a summer day. In winter the smell is usually just as bad thanks to clothing made damp by the winter rains. Sometimes the smell is from spicy food a passenger or two may be eating. But it doesn't take long to adjust to all that. Regular passengers hardly seem to notice it at all.

If you're tired or not feeling well, all the pained looks in the world aren't going to get another passenger to offer you a seat. Once in a while a pregnant woman or someone very old might get lucky, but chances are good that the offer of a seat will come from a tourist and not a native. About the best they'll do is to offer help to women with small babies. They'll offer to hold the child on their lap.

The Egged drivers are as much a part of Israel as Kosher food. They're thoroughly professional, and know exactly how to weave in and out of traffic without scratching the bus or dumping a passenger from his seat. It's one of the advantages of having owner-drivers.

But there's another kind of driver in the Israeli public transportation business. They're just as fascinating, but quite different. They drive the sherut taxis that take people between the cities and their suburbs and sometimes from city to city if there are enough people who want to go.

The word sherut means "service," and they've been providing reliable service since back in the days when there weren't too many cars in Israel. Most of the sheruts are American cars with the inside altered to hold more passengers, but some are more comfortable minibuses.

The drivers almost never own the cabs, but they split their profits with the people who do. That's probably why they seem so profit-oriented when they zip through traffic at the fastest possible speed.

Unlike the bus drivers, almost none of them are college educated. But all of them are graduates of the Israeli school of hard knocks, one of the toughest of its kind anywhere in the world. Most of them will tell you that they were once tank drivers in the army, and even those who weren't have told the story so often they believe it themselves. When you see how they drive, you don't doubt it for a minute.

Passengers are generally squeezed in, and it's a tight squeeze except for the one who's lucky enough to share the front seat with the driver. The cars have been modified to hold six across in the back seat. Compared to a sherut, a 747 jet is a private coach. (It even seems slower sometimes!)

For short distances, the squeezing is tolerable. But for the hour-long trip from Jerusalem to Tel Aviv, it's an unforgettable experience. And no sherut driver will even think of making the trip without a full load.

But like the bus drivers, they love to talk. They talk about inflation and taxes, how to cure the country's economic problems. The other passengers are just like the people on the buses. Start a conversation and they won't let it end, and in the process strangers become close friends. How could it be otherwise in the back seat of a sherut?!

. . . Thine health shall spring forth speedily.

– Isaiah 58:8

A great way to sample the fun of a sherut is to find one headed for Jericho. If you're lucky enough to get the front seat, and it's not so late in the day that the setting sun gets in your eyes, you'll see what might be the prettiest 15 miles in the country.

Jerusalem is more than 2,750 feet above sea level and Jericho is more than 800 feet below. The ride between the two is, therefore, mostly downhill and the hills are as rich in tradition as they are in beauty. The first hill is the Mount of Olives, the first drop the Kidron Valley. You'll pass the spot where so many passed and rejected the man who was finally saved by the Good Samaritan. You'll see an old monastery perched on the edge of a rocky cliff, and if the driver slows down, you'll see caves in the cliff wall where the monks go for a little peace and quiet and possibly some prayer. A little further on is a mosque which the

A field of wild flowers on the banks of the Sea of Galilee, at Ein Geir *above* seems a fitting contrast to the eloquent Hall of Remembrance *left,* a memorial to the millions of Jews who perished in the European Holocaust.

Moslems say is on the spot where Moses was buried.

The Bible says that Joshua put a curse on Jericho after he knocked down its walls with the sound of his ram's horns. But that hasn't stopped anyone from building there. The Jews themselves rebuilt it at one point in ancient times, in fact. But Alexander's followers, and then the Romans, built it again a little bit further west.

The latest buildings around the mound that was ancient Jericho are the crude brick structures that proliferate all over the country. Until the '67 war, the houses were home to more than 25,000 Palestinian Arabs, but they moved on into Jordan ahead of the Israeli army, and it seems today as though Joshua's curse may have had some teeth after all.

As far back as Roman times, Jericho has been a resort city and not far from it is the spectacular Hisham Palace, once the winter palace of the Caliph of Damascus, said to be a direct descendant of Mohammad.

It's one of several West Bank historic sites captured by the Israelis that's been incorporated into the National Parks system. The mosaics, well preserved in the dry heat, are among the best examples of Islamic art in the country.

There's a much newer mosaic floor in the sixth-century synagogue at Jericho. The inscription on it is in Aramaic rather than Hebrew, but some helpful person has tacked a translation to the wall for modern visitors. Some other helpful persons have penciled in their own criticism of the scholarship of the translation . . . a tradition among Jews that may be older than the floor itself.

It wasn't far from here that John the Baptist baptized Jesus in the waters of the Jordan River. But for the moment you'll have to take someone else's word for what the spot looks like. It's off-limits because it's so near the barbed-wire border. On the other side of town, though, it is possible to climb the high Mount of Temptation, where Saint Matthew tells us Jesus fasted for 40 days and 40 nights while resisting the temptation of Satan himself.

Possibly the least tempting spot on earth also happens to be the lowest. It's the Dead Sea Basin, some thousand feet below sea level and made to seem even deeper by the mountains that rise like something from another planet some 3,500 feet above it. But it's a very popular tourist attraction.

The hole is so deep that the pressure of the atmosphere is heavier and people with heart conditions are usually told to stay on higher ground. But some ignore the warning and find it's a lot easier to breathe once they get down there because the pressure condenses the air and increases its oxygen content.

To most of the people who come back to the Dead Sea year after year, that's a side benefit they hardly notice. What lures people here isn't even the sun, which gives you a glorious tan and almost never burns because it's filtered through that enriched air. The lure, of course, is the water itself. If you listen to any of the regulars, one of them sooner or later will tell you that Dead Sea water has magic powers.

The sea, or more accurately, lake, is fed by the Jordan River, but it has no outlet. The air around it is extremely dry, so it loses more water through evaporation than any ocean in the world. The result is that it's saltier than any of them, ten times saltier by actual measure. The evaporation causes a mist that's carried to the shore on a light breeze, and devotees say that chemicals in the mist soothe their nerves.

No wonder they spend more than $50 a day to be there!

Even if the water doesn't cure what you've got,

swimming in it is an odd experience, to say the least. It's impossible to sink. It isn't even easy to stand up in it because your body tends to float in a prone position. You could possibly go to sleep in it and not drown, but no one recommends it.

Ask anyone there why they're there and you'll probably find they do it every year and they'll probably recommend that you should do the same.

"Ten years ago, I couldn't get my arm over my head like this," one might tell you. "I used to have arthritis. Terrible pain all the time. The best doctors, they could do nothing for me. But after my first visit here . . . look!"

Another will tell you the sun and salt water eliminated "the heartbreak of psoriasis." It's been credited with doing away with the pain of slipped discs, pinched nerves and backaches. They say it helps mend broken bones, even slows the ageing process. And that's just the sun and the water.

The Dead Sea "treatment" includes more than that!

The mud, which is slightly radioactive, is said to relieve rheumatic pain, nerve disorders and some forms of paralysis. It apparently makes you more beautiful, too. At least Cleopatra thought so. She used to send slaves up to gather the mud for her, and it was said she never let her supply run low.

The Arabs sent their wives there to take a swim and thus become able to have more children. They may have been inspired by the Biblical story of Sarah who, after 90 years of barrenness, gave Abraham a son, Isaac. The event took place after she traveled to the Dead Sea to commiserate with her nephew, Lot, whose wife had recently been turned into a pillar of salt.

Yes, Sodom, and Gomorrah, too, were once in this part of the world. The town of Sodom today is home to a state-owned plant that processes the chemicals that are so abundant in the Dead Sea. More than 1,000 Israelis work there, and they're very happy as long as they can actually live in the hills above it. But when the plant was built, nobody wanted to go there. The government had to parole convicts to get enough workers to make the move.

Though much of the countryside is hostile and still seems to be scarred from the rain of fire and brimstone that destroyed Sodom and Gomorrah, one of the most beautiful natural sites in all Israel is on the Dead Sea shore at Ein Gedi.

There's a kibbutz there now, complete with a modern gas station, but the place has changed hardly at all since King Saul chased young David here and lost him in a cave. Waterfalls still cascade over the rocks and splash into deep cool pools where mountain goats and ibex come to have a drink. Wildflowers and luxurious green trees add an odd, but very welcome

touch to the desert outside.

But the kibbutzniks have added farms to the landscape producing everything from vegetables to cotton and even flowers to brighten the homes of city-dwellers. They've also added a hospitable touch to the sea shore – fresh water showers. Among the strange things that seem to happen to you when you swim in the Dead Sea, one of the strangest is that you come out of the water feeling sticky from all that salt. Fifty years ago promoters probably told bathers that the salt kept mosquitoes away, but it's nice not to have to stay sticky long if you can avoid it.

There's a modern highway stretching from the Dead Sea into the Sinai Peninsula and down to Eilat. It's one of the world's great engineering feats. It begins at more than a thousand feet below sea level and in less than 40 miles goes up to almost 1,500 feet above sea level, and there's hardly a gentle climb anywhere along the way. It took Israeli army engineers more than two years to build that first stretch, a man-made ridge that runs along the sides of cliffs, climbs steep hills in serpentines and runs along the tops of mountains that only mountain goats ought to be running along.

It was back-breaking work with the sun beating down without mercy and the constant danger of hit and

The colorful and happy scenes *on these pages* shows the domestic side of life on Degania kibbutz, the "Mother of the Collective Villages", which was started in 1909.

run attacks by Arabs out on mischief-making sorties from Jordan. Water had to be brought to them across the desert in tank trucks and except for other truckers bringing them supplies, it was their only contact with civilization for weeks at a time. But they moved mountains to connect the Negev with the civilized world.

Or is it the other way around?

The pastures are clothed with flocks;
The valleys also are covered with corn.

– Psalms 65:13

The Negev was one of the first places in the world to be touched by civilization. When the Jews marched through it to conquer the Canaanites they had to fend off attacks from people already established in the desert, much in the same way their 20th-century descendants had to do.

In the early 1960s, scientists from the Hebrew University found an Israelite settlement in the Negev they're sure was thriving in the 7th century B.C. And other discoveries in the area uncovered traces of huge numbers of people living there as far back as 600 years before that, in the era known as the Iron Age.

But for long centuries, the place was deserted. Even the Arab caravans preferred to go around the Negev. And who could blame them? On a breezy summer day, the temperature goes up as high as 115 degrees. When there's no breeze, it's even hotter. At night it gets almost cold enough to freeze water. Except there isn't any water to freeze. It rains sometimes, but the sun is so hot it evaporates the water before it can get to the ground. No wonder the prophet Jeremiah called it "a land wherein no man dwelleth, nor doth any son of man pass thereby." Who would want to?

Israeli pioneers, that's who!

Back in 1938, a band of pioneers established a kibbutz north of there above the Dead Sea. They called it Beth Ha'arava. They were proud of the fact that it was the lowest town on the face of the earth, but that was about all anyone could say about it. The countryside was flat and the soil was an odd blue-gray color. What water there was, was brackish and the plants they tried to grow withered and died.

They supported themselves by working in a potash factory, and in their spare time experimented with a little garden. They started by building a retaining wall around a plot of ground and they kept it filled with fresh water carried overland from the Jordan River. Every night on the way home from work in the factory, each worker carried his share of water to be dumped into the garden. Overnight the water soaked into the ground and after several months it soaked away the salt in the soil.

When they felt the salinity had been reduced enough, they started adding nitrates to replace the chloride and in a matter of weeks were ready to fill the plot with tomato plants.

The soil hadn't supported plant growth at any time in recorded history, so it was rich in nutrients. The tomatoes, tended with loving care, were possibly the healthiest plants anywhere in creation. And the pioneers of Beth Ha'arava were the happiest farmers.

Their quarter acre garden began growing by leaps and bounds now that they knew how to reclaim the desert and within ten years of its founding, the kibbutz had a 30-acre farm with one of the greatest yields per

Agriculture plays an extremely important part in the economy of Israel and thanks to massive irrigation projects the inhospitable desert has been made to bloom again and bear an abundance of crops.

In pensive mood a small Arab
girl *right* sits on a step in
Jerusalem's Old City.

acre in the world. They planted trees as well as vegetables, but, more important, they planted hope in the minds of other Jewish settlers that the desert could indeed be made to bloom if you gave it enough hard work and imagination.

Beth Ha'arava had to be abandoned when the Arab Legion swept through in 1947 and it was eventually returned to the desert it had been. But even the Arabs couldn't destroy the memory of the place. It still lives, and it has been duplicated in dozens of places all over the country.

Until the 1950s immigrants to Israel much preferred to settle along the coast rather than facing the hostile desert. To spread them out a bit, the government began establishing new towns in the Negev that were envisioned as suppliers of the smaller settlements around them. In that way, they hoped, they could make life more attractive in the desert areas and at the same time provide more places for more people to live. The new towns have office buildings and warehouses, stores and factories. They refine sugar, mill cotton, process peanuts and put together complicated electronic equipment.

But not all the "new towns" are all that new. The biggest of them, Beersheba, is the place Abraham considered his home base during his days of wanderings through the desert. It's where God spoke to Jacob to reassure him that He would be with them when the Hebrews migrated into Egypt and that He would one day lead them back home again.

Neither Abraham nor Jacob would recognize the place today. It's been transformed from a desert watering hole into a city that boasts it will be home to 250,000 in the next decade or so; a city that's passionate about being modern and up-to-date; a city that calls itself the "Cinderella City of the Negev."

When the State of Israel was established the city was still not much more than a sleepy little town in the desert. It's been growing outward ever since, following what the city fathers call a plan. The plan calls for buildings suited to the environment, punctuated by parks and surrounded by a greenbelt. Unfortunately, much of the growth took place in the '50s and '60s when designers of buildings thought drab was another word for dramatic. But the immigrants who came to live in them expressed their own individuality with touches of paint and stucco to give some relief from the sea of sameness.

One of the men assigned to the job of planning new towns for the Negev has called Beersheba "a museum of planning errors." The original plan came to Israel from England in the form of the idea that every man was entitled to his own green plot and a house set on a winding country lane a respectable distance from his nearest neighbor.

It was a great idea back in England. So are umbrella factories. Where green plots were planned in Beersheba, desert sand filled the open spaces. Getting lawns established was too tough even for the Israelis, and every man's "green plot" is much more likely to be brown and disheartening.

Yet, to many of the people who live there it's a good city. One woman who migrated to Israel from Poland was sent to Beersheba to live and decided when she first saw the place that she would never stay long. That was 20 years ago. Now she feels she and the city have grown up together and nothing would make her want to move again.

On the other hand, a young Israeli soldier from Tel Aviv, just passing through, had an impression of the "Cinderella City" that makes it apparent he doesn't want to move either.

"It's a frightful dump," he reported. "I have a 48-hour furlough from my unit and spending the time in Beersheba is the last thing I want. It's much too staid.

"You can go to the swimming pool or watch television . . . and, oh, yes, I forgot. You can have your picture taken with the bored camel that they keep outside the Desert Inn Hotel for the tourists. And you can go with the tourists to the Bedouin market early in the morning on Thursday and buy some copper ornaments."

His problem probably was that he didn't bother looking beyond the landscape to find the people who make the city work. They've come here from all over the world, from Africa and Asia, from Russia, and from the surrounding desert itself. Thousands of Bedouin have decided to stop their wandering and settle down in their own community a few miles out of town. Some of their relatives still prefer to wander, and once a week they file into Beersheba at sunrise, their camels and goats loaded down with bargains to be offered for sale in the marketplace. Their ancestors traded sheep and goats here, now they deal in used cars and heavy trucks.

And what brings all these diverse people together and unifies them? Education is one of the things. Beersheba is the home of David Ben-Gurion University, an institution established to advance settlement. Most of its students, and the faculty, too, are new immigrants interested in natural sciences and engineering. It also supports other schools that teach Hebrew, an effort many consider more important than anything else to help new arrivals assimilate into the Israeli culture.

Most of the new arrivals these days are from the

Monuments of war: a burnt-out enemy tank *below,*
south of Beersheba, and *below right,* also south
of Beersheba, the monument to the Six Day War.

Soviet Union, and that's entirely appropriate. People have been migrating here from Russia since the early 1940s when a hopeful band arrived to establish the first pioneer settlement in the Negev at a God-forsaken spot called Gevulot. They had bought the right to settle on 150 acres of dust and rocks, and though they knew the place would be inhospitable, nothing could have prepared them for what they found there.

There was no water on their tract, but fortunately there was an oasis not far away and the Arabs who lived around it were willing to share its water, for a price, until they could dig their own well. They dug several before they finally hit water that was fit to drink, and the time it took ran up quite a huge bill with the water-sellers down the road.

It put a big dent in their financial resources, but each of them had two hands and willing backs and while the well-digging was going on, they built a comfortable, but crude, blockhouse and watchtower and they lived in reasonable security behind a fence they built around their little tent city and the fields that extended out from it.

What they had in mind was farming. In the desert.

They had done their homework, and they knew that when winter came so would the rain. When it did, they would be ready for it with three huge reservoirs they built over the summer. They would also be ready with plowed fields and the seeds of their first crop already planted.

When it rained, it rained hard for several days.

away, and that was a pitiful collection itself.

They found their answer in the Bible. Their forefathers had recorded that pomegranate and figs, acacia and carob grew in the area two thousand years ago, so they took a chance and planted those along with other trees mentioned in the Scriptures. Trees don't grow overnight, of course, but before long they had natural windscreens that also shaded them from the hot sun and protected their crops. Before too long, they were even growing watermelons.

By experimentation with crop rotation they were able to outproduce many of the farms in the North, which any experienced farmer would have said was impossible.

But then, anybody who had experienced the spirit of those pioneers of the '40s would have known better. To them, nothing was impossible.

On the other hand, if they had been able to look 40 years into the future, they might not have believed what has become of some of the towns they started. There are more than 225 kibbutzim in Israel today, and though some of them are very much like the originals, a great many could easily be small towns in the American Midwest. The biggest and possibly most affluent of all of them is Kibbutz Afikim in the Jordan Valley.

Most of the homes there are air-conditioned, an amenity the old pioneers never even dreamed of. It has a community swimming pool, too, and another pool just for divers. Its herd of cows, kept contented with piped-in music, is milked twice a day by electric milking machines. There are huge ponds just outside town where carp are fattened to make gefilte fish, and the commune has a zoo where camels and monkeys are fattened for the amusement of the children who live there.

Their plywood factory, their dairy, their fish farm and the irrigation system that keeps their fields green are all controlled from a computer center that also keeps track of the profits that are divided among the members of the community as well as handling the payroll of the Arab laborers who help free them from drudgery.

It also keeps tracks of the stock in the supermarket that would be the pride of Peoria. It's more department store than food store, dispensing everything from furniture to fine wine.

A few years ago Afikim's members voted to allow their children to sleep in the homes of their parents and that started a boom in remodeling their houses to add extra rooms. They didn't have to add dining rooms, though, because most of the residents still gather at the community dining hall at mealtimes. Most of the

Some of them jokingly said their next construction project ought to be the building of an ark. The reservoirs were filled to overflowing and by spring little plants began appearing in the fields.

But it only rains in the winter in the Negev. Nature spends the rest of the year re-establishing the desert. In the spring the winds came and with the wind, dust and more dryness. The little plants never had a chance. If this corner of the desert was ever going to be reclaimed, something had to be done about that wind. The answer was trees, but their original research hadn't covered that. They had been studying to be farmers, not foresters. It didn't help to look around them to find out what sort of trees would survive in a place like this. The nearest trees were at the waterhole four miles

All young Israelis are subject to a
period of active military service,
and rigorous training ensures the
country's capability to defend itself
at all times.

homes, however, have tiny kitchens and the women of Afikim are discovering the joy of cooking, with the result that the dining hall is less crowded at dinner time than it once was.

The dining hall of any kibbutz is also its social center. Afikim is no exception, but their bomb shelter, which doubles as an art gallery, is almost as popular. On a typical Friday evening, women in long dresses, fresh from an afternoon in the beauty parlor, add a nice touch of loveliness to the place and put to rest the popular image of kibbutzniks with dirty faces, dressed in sandals and shorts.

Not everyone agrees that this is what kibbutz life ought to be like, and some of the younger people have left home for the challenge of a less comfortable life. On the other hand, the life is attractive to many immigrants, and Afikim boasts a population drawn from 36 different countries as diverse as India and Argentina.

Some of the old-timers miss the days when their kibbutz was a big happy family and complain that you can't socialize with a thousand people at once. But others are more philosophical. The community's unofficial historian, who has lived in Israel for 50 years, summed it up for them in an interview in The New York Times:

"When we came here we had Utopian ideas. We thought we could live in a small intimate circle. Today I know this can't go on. Now I prefer the large community with all the possibilities it gives one. When we started we had other demands. We ennobled physical labor.

"If we weren't successful economically, we'd have to say our way had failed. Life changes, but not the principles, and though some leave, others come.

"Growing materialism has its perils. There is a price. . . . But I consciously accept the change."

Change has always been the operative word for settlement in Israel. The painstakingly established communities in the Negev were in the thick of the battle during the 1948 War for Independence and many were wiped out as the Arab Legion and the Israeli Army marched across them. But the war had its good effects, too. Many of the young men and women from Tel Aviv and Haifa saw the Negev for the first time during the fighting, and as they fought they became obsessed with the idea that the future of their country was here. After the war was over, thousands went south to be part of that future.

When they came back they found the war wasn't quite over. The Egyptians had retreated to the Gaza Strip and had taken hordes of vengeful refugees with them. They appeared to be quiet, but the situation was tense, and the only sure way to keep things peaceful was to establish new settlements in the Negev to keep a close watch on the greenbelt along the coast.

Dozens of new communities were established and provided homes for many of the quarter of a million refugees who arrived in the first year of independence. By the early 1950s there were nearly 70 villages in an area that had supported less than 20 before the war began. Life was made easier for them by a network of new roads that connected them, and a pipeline that took precious water deeper into the desert.

The new settlers came from all over the world and even from the Israeli cities in the North. But the overwhelming majority who were establishing orchards and farms were from North Africa and other parts of the Middle East, particularly Yemen, brought to Israel in a massive airlift called "Operation Magic Carpet."

Across the border in Egyptian Gaza, more than 200,000 Palestinian Arabs were crowded into displaced persons camps strategically placed near the border so they wouldn't miss what was going on in their former homeland.

What they couldn't see for themselves was carefully reported to them. They were told that the farmers in the Negev were mostly Arabs like themselves who were working against their brothers to prevent them from ever returning. They were told that the only way they ever could return was to fight for what was rightfully theirs. To mount the fight, they were loosely organized into terrorist units called fedayeen.

They usually attacked by night, cutting electrical wires, mining roads, burning crops and setting bombs in settlers' homes. During the day when the farmers were restoring the damage, they retreated to their camps across the border under the protection of a special U.N. peace-keeping force. Since there wasn't much else to do in their camps, they used the time to plan new attacks and to train others to join them.

It's been estimated that in the first five years of the "peace" that followed the War of Independence, the Israelis sustained more than 1,300 casualties from nearly 12,000 fedayeen raids. In towns close to the border a normal fact of life was that you simply didn't go outside after dark. Every town was completely surrounded with tightly-coiled barbed wire and the windows of every house had thick steel shutters that were closed and locked before sundown each day.

But in spite of it all, new settlers kept arriving

The imposing walls of the Citadel
and its 14th-century minaret soar
into the clear blue sky *left*.

willing to take a chance. Golda Meir explained their willingness to take on such burdens by saying:

"Security represents an extreme burden for Israel, and if we have to do even more the burden will increase. Yet there is no limit to what we can take. How much pain can one bear before one dies? This nation won't die, won't commit suicide."

. . . I will promote thee unto very great honor.

– Numbers 22:17

The burden was pushed to new limits in 1956 when President Nasser of Egypt announced to the world that the Suez Canal was the sole property of the Egyptian nation and was off-limits to ships going to or from Israeli ports. The move made Nasser an enemy of both France and England, who had considered themselves the masters of Suez. The United States wasn't too pleased, either, and with the international situation tilted in a new direction, the Ben-Gurion Government decided it was time to do something about Israel's situation.

On the morning of October 29, 1956, a force of Israeli paratroopers dropped in on the Mitla Pass, within easy walking distance of the Canal.

Israel had mobilized 90,000 men from its well-trained reserve units within just three days, and all of them were in place and battle-ready before the first parachutes appeared over the Canal. Some were deployed to the Jordanian and Syrian borders just in case those countries decided to get in on the fight, but the main force was moved quickly into the Sinai.

They had been well-armed by the French, who considered the Suez Canal vital to their own interests and the Israeli Army a convenient way to secure it. The Egyptian forces in the Sinai, some of whom had been moved to the Canal area to defend it against an expected Anglo-French attack, had been equipped with Russian weapons they didn't quite understand. Nasser had been expecting an eventual Israeli attack in the Sinai, but not so soon, and training on the new equipment hadn't been done with any sense of urgency.

After the first Israeli attack, the British and French, who had forces ready to move from Cyprus, ordered both sides to stop firing and to retreat from the Canal. Israel followed the order, but Egypt did not, with the result that bombs began falling around Port Said and word reached Cairo that a joint British-French force would land there soon.

When the Egyptian troops moved south to counter the strike, the Israeli forces were right on their heels. The Egyptians hadn't really been retreating, but to any but the most-informed observer it certainly looked that way. Even the Egyptian troops themselves felt like they were being pushed off the Sinai Peninsula, and that was the psychological advantage the Israelis had counted on.

There was resistance, some of it stiff, but in less than a week the Israelis controlled the whole of the Sinai as well as the Straits of Tiran. They did it with a loss of less than 175 soldiers and proved to the world that their army was fast and well-organized. More important, they showed the world that they were resourceful and creative as well as dedicated.

The message wasn't lost on the Egyptians.

The British and French didn't press their threat to retake the Suez by force and, after the cease-fire was signed, the world turned to see what Israel would do next.

Israeli public opinion said to do nothing but stay put in the territories they had captured. But the U.S. brought pressure on Ben-Gurion to pull out and the British backed them. The Russians began making threatening noises, too, but they were having so much trouble in Hungary at the moment, nobody took them too seriously.

The Israeli Government finally agreed to pull back from the Sinai, but insisted that Egypt should also pull out of the Gaza Strip and take the fedayeen with them. They were already operating shipping through the Straits of Tiran, the gateway to Akaba, a port vital to the development of the Negev, and made that part of their price as well.

But the superpowers considered the price too high. They eventually settled for an agreement for Israeli withdrawal in exchange for a U.N. peace-keeping force in Gaza and overlooking the Straits of Tiran. It wasn't perfect, but the situation was much less tense at the border, and the basic attitude of all Israelis, particularly in the Negev, became dramatically different.

It had been a problem right from the beginning that the longer a person had been an Israeli, the less likely he was to accept newcomers as equals. The veterans of the '48 war who had moved in to tame the Negev had a mystique about them that amounted to a hard shell that most newcomers found impossible to crack. Men and women who had come here when there was nothing felt a certain resentment towards people who followed them. But now many of the people who followed were veterans themselves, and they were veterans of a new army the whole world was saying was among the best any country, even Israel herself, had ever produced.

Something new had happened to the children of Israel.

Fighting together had brought the young people of Israel closer together, and the personality that emerged was more self-confident, even arrogant, than any pioneer could ever have been.

The years following the Sinai campaign were relatively quiet, at least on the surface. Arab raids slowed to a trickle, the economy expanded, and for the first time, the Israeli people knew for sure that their country was going to make it.

Politically, though, it was a country in turmoil. It was a classic case of youth versus age, with the younger generation pitted against the older institutions who read the message clearly: change or die. They changed.

Ironically, the older generation was personified by David Ben-Gurion and others who had shaped the country as teenagers themselves. The battle cries of the young called for sweeping away the dreamy ideals of

In the grounds of the Hoyland Hotel, in Jerusalem, stands the excellent and informative model of the city at the time of the Second Temple *above left and right,* while *above* is shown the real city at night, with the Jaffa Gate at the far left and the Mount of Olives beyond the city.

Zionism and replacing them with ideas suited to the times. Socialism had to go, too, they shouted, and be replaced with efficiency and a system based on merit. They won their points, and the man who helped them win was the man most credited with the success against the Egyptians in the Sinai, a Sabra army officer named Moshe Dayan.

As the old ways of living began to change, the young country kept growing. Cattle ranches were beginning to appear in the Negev along with new farms and factories and, of course, new towns were added almost every week. The generation gap was felt as strongly in individual families as it was in any public

institution. Children returning from their military service as adults were bringing strong new ideas with them. They had learned to read and write, to sing and to dance. Most important, they brought back the idea that this country was theirs . . . theirs to fight and die for, but also theirs to profit by. The older generation had believed in working for a common goal, too, but their horizons had never been as broad as this!

> . . . *Gathereth together the outcasts of Israel.*
> – Psalm 147:2

But at least they all had one thing in common. They were all Jewish. But now the young people were beginning to question even that. "What is a Jew?" they asked, and young and old alike turned to the government for an answer.

It was a question the Zionists had never had to ask.

122

They had strong bonds and a common experience with the Jews of the world, and a dream of a National Home, which to them meant a nation of Jews. What they got instead was a Jewish nation with a younger generation which had grown up in a much different world.

Their roots and their ideas had come from the European ghettoes, yet many of the citizens of their country had come from the other side of the world, where experiences were different; many others had come to Israel as a place of refuge and had never given any thought to the ideas that made Zionism such an important force.

What they had in common, the government was sure, was the Holocaust. And when Israeli agents in Argentina arrested Adolph Eichmann, the former head of the Gestapo's Jewish Department, in 1960, it was decided to hold a trial under Jewish law in Jerusalem.

Eichman was found guilty and executed after a trial that turned the world's attention one more time on what the Jews had gone through 15 years before, and public opinion throughout the world came that much closer to the support of the Jewish nation.

But the people the country's leaders wanted most to impress reacted in a different way. The youth of Israel who had been personally untouched by the Holocaust weren't unimpressed by it, but it solidified another resolve: if Jews were alone in the world, as their treatment in other lands seemed to prove, they were together as Israelis, and together they would fight. But they were Israelis first, and asked their government once again: "what is a Jew?"

The Law of Return enacted by the Knesset in 1950 gave all Jews the right to immigrate as long as they didn't have a criminal record or present a danger to the public health or safety. It made citizenship automatic unless the immigrant formally refused it. A Nationality Law, passed two years later, added that anyone living there at the time of Statehood, including non-Jews, also had the right of citizenship.

They came closer to defining Jewishness in 1960 with a law that said anyone born of a Jewish mother or a convert to Judaism with no other formal religious ties was legally a Jew in Israel.

It sounds simple, but questions of religion almost never are. There are some 12,000 Israelis who came from India. They are descendants of Jews who went there in the second century and who have for generations been indistinguishable from the Hindus, even to the point of following a caste system. But for all that, they still considered themselves Jewish, keeping the Sabbath, saying prayers in Hebrew and observing many of the traditional festivals. When they got to Israel, though, no one recognized them. The average man in the street accepted them, but the rabbis were more cautious, and ordered that they were not to marry outside their own sect. In 1961 they finally admitted that the Bene Israel, as they are called, were bone fide Jews, but they added that they were still subject to special restrictions. If one of them wanted to marry outside their own community, they had to prove that neither their mother nor grandmother had married non-Jews or had ever remarried after a divorce. If records were available, rabbis were also required to dig further back into family histories to see if any of their women had been guilty of such things.

Needless to say, the Indians were furious. The situation came to a head when they poured into Jerusalem and staged a hunger strike. The issue, and all other such questions, had been decided by the Chief Rabbinate. But the Bene Israel took its case to the government, and that raised a lot of eyebrows as well as tempers. The debate that finally took place in the Knesset was one of the stormiest Israel has ever seen. When the storm settled, the Bene Israel had the right to marry anybody without having their ancestry checked. But the rule remained in force for anyone else whose heritage might be questionable.

In the days when the great-grandparents of today's Jews were thinking about getting married, the idea of being Jewish but not religious was out of the question. Any Jew who didn't observe the Holy Laws wasn't recognized as part of the fold, and was simply no longer considered Jewish. But in the 19th century a new breed appeared. They called themselves "Reformed." People who followed the laws strictly were known as "Conservatives," later to be called "Orthodox," to keep them separate in people's minds from an offshoot of the Reform movement that fell somewhere between radical and classical.

By the time the State of Israel was established, a Jew had at least four options . . . to be strictly Orthodox, Conservative or Reform or not to be committed to any of them. The religious establishment is Orthodox, but Israeli citizens still have those four options. A convert to Judaism, on the other hand, may not be recognized as Jewish in Israel unless the conversion was done by an Orthodox rabbi. Marriages and divorces aren't legal unless performed by Orthodox rules, and Reform and Conservative congregations don't get financial support from the religious councils.

Neither Reform nor Conservative Judaism is officially recognized by the State, but both exist in freedom. They've been promised official status once

Jews from all over the world come to Jerusalem to pray at the Western Wall *these pages,* where the sexes are strictly segregated *left.*

large numbers of them immigrate, but nobody's taking any bets on when that will happen.

By law, Saturday is a day of rest, but the law also provides for the rights of non-Jews to celebrate their own Sabbath. Usually the issue is handled by local option, and in some places you can ride a bus or buy a loaf of bread on a Saturday, but in some others you can't. But it isn't possible to find a train running anywhere in the country on Saturday and it isn't possible to send a telegram, nor to leave the country on an El Al jet or an Israeli ship.

But that's just one of the things that makes the country so fascinating.

New immigrants find out a lot of fascinating things about Israel at special centers that have been established all over the country to help them assimilate into the society. The centers, called ulpanim, basically teach Hebrew, but new Israeli citizens learn a lot more from them than a new language. Professional people live at an ulpan for five months, immigrants on their way to live in a kibbutz take a six-month course first.

Immigrants in more of a hurry often prefer to take advantage of an ulpan program that offers 16 hours a week of training over a four-month period. They augment that by participating in the Hebrew lessons that are given on the radio.

Either way, everybody has a chance to find out about their new world before they become a part of it. More important, they learn the language before they have to live with it, and that's an idea for helping immigrants that's unique in all the world.

But there's one group of Israeli citizens who may never be completely integrated into Israeli society. Among them are the members of some 30 Christian denominations, including Catholics, both Roman and Greek, and a substantial colony of Mennonites. Israel is important to the world's Christians as the place where their religion began, and all the Holy Sites recognized by all the Christian religions are within Israel's borders. Of the close to 100,000 Christians living in Israel, the huge majority are members of the Greek Orthodox Church, who, with the Roman Catholics, maintain most of those Holy Places. There are some Protestants, of course, but they seem to have been late bloomers in the Holy Land. Almost none were there before the 1820s, and they came mostly as missionaries looking for converts. It wasn't easy for them then, and it's impossible today because of an Israeli law that requires a five-year prison sentence of anyone who uses "material means" of gathering converts. Worse, the converts themselves face three years in jail for accepting.

There are dozens of Protestant sects loosely banded together as the United Christian Church. But in general, most of the Christians aren't banded together at all. Officially, the government recognizes three religions in Israel: Christian, Jewish and Moslem. Matters like marriage and divorce for their followers are handled by ecclesiastical courts, whose decisions are recognized as law. With so many different points of view among the Christians, it takes the talents of a Philadelphia lawyer to reach decisions everyone can agree on.

Each of the churches normally provides religious education for young people. But when for one reason or another they don't, parents can ask for, and get, religious training in government-operated schools.

The biggest minority within the Israeli society actually makes up the majority of the country's population and all of its members are Jewish.

After the creation of the State of Israel huge waves of people began arriving from Eastern countries and they didn't slow their coming until the mid-1970s.

Most of them had come from places where they had been totally isolated from other Jews. Some were so isolated they accepted as an article of faith that their community was the last remnant on earth of a once-proud race of men. They had integrated more into local societies than their cousins in the West and the only thing that distinguished them from their non-Jewish neighbors was the fact that they followed the old Jewish laws and kept their identity in spite of generations of integration.

When they began arriving in Israel, it was obvious they were different. To people from Poland and Russia, they didn't even look like Jews. Modern technology was alien to them and so was the concept of living in large cities. They were very happy to be settled in remote farm country, which the Ashkenazic Jews usually left for life in the city once the romance of the great outdoors wore thin.

The Sephardim, possibly because they live in rural areas, have a much higher birthrate than immigrants from the West. They started by scratching out a living, and many of them haven't been able to scratch fast enough to keep up with their growing families. The result is often overcrowding, poverty and worse.

In the countries they had come from, discrimination hadn't been a serious problem. They were second-class citizens, to be sure, but there were usually third- or fourth-class citizens beneath them. They were used to being called Jews by the people around them, often even scornfully. But they were never called Iraqui-Jews or Syrian-Jews in the way the Ashkenazim had been labeled German-Jews or Russian-Jews. Not until they came to Israel hoping to be called, simply, Israelis.

129

Some find the emotional experience
of a visit to the Western Wall almost
too much to bear *below and right,*
while for others a ceremony can be
a time of great rejoicing *overleaf.*

It's the kind of discrimination that hurts most. But the country had been established on Western models and discrimination was probably inevitable. The gap is closing today as programs for their benefit have expanded their skills and their outlook. A lot of the bitterness evaporates as young people from both groups meet during their required time in military service. Still more disappears when Orientals move into more comfortable neighborhoods, as more of them are doing, and send their children to the same schools as the Western immigrants. Little by little, understanding is making life pleasanter for both sides of what was once a much wider gulf.

Both Ashkenazim and Sephardim alike agree that Arabs don't have a place in the Israeli melting pot, and most Israeli Arabs agree, too. There usually isn't any open hostility between them, but every Israeli knows that the average Arab heart isn't tuned to the Jewish State, so all they ask is to live in peace together.

The Arab citizens of Israel have exactly the same rights as the Jewish citizens on paper. But mostly they live isolated in their own communities and the only jobs open to them are usually at manual labor. In the beginning, every Arab in Israel was required to carry an identity card at all times and needed special permission to move between one village and the next. In the last few years, the requirement has been softened to include only Arabs suspected of being trouble-makers. Their identity cards are especially imprinted so police can spot them quickly.

Though they are citizens of Israel they can't buy land. The Jewish National Fund, which controls most of Israel's land, is forbidden by law to sell any of it to anyone who is not Jewish. When they are able to keep some of their land in the Arab towns, they can't develop it with government money as is the case in Jewish towns.

But not every Arab in Israel is looked down upon, or considered a potential enemy. One of them has even managed to rise to ministerial level in the national government. He is a member of a secret sect the Moslems once called brothers but now call heretics. The Israelis call them what they call themselves: Druses. They've been outsiders in the Islamic world for a thousand years, ever since a group of them began accepting the idea that the Egyptian Caliph was divine. They believe that Jesus and Moses were important prophets, just as important as Mohammad, and the central figure in their religion is Moses' father-in-law, Jethro.

A large group of Druses migrated into the upper Galilee region in the 16th century and they're still there. They didn't fare too well during the years of

Turkish rule, and welcomed the 19th-century Jewish immigrants with open arms. They've been generally friendly ever since. Druses were among the first to join Haganah, and they're the only Arabs who are drafted into the Israeli Army now.

Their finest hour as Israeli soldiers was during the 1967 war . . . the one they call the Six Day War.

They that war against thee shall be as nothing, and as a thing of naught.

– Isaiah 41:12

In the years after the Sinai campaign, the Israeli defense establishment built up its arsenal and quietly planned for the next war, which everybody on both sides knew wasn't too far in the future. Lessons they learned in 1956 told them that their wars would need to be fought by fast, highly maneuverable armored divisions. They also knew that any war had to be as short as possible so the enemies on both sides of them wouldn't have time to get together.

The Egyptians, who had been demoralized and virtually stripped of all their weapons in '56, were planning for the next war, too. As fast as the Israelis added to their arsenal, so did the Egyptians. If one side

The dividing screen between the men's and women's sections of the Western Wall is shown *right,* where a small group of tourists gather in the women's section, listening intently to their guide.

added a faster jet plane, the other responded with one that was faster still. A new tank would be matched by another that could turn faster and move faster. It's an arms race that's still going on, but it was moving at an almost terrifying pace in those days. It was only a matter of time before one side or the other decided to put all this new power to the test.

The Israeli air force made the first move. The Arabs knew that the attack would come, but obviously hadn't learned from the previous war that they were dealing with an inventive enemy who made it normal procedure not to fight by the traditional rules of warfare. The first Israeli objective was to knock out Arab airpower, a perfectly normal thing to do. But an ordinary military power would have done it with one massive attack and held back some planes for reserve security. The Israelis put every plane they owned into the air and brought them in low in small waves over nearly 20 Egyptian airfields. As each wave moved on, another followed it. They kept the strike intense over a period that was measured in hours rather than minutes. At the same time, they did the same thing to the Syrian and Jordanian air forces.

Once having eliminated the threat of being attacked by enemy planes, Israeli armored divisions rushed into the Sinai and Gaza. The Egyptians fought hard, and it took the Israelis four days to send them packing. But, for their efforts, they occupied all of the Sinai again and all of the Gaza Strip. More important, they removed the threat of a well-armed Egyptian army for the second time.

But that was just one phase of the war. The Jordanians had attacked at several points along their border, including Jerusalem. It was a much tougher battleground for the Israelis because the mountains restricted movement of their armored divisions. It was also heavily populated, making it impossible to bull their way through the enemy's lines.

It took the Israelis three days to move the Jordanian border back across the Jordan River. In the process, they captured all of the Jordan's West Bank, including the coveted Holy Sites in Jerusalem itself.

The only Arab movement inside the existing boundaries of Israel itself was a Syrian attack on some settlements in the far north. Once the Jordanians had been pushed back, Israeli units went on the offensive in the Golan Heights. The Syrians had been building up defenses there almost continuously since Israel had become a country. The Israeli strategy was to move in from the north rather than hit the defenses head-on. Another force from the south planned to meet it and send the Syrians back to Damascus. It wasn't quite that easy.

Outside the wall that flanks the blocked-up Golden Gate, or Gate of Mercy, are the tombs of the Moslem Cemetery *left*.

The Syrians took heavy losses, as many as 2,500 of them were killed, but they kept right on fighting. They may have fought to the last man, but the Syrian propaganda machine broadcast a false announcement that a city more than 15 miles inside their country had been overrun by Israeli troops who seemed headed for Damascus. It was an attempt to get help from other countries, but when their own soldiers heard the report, they assumed they had been surrounded and ran for the safety of the interior.

If the world had been impressed by the performance of the Israeli fighting machine ten years earlier, it was overwhelmed with admiration in '67. Military experts still use the war as a textbook example of classical planning, and one of history's great examples of making military plans work.

The enthusiasm began almost at the moment the first shot was fired. On the second day of the Six Day War hundreds of volunteers arrived in Israel from all over the world to do anything they could to help. Israeli embassies and consulates were flooded with people who intended to do the same. Others sent money, and those who couldn't sent encouraging words.

With a war going on, the tourist industry braced itself for a slump. And that's probably the only example of planning in the Six Day War that didn't work. Before it ended they began to feel a surge and during the summer after it was over, the industry broke all its previous records.

And the enthusiasm had its effect on the Israelis, too. In the early '60s, Jews in Israel had begun drifting away from world Jewry. They felt isolated but content to create their own future without any help from the outside world. But when the outside world helped anyway, and so willingly, a lot of Israelis did a lot of soul-searching and a great many who had abandoned their religion became interested in their heritage again and began to investigate the bonds they had with Jews everywhere in the world.

The return to religion and the search for roots, possibly even the surge in tourism, was also tied to the fact that so many of the old Biblical sites had now become part of their country. Its size had grown from less than 8,000 square miles, not much bigger than the State of New Jersey, to 34,000 square miles, slightly smaller than Portugal.

They had annexed all of the Sinai, Judea, Sumaria and the Golan Heights; and they had made Jerusalem whole again.

But though they had breathing space, they were still surrounded by hostile neighbors. As Golda Meir put it:

"We have our backs against the wall. We don't even

Small shops and stalls and goods-laden donkeys *overleaf* abound in the Old City. Colorful scarves hang in the bright sunshine *above,* while traders flank the gloom of one of the numerous narrow alleys *left* that lead to the Temple area.

have a wall. We have a sea. The only friendly neighbor we have is the Mediterranean."

. . . Reserved against the time of trouble, against the day of battle and war.

– Job 38:23

It makes Israel one of the most security-conscious countries in the world. On one side of the coin, it gives them military censorship; on the other it gives them pride in their defense establishment that almost no country has seen in the history of the world.

The woman who had difficulty getting aboard an Egged bus outside Jerusalem would have stepped down and out of the way if a healthy 20-year-old in uniform came along. It's an Israeli custom that goes right back to the beginnings of the country.

On special occasions where pictures of the country's leaders are trotted out to be displayed and admired, the Chief of Staff of the military is usually the most adored of all.

What outsiders admire most about the Israeli military is the fact that it's largely a civilian army. In the '67 War, more than half the fighters were reserve troops called up just hours before the first shots were fired. But there was no period of confusion while they got into fighting shape. Their morale was legendary, their determination and inventiveness was of a sort that had never before existed in a reserve army. In fact, they were up to fighting trim in less time than the enemy army that was composed entirely of professional soldiers. Add to that the fact that just one of the armies they were fighting, and they were up against four, was bigger than they were, and as well-equipped.

The professionals in the Israeli army reflect the makeup of the country itself and often migrated after having been trained in the military traditions of countries as diverse as Russia and the United States. But there are others. like Moshe Dayan, who were trained in the school of hard knocks.

He began his career as a teenage kibbutz guard back in the 1930s. In four wars he served as a battalion commander, Chief of Staff and Minister of Defense. Like other Sabra soldiers, he has usually taken the best ideas from his foreign-trained staff and adapted them to Israel's own problems, then adapted them even further with an almost uncanny understanding of the enemy.

The real training ground for the founders of the Israeli army was the Haganah, and the defense forces today are more like the old underground army than like any other army in the world.

More than half of all the Israeli men and a large number of women, too, over 18 and under 54 are members of Zahal, the Israeli Defense Force. Some are regular soldiers, but most are ordinary citizens who work in banks, drive buses or run small shops. Many of them even work in factories that turn out the weapons they use. Much of their armor comes from the United States, but they also buy from Britain and West Germany, and every time they clash with an Arab army, they add Soviet-made equipment to their collection.

The navy and air force are integrated into the IDF. The Sea Corps concentrates on small, fast, missile-equipped patrol boats, but it does operate a pair of submarines. The Air Corps, as it is in most countries, is the elite of the military, with more career professionals than the other branches.

Every Israeli citizen, and every alien who lives in Israel, serves in the military when they become 18 years old. Men serve for three years and unmarried women

Carrying his wares firmly strapped to his body, like some ancient weaponry, an Arab tea vendor *left* dispenses hot, sweet tea to passers-by just inside the Old City, near Herod's Gate, and deeper within the city two small boys *above* sell their goods from a bench.

for two. After that men serve as reservists until they reach 55. Women have the same duty, if they don't get married, until their 34th birthday.

Male immigrants under 29 and females under 26 are drafted in the same way. If they're older, they're still subject to military service, but for a shorter time.

Except for the Druses, Israeli Arabs get an automatic exemption from the draft. But very few other Israelis have any choice but to serve. Ultra-Orthodox Jews studying to be rabbis are usually excluded, but there's almost no such thing as a conscientious objector or a young person exempted for flat feet or punctured ear drums. Less than 10 per cent of the men are able to avoid the compulsory three years of service.

On the other hand, more than half the eligible women are excused for a variety of reasons. Some are married, of course, and get exemption as potential child-bearers. Some others simply sign statements that they can't serve for "religious reasons." If they do that, they are required to put in time doing social work.

Women who do serve go into the Women's Army Corps right from high school and, after a month of basic training, they are usually assigned to such jobs as maintenance worker or mechanic. During their training, they are taught to handle a rifle and a sub-

machine gun, but no one expects them ever to use either one. Their role in the military is to allow more men to take on combat duty while they stay behind the lines.

Though men and women don't train together, there is a growing trend to use women to train men. They've discovered that men try harder when they're asked to run for three miles and the person who's doing the asking is a former ballerina who stays ahead of the column without even seeming to be trying hard. When a man watches a little slip of a girl take a rifle apart and put it back together with the ease of handling a hair roller, it naturally makes them want to do better.

Most Israeli women are content with their role in the military and they serve willingly and well. But there's a growing number who are asking for equality and more chance for advancement. They look at the United States Army where women train alongside men and share the same opportunities not only for combat but for advancement. They've been successful in convincing the authorities to allow them to take on technical jobs. But that seems to be as far as the movement will take them. The Israeli point of view is that women have a deeper obligation to raise the future generations of the country, and that's as important to Israel's survival as success on any battlefield.

Many of the young IDF recruits choose to serve in Nahal, which gives them a chance to get some agricultural training along with their basic military skills. They function in much the same way as the original pioneers by moving into virgin territory to establish new settlements which are also a line of defense along the country's borders. It isn't unusual for their bases eventually to become permanent settlements, nor for them to become the citizens of these settlements.

Before they serve in the military, a lot of Israeli young people get a taste of the services while they're still in high school by joining such organizations as Gadna, the IDF-administered youth corps. They start out at 14 spending an hour a week in training and two weeks in a special camp. By the time they are 17 and on the verge of being drafted, they spend more than a month in the field learning military discipline. They were put on alert during the '48 war, but their traditional role involves more training than fighting

Once their full-time military service is over, Israelis automatically become, as has been mentioned, members of the reserve force. That means they are required to train one day a month plus one month a year, some even more. It's the most demanding military system of just about any country in the world.

Career soldiers are paid about the same as workers in civilian life, but conscripts get a bare minimum.

The bustling market scenes *on these pages,* taken inside the Old City, near the Damascus Gate, are typical of many such scenes throughout the Middle East.

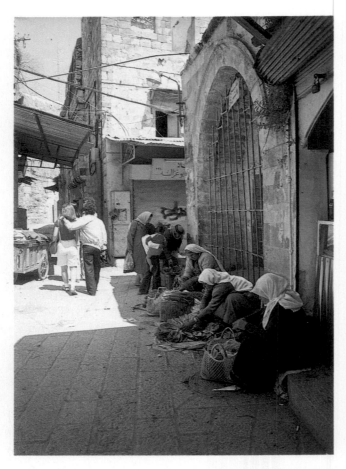

Outside the Damascus Gate traders *left* spread their wares on one of the ramps leading up to it. Fascinating little streets and alleys *below and below right* are to be discovered round almost every corner in the labyrinthine Old City.

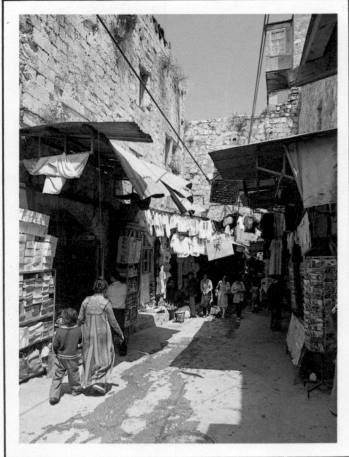

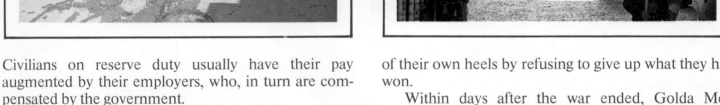

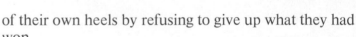

Civilians on reserve duty usually have their pay augmented by their employers, who, in turn are compensated by the government.

Spending all that time in uniform makes Israeli fighting people feel like part of a very special family. Officers and men don't have the usual gulf between them. In fact, of all the words Ben Yehuda added to the Hebrew language, he never got around to coining the equivalent of "sir." No one since has found it necessary, either. Military decorum exists, but it isn't a traditional part of discipline in Israel as it is in other military organizations. Rank doesn't seem to impress them until they get into battle. One of the reasons is that the official policy of the IDF is that an officer never asks his men to go into battle except with the command to "follow me."

Commanders get their rank by training as commandos or as paratroopers. There is almost no other way to get into a position to lead. They get to keep their jobs by setting examples their men will follow willingly. It's a system that works. Ask any Arab.

After the Six Day War, the Arab countries dug in. The UN issued a call for Israel to withdraw from territories she had occupied. But the Israelis were ready to meet the Arab threat, and they did some digging-in

of their own heels by refusing to give up what they had won.

Within days after the war ended, Golda Meir addressed a huge rally in New York's Madison Square Garden:

"I want to describe for you briefly the spirit of our people," she said. "One Israeli family that left Israel about a half a year ago, due to economic difficulties, returned with their children just a week before the war broke out. At the airport, the father was asked, 'Why did you come back now?' He answered, 'I have returned to live in peace!' And that was true.

"If you went through the streets of Tel Aviv and Jerusalem and Haifa and Beersheba, or through the settlements, during those weeks of tension, you would see no signs of panic. No mother, no grandmother tried to keep her son or grandson back. Everybody was mobilized. In one place when the reserves came up and reported, there was disorder. One hundred and ten per cent of the reserves had reported; hence, there was trouble. Everybody wanted to be in it, to have a share in the battle.

"Now the war on the battlefield is over; the battle in the United Nations has begun. On your television, on your radio, you hear falsehood and distortion. One

would imagine that we were 40 million who attacked a poor little nation of 20 million. We are called criminals! Nazis! What crime have we committed? We won the war!

"While this new battle is getting underway, we must immediately begin to rebuild everything that was destroyed in the Old City, in the Northern settlements, in the South, in the houses of the New City of Jerusalem . . . wherever the shells struck. I am sure that pretty soon you will hear that Jerusalem is a Holy City for all religions. Yet when Jerusalem was shelled in 1948, nobody defended Jerusalem, this Holy City of all religions! The only people who defended Jerusalem and its sanctuaries at that time were the Jews.

"The same took place now. When Jerusalem was shelled, our boys recaptured it by fighting hand-to-hand in the narrow streets, suffering heavy casualties so as not to demolish the ancient Holy Places with mortars. But we must begin to rebuild. We have much to do for those who are in Israel now and for those who will come. We must do it together with you, for everything that we have done in Israel until now we have done together.

"During the fighting and the week before the fighting, young Jews from all over the world were trying to reach Israel. At the London airport there were riots because El Al, the only airline flying to Israel during the war, could not possibly take all those who wanted to come. Therefore, I ask the youth of America, if you came in war, why not in peace? The settlements must be reconstructed. In Gadot, not one building remains. In all the settlements on the Syrian border much work needs to be done as well as in the other settlements along the borders. We want more strength, not only in arms . . . but in people in the settlements, in the schools, in the universities, in the cities. You are filled with joy because we have remained alive. You want us to be safe in the future, too. Can we not work close together rather than at a long distance? Can we not build together in Ein Gev, in Tel Katzir, in Jerusalem, in Tel Aviv?

"And so Israel goes on . . . in peace, we hope. But nobody can be mistaken any longer. This nation, this Jewish people, this State of Israel, has exactly the same right of self-defense as any other people in the world . . . no more, but no less. We pray that we will never more have to send our sons into battle. We pray that our

Beyond the tombs and monuments in the Kidron Valley *previous page* rises the Mount of Olives, on the lower slopes of which stands the impressively beautiful Gethsemane Church of All Nations *left,* built on the site of two earlier churches and so-named because its building was sponsored by several countries.

Arab neighbors will finally realize that peace is as necessary for them as it is for us."

Within two months, the Arabs held a summit meeting and announced to the world that there would be no negotiations with Israel, no recognition, and no peace.

Obviously, they weren't listening to Mrs Meir. And they hadn't learned anything from the wars they had already fought with this new nation.

He sitteth in the lurking places of the villages: in the secret places doth he murder the innocent.

– Psalms 10:8

The Arab countries weren't too convincing at sabre-rattling in the summer of 1967. The Egyptians had lost as much as 80 per cent of their strength and most of the weapons they lost were being adapted to be used against them. The Syrians had lost their position in the Golan Heights, which had been a perfect spot for shelling Israeli towns in the North, and having the Israelis in control there made their own territory more vulnerable. The Jordanians found the Israeli threat more real, too, and couldn't rely on Egyptian help in a crisis any more because Egypt was suddenly a lot further away. On the Israeli side, they not only controlled more territory, but by a trick of geography they had one-third fewer miles of border to defend.

Almost no one would have believed that there could be another war with the Arab States in their lifetime. What made peace seem so secure was the fact of Israel's occupation of the territories she had fought for and won. And that was the cause of new trouble for Israel.

To the average Arab man in the street, Israel had always been a neighboring country his leaders didn't much like, but only an abstract threat at best. In the spring of 1967, the neighbor had suddenly become a military presence in his streets. People who had been indifferent about Israel, even potentially friendly, didn't much like living as conquered people in occupied territory. It didn't take long for them to get militant ideas along with the conviction that the only way they'd ever get back the lands they thought belonged to them was by going to war.

Suddenly Israel had a new Arab enemy to deal with: The Palestine Liberation Organization. The Arab countries, especially Egypt and Syria, had used Palestinian refugees as arms of terror in the past, but now that the Palestinians were able to organize on their own, they represented much more of a threat than ever.

Higher on the slopes of the Mount of Olives, behind high walls, is the Church of Mary Magdalene *left and below,* with its characteristically Russian, onion-shaped domes.

They weren't able to meet the Israeli army head-on in the field, so they turned to terror as a means of waging their war.

Using a "let's you and them fight" policy, the Egyptians gave the terrorists as much help as they could to keep the Israelis occupied while they rebuilt their war machine. Meanwhile, the Israelis were improving their war machine, too, as the Egyptians discovered when they started a new war in 1969. They called it a 'War of Attrition." Before it was over, the following summer, the Arab countries, even with Soviet help, sustained losses greater than in any war up to that point. And they lost another war.

Through it all, though, the fedayeen, as the Palestinian guerillas were called, were growing in numbers and were being well-equipped by Arab oil millionaires. To counter the potential threat, Defense Minister

154

Moshe Dayan suggested relaxing a lot of the rules in order to make Israel look less like a military occupier. The authorities took his suggestion and began allowing free Arab movement across the Jordan River as well as through all of Israel. They began to allow Arab tourists to come into the country, and hundreds of thousands did. And finally they encouraged Arabs in occupied territories to take jobs at the same rate of pay as Jewish workers.

It was good for the economy of the occupied territories, obviously, and it expanded the labor force that was needed to rebuild and to stimulate growth. It also had the desired effect of reducing terrorism. Arabs whose opportunities for a better life were suddenly better than at any time in their lives were more than willing to oppose the recruitment efforts of Al Fatah, the Syrian-supported terrorist group, or even the home-grown PLO. One at a time, nests of terrorists were uncovered and deported and their threat was greatly diminished.

To make sure they didn't come back in the dark at night, new settlements of Nahal were established at strategic points along the Jordanian border. By day they

It is difficult to imagine that the assortment of buildings, towers and domes *previous page* that make up the Church of the Holy Sepulcher in fact mark the site of a small hill, Calvary, and a garden tomb. Through the centuries buildings have been added, knocked down and altered so as to disguise its identity entirely; yet this is the holiest shrine of Christianity, where worshippers regularly gather, particularly at such times as Good Friday *above and right*.

From the vantage point of the tower of the Church of the Redeemer may be seen the splendid view of the Old City *overleaf,* with the Dome of the Rock as the focal point and the Mount of Olives rising to the horizon.

attacked fedayeen bases established anywhere within a day's journey of the Israel border to make sure a night attack would be difficult at best.

The deeper the Israelis drove the fedayeen into Jordan, the deeper they went as a thorn in King Hussein's side. When he agreed to stop his war against Israel, the refugees in his country told him not to include them in his agreement and went right on trying to slip across the border to do their dirty work.

He was eventually forced to turn his own army loose on them and after what turned out to be a near-

The lovely Church called Dominus Flevit – The Lord Wept – stands about half-way up the Mount of Olives, seen *right* through the arches of the Temple area, and affords not only a welcome respite on the steep climb to the top but also a magnificent view over the Old City, particularly when viewed across the altar and through the wrought-iron-work *above*.

slaughter, managed to ship them off to Lebanon. The authorities there forced them to stay in the South, not to make raiding Israel easier, but to make Israeli retaliation easier.

None of that removed the threat of clandestine Arab raids, of course, but it did help to localize the problem. On the other hand, it also expanded the PLO's ambitions. The border with Egypt was off-limits to them because of the huge desert they had to cross before they could do any damage; Jordan's king was gunning for them, so that border was closed; the short Syrian border was too well-defended and the seacoast

At the foot of the Mount of Olives, to the left of the Basilica of the Agony, or Church of All Nations *overleaf,* stands the Tomb of the Virgin, the bells of which are shown *below.*

hid too many Israeli patrol boats. Out of frustration, they hit where they could . . . anywhere in the world.

One of their first adventures outside their own or Israeli territories was in the fall of 1970 when PLO activists in Europe hijacked four airliners at the same time. Ironically, only one of the four planes was an El Al jet, and that was the only attempt that failed. The Israeli crew managed to overpower the hijackers and take them home as prisoners. An American plane was diverted to Cairo where it was blown up after the passengers had been removed. Another American plane and jets belonging to Swissair and BOAC were forced to land in the Jordanian desert where the passengers were held as hostages. They held them there for nearly a week, threatening to kill them all if PLO "political prisoners" weren't released from prison.

They finally backed down; no prisoners were released and they let their hostages go. But they did blow up the planes, and they did call a lot of attention to themselves, which had been their intention all along. But obviously, there wasn't a PR man in the bunch. It was the straw that broke the camel's back as far as King Hussein was concerned, and the incident was the start of the campaign that drove the guerillas out of Jordan.

It also made the Palestinians look more like heartless gangsters than displaced people in the eyes of the world.

But in dozens of similar incidents over the years since, in spite of merciless Israeli retaliation every time, they still seem to feel that terror is their one best hope for recognition and sympathy.

In all the wars they had fought against the Arabs, the Israelis had come out of each more confident and stronger than before. Even in the War of Attrition, where the Arabs had a chance to dictate some of the rules for a change, they still won soundly and walked away with even more pride.

But that war had its bad effects. It had cost more in money and lives and it dragged on for months. For the first time there were doves as well as hawks in Israeli politics. But their debates were suspended for a while in 1973. The Arabs were at it again.

The strongholds are surprised . . .

– Jeremiah 48:41

After the Six Day War, the Egyptians knew they were going to have to do a lot of homework if they wanted to take back all that territory by force. Their studies showed them they couldn't do it. They knew how strong Israel was in the air from bitter experience and they had seen how fast she could be on the ground. But they also knew there would be more ground to defend this time around, and bigger distances to move supplies and troops. It was a big advantage, big enough to make a difference. But there was only one way to get any advantage against the Israelis . . . they had to be caught napping.

And that was almost impossible. Almost.

Naturally, Israel knew that the Egyptians were getting ready for yet another war. Their agents were feeding them facts almost hourly. Even United States agents in the area saw the signs and reported them. But Israeli intelligence, working from long experience with this enemy, insisted that the buildup was nowhere near complete and no attack would take place any time soon. Air reserves were called up, just in case, and army reserves were put on alert. They weren't called up until a few hours before the attack came.

It came early in the afternoon on October 6, 1973, the Sabbath in Israel as well as Yom Kippur, the Day of Atonement. It began with an Egyptian air attack on the Sinai, followed by an artillery barrage that preceded an infantry assault across the Suez Canal. Israeli planes were in the air quickly, but with only a few hours of

Pilgrims with lighted candles
pack the Church of the
Holy Sepulcher *right*.

daylight left, they were forced to stay on the defensive. Ground forces shared the same problem and faced the added problem of getting themselves into position. In the confusion, the Egyptians clearly had the day.

Up north, the Syrians were having their way in the Golan, even managing to capture the Israeli listening post on Mount Hermon. By the end of the day, the Israelis were in a very unfamiliar position, offbalanced on two fronts.

They didn't stay that way long. They counter-attacked against the Syrians and pushed them back beyond the old ceasefire line in less than ten days. It took them ten days more to force the Egyptians back across the Canal, and they might have made it all the way to Cairo if the UN hadn't called for a ceasefire.

After the negotiations that followed, a buffer zone was set up in the Sinai to separate Egypt and Israel and another established in the Golan Heights to keep the Israelis and the Syrians apart.

A lot more than negotiations followed the Yom Kippur War. Almost 2,500 Israelis had lost their lives fighting it and more than $5 billion were spent. For the first time, Israelis began to wonder if it was worth it.

They were still determined to defend their country no matter what it cost. And military superiority still made Israelis feel like a superior people. But they were beginning to think more positively about building the good life their parents had come there to find. There were still wars to be fought, but there were lives to be led, too, and most Israelis were anxious to get on with it. It was clear to everyone by then that there would never be a danger of their country becoming a completely military state, as many in history have with lesser reasons.

Make sweet melody, sing many songs . . .

Isaiah 35:2

When the Yom Kippur War broke out, the American violinist Isaac Stern was on his way to Israel for one of his many concert tours. He didn't turn back and he didn't cancel the concerts, either. In Israel, wars come and go, but the music never stops.

The Israel Philharmonic has almost never played to an empty seat since the day Arturo Toscanini took over as its first conductor in the 1935 season. Among the conductors who have filled his shoes in the years since, Indian-born Zubin Mehta was the orchestra's music director for 16 years before going to New York to take over the New York Philharmonic. During his years

with the Los Angeles Philharmonic, he still insisted on commuting back and forth between Israel and California, which made him all the more popular among the Israelis, most of whom also hold down two jobs.

When he gave up some of the commuting to give his attention to the New York orchestra, his first consideration on moving to New York was to find a place to live as close as possible to two close Israeli friends, Daniel Barenboim the conductor and Pinchas Zuckerman the violinist, two of the world's finest, and therefore most popular, musicians. He said later that it was the only way he could get his wife to live on Manhattan's West Side, "so far from Bloomingdale's!"

The Israeli Philharmonic plays one of the heaviest schedules of any major orchestra in the world. But even though they give more than 200 concerts a year in Israel, it's just about impossible to get a seat for any of them. Subscribers usually re-subscribe season after season and they leave their tickets to their children in their wills.

There's a story that may or may not be true about a man who wanted to get a subscription for his daughter, but not badly enough to give up his own seat or his wife's. Then he began to notice an empty seat in the row in front of his every time he went to a concert. After five performances, always with the empty seat, he went to the orchestra management to get the address of the no-show. Though they were reluctant, his story touched them and they gave him a woman's telephone number.

When he called the number, a man answered. He didn't hang up, but stammered out condolences to the man who he assumed must recently have lost his wife.

No, he was assured, the woman was not dead. On the contrary, she was quite healthy and in recent months had even been given to smiling a lot more than usual.

"Oh," said the caller, "I was sure she had died because her seat at the Philharmonic concerts has been empty for so long. I was calling to see if you would sell me her ticket."

That was answered by a long silence. Finally the husband said he would be willing to sell the ticket, but there was a legal matter that needed attending to first. He told him to call a certain lawyer in a week.

The lawyer turned out to be unusually friendly, even offering to sell the ticket at a discount. But there was a catch. The would-be subscriber would have to appear as a witness before a Rabbinical Court in a divorce case.

It developed that the woman who was supposed to be at the concerts was out playing around instead. The

A Palm Sunday procession *left* makes
its way up to the St. Stephen's
Gate entrance to the Old City.

divorce was granted and the seat wasn't empty again
for the rest of the season.

Back in 1945 a group of New Yorkers organized
what they hoped would become an annual event called
Jewish Music Week. Thirty-five years later it was still
going strong, but as Jewish Music Month. They
discovered early in the game that it isn't possible to
squeeze it all into a week.

In Israel, even a month isn't enough. Everybody
there is into the act. The Philharmonic is only part of it.
There are choirs in almost every city and in a great
many small towns that wouldn't seem big enough to
muster a good bass section. There are more than 600
high school choirs that compete with each other in
much the same way high school football teams do in
the United States. And there are dozens of professional
vocal groups and choirs that give them a standard to
aim for. Everybody seems to participate in the singing
and they do it with an enthusiasm anyone would say
couldn't be matched anywhere in the world.

Anywhere, that is, but in Israel itself. It can be
matched in the Haifa Symphony, the youth orchestra at
Holon or any kibbutz in the country where there is
usually either a symphony orchestra or at least a
chamber group. The Police Force Band, or any of
dozens of woodwind ensembles, doesn't take a back
seat to anyone in the enthusiasm department. And
don't forget the National Opera and all those groups
connected with all those music schools.

Enthusiasm? Passion? The words aren't strong
enough to describe how Israelis feel about music.

But for all that, Israel's musical heritage is as
diverse as the people themselves. The country has
produced an impressive number of composers
including Noam Sheriff and Joseph Tal, Robert Starer
and Marc Lavry. And some 15 conservatories, two
academies and a first-rate university music department are turning out even more. But most music that's
Israeli has strong roots in the music of the places the
Israelis migrated from. Even the Israeli national
anthem is built around a theme by the Czech
composer, Bedrich Smetana. But it's only a matter of
time before they build solid themes of their own.

Almost as much as music, dance in all its forms
abounds everywhere in the country. Just about
everybody is both a participant in and an expert about
folk dancing. Inhal, an ethnic dance company, is
known and hugely respected in just about every part of
the world, and so are two Israeli modern dance companies, Bat-Door and Batsheva. The country also has a
first-rate classical ballet company, the Israel Ballet.

And how can a people who created the Yiddish
theater not have a great theater company? There is no

way, and of course Israel has one. It's called Habimah, the Israel National Theater, and it's a good bit older than modern Israel itself.

Habimah was founded in 1917 during the Russian Revolution in Moscow. It was created by Jewish actors as the world's first Hebrew theater.

Habimah earned international recognition under the direction of Eugheny Vakhtangov, a disciple of Stanislavski. By the time they pulled up stakes and moved to Palestine in 1928, people like Maxim Gorky were hailing their work as "magic."

Almost every theatrical enterprise in Israel for the next 40 years or more looked to Habimah for direction, for advice and for support. Naturally, young actors eventually began to rebel against such hard-bound tradition and began to mutter about being tired of

having to speak Hebrew on stage with a Russian accent.

A new breed of rebels started to emerge and Israeli playwrights began writing original material for them. It gave Israel a theatrical alternative. But the government supports Habimah, so it's still the dominant force.

Israeli citizens support theater in general. About a quarter of them see at least one theatrical production a year, a much higher average than most countries. It's not a bad way for newcomers to brush up on their Hebrew. Reviews and musicals are most popular, but there is a growing repertoire of original plays by Israeli writers and younger audiences are taking to them like ducks to water.

That in turn is leading to a new film industry, and that's a perfect way to get the whole country involved in developing a whole new culture.

In the long history of Jewish art, sculpture is about the only form that was ever neglected, possibly because of the Biblical caution against making graven images. But Israelis are closing the gap fast. One of the things that inspires them is the sculpture garden at the Israel Museum in Jerusalem. It's named for the American showman Billy Rose, who left his personal sculpture collection in his will to the Israeli people. It's a collection that includes work by Rodin, Henry Moore, Daumier and other contemporary and abstract sculptors.

There are growing artists' colonies in Jaffa, Ein Hod and Safad, but there is hardly a town anywhere in the country that doesn't have galleries and museums; hardly a kibbutz whose bomb shelter doesn't double as exhibition space for its members who paint, sculpt or make great photographs.

That which hath been is now; and that which is to be hath already been.

– Ecclesiastes 3:15

Of the 98 museums in the country 15 are for art. Twice that many are archaeological museums. Probably the best way to make an Israeli happy is to hand him a shovel. There are "digs" everywhere in the country and people sifting through the rubble have found traces of civilizations that were thriving more than 5,000 years ago.

It's a game anybody can play once they've gotten a permit from the Department of Antiquities, and it's a game not restricted to Israelis. Some 6,000 foreign tourists show up every summer to volunteer to poke around in Israel's past. They do it in spite of warnings like this one that was sent out to prospective volunteers by the Hebrew Union College in Jerusalem:

"It is hard, dirty physical labor requiring stooping, picking, hoeing, lifting stones and heavy baskets to shoulder height, etc. Both men and women do the same kind of work.

"There is, of course, much fine hand work as well, but this can be tedious and is often in the hottest, most airless part of the area.

"And when you do get a chance to raise your head into the breeze, you may well get a faceful of flying dust. The mixture of dust and sweat produces

It was through the majestic Golden Gate *overleaf* that Jesus is believed to have made His triumphant entry into Jerusalem on Palm Sunday. It was blocked up by the Turks in 1530 and remains so to this day.

Excavation, restoration and rebuilding seem part of everyday life in many parts of Israel but particularly in Jerusalem, where the site of the original City of David comes to light *left*.

From the walls of Jerusalem, the Valley of Kidron drops away, and then the ground rises to the summit of the Mount of Olives *above*.

charming little rivulets of mud that trickles down your back and off your nose.

"Those who find 'romance' in this process must look for it in terms of the contribution of the entire enterprise to the recovery of man's past; the individual task assigned to you may well be difficult and unglamorous."

About two-thirds of the people who accept challenges like that are women. Many are students, some are Christian fundamentalists, some are simply fascinated by the idea of digging up the past. To a few, it represents a cheap vacation. It's a way to visit Israel for as little as $10 a day, and for some, a way to earn college credit in the bargain.

Many of the excavations couldn't exist without volunteer labor, but the people who run them often long for people with a more archaeological background. They also can't help wondering why such a large percentage of the volunteers are women. One explanation could be that all that backbreaking work in

all that heat can help a person lose as much as 40 pounds in a summer.

Tourist-volunteers are usually carefully screened before they are accepted for work. Most expeditions require a physical examination, too, and almost none will accept volunteers for less than two full weeks. The daily routine most likely begins at four in the morning to beat the heat of the day. But work goes on all day, and lectures go on into the night.

But still they keep coming, often in groups on package tours. And some come back year after year. For some of them the thrill of potential discovery is the lure, but for others like a New Yorker who's been at it enough summers to be something of an expert, the lure is the combination of something interesting and something physical. "I sit at a desk all year," he says, "so this is a change. And I don't want to have a big belly by the time I'm 25. But it's not just the sweating; you can learn quite a bit here."

And there's still a lot to learn. There are more than 400 tels, as the ancient mounds are called, in Israel and less than 50 have given up their secrets. Little children are forever finding bits of pottery or chunks of flint and one of the first lessons they learn in school is to handle them carefully and take them to class with them, not for show and tell, but to be forwarded to the Department of Antiquities for identification.

Archaeology in Palestine began in earnest more than 60 years ago with important excavations in Jerusalem and Jericho and in Samaria and Galilee. Under British control, American and British scholars kept the work going at several sites, including the old 12th-century port city of Atlit where they found a fort that had been built by the Crusaders.

In the 1920s, Jewish archaeologists uncovered part of the fortifications of Jerusalem and work there has been going on almost without stop ever since. In fact, the dig at Temple Mount is the only year-round expedition open to volunteers, and it's by far the simplest to get accepted in.

Not much has been left to uncover at Caesaria, but it's a paradise for archaeologists anyway. When Herod was king, he developed it as one of the great seaports of the world, and to show the Romans his heart was in the right place, he named it after Caesar Augustus. It was obviously very beautiful and very Roman, with wide streets running from the waterfront past glorious marble buildings toward a huge theater and an even greater Hippodrome that was used primarily as a race track. It was said that Herod placed highly polished marble at strategic spots so the sun would reflect off it to get the horses excited.

After Herod died, the Romans made Caesaria their

headquarters. And why not? The architecture was a good cure for homesickness. Caesaria was where the War of the Jews began in AD 66, and after the destruction of Jerusalem, it became the capital of Palestine, which it remained for 500 years.

It was an Arab city for another 450 years before the Crusaders moved in and moved the Arabs out in 1099. Each succeeding occupier recycled buildings they found there. The Arabs used Roman marble for the floors of their houses, the Crusaders used it to repair the streets. Under the direction of Louis IX, King of France (later to be canonised by Pope Boniface VIII), they also used remnants of Roman buildings to build a fortress around the city.

In more modern times, Jewish settlers established a collective farm just outside the walls. Their plows uncovered the remnants of a 4th-century synagogue. That was in 1927, and though it caused quite a stir at the time, no one began to dig with any seriousness until 1951, when other farmers uncovered the remains of two huge Roman statues. That prompted the government to organize an excavation that uncovered a Byzantine city. In the years since, they've found most of the fortifications Louis built in the 12th century as well as the ruins of a Christian cathedral built on the foundations of a Roman temple. They've uncovered and restored the Roman aqueduct and the Roman theater, which they've also "modernized." And to make the place more attractive, they've built what everyone agrees is the best golf course in all Israel. The fascination of Caesaria stems from the fact that it includes the artifacts of several civilizations, each determined to wipe out traces of the other. Fortunately none was completely successful.

If Caesaria is history restored, Acre, which the Israelis usually call Akko, is history alive and untouched. It's been an important city ever since a Phoenician sailor built a fire on the beach and was amazed to find that if you get sand hot enough it becomes glass. For generations they believed it could only happen with sand from Acre. It was also the place where they found those little shellfish that produce the purple dye that made the Phoenicians rich.

It's been under siege 17 different times and under control of 12 different races of men. The last time a battle was fought for control of Acre, it was fought and won by Jews. The first battle was fought by Joshua, but the city held out against him. In the seventh century, Mohammedans overran all of the Holy Land and took control of Acre along with every other city, including Jerusalem. When that happened, Europeans were incensed and began the great Crusades to drive the

The golden Dome of the Rock *left and previous page* must surely rank as one of the finest examples of religious building anywhere in the world, its mosaic-covered walls constantly delighting the eye as the intensity of color changes according to the strength and direction of the sunlight.

A high viewpoint allows the Dome of the Rock *below* to be seen against the Mount of Olives in the background and a low angle *right* adds to its impression of majesty.

Near the great mosque is El Kas *left,* the ablution fountain fed by the waters of Solomon's aqueduct, at which the faithful ritually wash before prayer.

Some idea of the beauty of the interior of the Dome of the Rock may be gathered from the illustrations *overleaf*. The niche *at the bottom right of page 180* indicates the direction of Mecca.

Infidel out. The first place they captured was Acre, which was their capital for more than 75 years.

Saladin took it from them, but Richard of England and Philip Augustus of France took it back and it remained a Christian citadel for two centuries. The Knights Templar and Knights of Saint John built their headquarters there and in those days Acre's streets were filled with knights in clanking armor and camp-following merchants from all parts of Europe.

When the Crusaders and their retinues went home, Arabs took over and then the Turks, but not much happened in Acre until 1799 when Napoleon passed by on his way back from beating the Egyptians. He decided to take on the Turks and take Acre from them,

but after two months of shelling, the Turks were still inside the walls and not even considering surrender. Napoleon packed up his army and went back to France in disgust. It was the first time he was ever defeated.

The city walls and many of the wonderful buildings inside, including a mosque that's easily the most beautiful Islamic building in Israel outside Jerusalem, were built by Pasha Jami El Jazzar. He was more than a builder. His name translates into English as Ahmed the Butcher. His mosque, which has been recently restored, is a strange monument to a man with a reputation like that. The courtyard outside it is decorated with soft palm trees, its walls are whitewashed, graceful arches carry the eye toward heaven. Inside, the walls are decorated with striking brown and white murals, the entire floor is covered with a wall-to-wall Persian carpet, and it's as peaceful a spot as you'll find anywhere.

Just as peaceful is the wondrous Crypt of Saint John, built at the lowest level of the fortress by Crusaders more than 700 years ago. Only the Cathedral of St. Denis in France, built four years earlier, is an older example of Gothic architecture. Huge Gothic arches support the high ceiling and the walls are decorated with reliefs of the English lion and the French fleur-de-lis. It doesn't take a lot of imagination to picture the room, which was probably built as dining room and reception hall, filled with long tables and raucous knights relaxing after a hot day chasing after the Infidel.

The entrance to the Crypt, 25 feet above it, is in a building that was built by the Turks on top of the Crusader buildings. The Crusaders had built their city on top of another the Romans had built. And, of course, the Romans built on foundations set in place by Greeks who had built on top of the Phoenician city.

In its glory days, Acre was a crossroads on trade routes between East and West. Marco Polo stopped over for a few days on his way to China, and it's likely the place he stopped was the Khan of Venice. A four-star hotel at the time, it was surely a must for any Italian on the move. There were six such places in the city and four are still there. One of them, Khan el-Umdan, named for the beautiful columns its builders took from a Caesaria ruin, is being converted into a modern hotel by the Israeli Government.

Even without its odd mixture of monuments, Acre would still be fascinating. The city's streets are narrow, a holdover from the Crusaders who purposely made them that way so a single knight could block the way to any hostile intruder. The Arab buildings that line them keep hostile intruders out with tightly-shut doors and a complete absence of windows. Just about every street in town eventually leads to the souk, the Arab marketplace. It's a place filled with cafes and shops and endless crowds of people haggling over the price of a bunch of grapes and arguing about whether it's legal to charge Value Added Tax on the price of fresh fruit.

During the days of British rule, the Citadel at Acre, one of the city's most dominant buildings, was used as a top-security prison for Jewish troublemakers. In 1947 an Irgun band broke in and released nearly 30 of their co-members who were being held there, and while they were at it, they held the door open for 200 more. It was one of the most spectacular prison breaks of all time. Except for a small portion of the building that's been converted to a mental institution, the Citadel is a national shrine dedicated to the memory of the freedom fighters who helped make Israel possible.

The archaeologists haven't done much digging at Acre, but it's only a matter of time before they do. When they do, they'll have plenty of signs to follow because it's still a thriving city.

It isn't always that easy to know where to dig. Some of the ancient cities have vanished without a trace. One of them is Hatzor, once the biggest of the Canaanite cities. Today it's Israel's biggest archaeological site.

It was uncovered in the late 1950's by Yigael Yadin, the former soldier who supervised the work at Masada. His work here proved that Joshua took the city in the 13th century B.C. and burned it to the ground; that Solomon had rebuilt it as a fortress and successive kings, notably Ahab in the 9th century B.C., had strengthened it.

The Yadin expedition found 21 different strata under the tel that hid the remains of Hatzor, and the stories in the dust went back more than 2,500 years beyond the last settlement that was destroyed there in the second century B.C.

Professor Yadin has also done a great deal of work at Megiddo, a similar fortress also built by Solomon and expanded by Ahab. Digging began there in 1925 and has since uncovered remains of 20 different settlements including Canaanite temples built about 4,000 B.C. Solomon used it as a cavalry base, with stables big enough for hundreds of horses and storage areas for as many chariots. His fortress, much like Masada, was built to hold up under a long seige. A secret water tunnel leads to a spring some distance away to guarantee that the defenders wouldn't die of thirst, and a huge silo held enough grain to ensure against starvation.

Megiddo, by the way, is where the New Testament's Book of Revelation tells us "the kings of the earth and of the whole world will be gathered together for the battle of the great day of God Almighty . . . a place called in the Hebrew tongue Armageddon." In the

Markets and cave-like shops *these pages*,
filled with goods of every description,
jostle for space in the narrow streets
of Jerusalem's Old City *overleaf*.

Outside the Knesset – the seat of
the Israeli Parliament – stands
Benno Elkan's Menorah *right,* carved
with scenes from Jewish history.

Dawn brings its soft pink glow to the landscape *above.*

Hebrew language the words are really Har Megiddo, "the Hill of Megiddo."

It was the scene of a bitter battle in World War I when the British Field Marshal Viscount Allenby defeated the Turks. And in the 1948 Israeli War for Independence, Megiddo was where the Israeli Army stopped the Arabs on their way to Haifa.

But if the words of the prophesying angel of Revelation have yet to be proven, the archaeologists in Israel are hard at work proving other things the Bible says.

They've found the battlefield at Tel Gezer where Joshua ordered the sun to stand still and where David and Saul beat the Philistines. They've uncovered 18 cities under a hill at Bet Shean and explored Mount Gilboa where King Saul died. They've probed the Valley of Soreq where Delilah was born and the area around Ashquelon where she and Samson played.

They've dug in King Solomon's mines and they've read letters at Lachish about the city's defense against the Babylonian King Nebuchadnezzar.

They haven't found Eden yet, but they're busy creating a new one. Meanwhile, who knows? The original might be just under the surface or at the bottom of some deep canyon. If it's there, it will be found. And who knows what else will be found in the meantime? That's what makes it so exciting. It's why archaeology is the national pastime.

Provide me now a man that can play well.

– I Samuel 16:17

But it's not the only one. Not by a long shot. Back in 1977 all Israel turned out to see and cheer Tel Aviv Maccabi, a basketball team. It was practically a national holiday. The outpouring of pride came after they beat the Italian champions, Mobil Girgi from Varese, at

188

Belgrade. The victory earned them the European Cup of Champions and officially put Israel on the map of the world of sport.

In the same way Americans promoted understanding between themselves and the People's Republic of China by meeting them across ping pong tables, some Israelis are promoting the idea that basketball may be a perfect link between them and the Arab countries. Taking advantage of the new contacts between Israel and Egypt, their plan is to start there, which they've already done, and see where the competition takes them. It's one of those simple ideas that makes perfect sense. And to show that the Arabs take it seriously, consider the fact that to get in shape for their first meeting on the basketball court, the Egyptians hired a Jewish coach from America.

Soccer is almost as important as basketball to Israeli sports fans. Officially it's called an amateur sport, but at the very least it's semi-professional and a major soccer match can tie up traffic all day. There are four major leagues representing more than 100 teams and each has a following that can only be described as fanatical. They sent a team to the Montreal Olympics in 1976 and anybody who saw the finals knew why the folks back home were so excited about soccer.

The excitement comes from the fact the teams are good, of course, but there's another reason for it that's just as good: the football pool. It's practically a major industry in Israel, with little glass booths everywhere you go. On Fridays when the results are posted, anxious people of every size and shape elbow each other out of the way for a chance to scrutinize the numbers. It's a

mark of the Israeli character that almost none of them is there to find out if he won, what they're looking for is how much they won. Not a single bettor in Israel ever expects to lose, and when they do they feel that they have been cheated. But they're not so angry that they won't put down another bet next week.

Once a year thousands of Israelis walk off that kind of frustration in the annual four-day march to Jerusalem, Tza'ada. Everyone over 18 and under 40 walks 25 miles on each of the days, people younger or older walk 19 miles a day for two days. In the fall, thousands more converge on the Sea of Galilee to see if they can swim the 2.8 miles across it. And serious runners show their stuff every year in a race around Mount Tabor.

Once every fours years, Jews from all over the

Basking in the afternoon sun lies Jerusalem the Golden, a city of crenellated walls, domes, spires and minarets *above and overleaf.*

world show their stuff in Israel in a competition officially known as the Maccabiah, but popularly called "the Jewish Olympics." It's held in the giant Ramat Gan Sports Stadium in Tel Aviv. The rest of the time it's where major soccer teams take on all comers from other countries.

For years events like the Maccabiah and the soccer games were described for people who couldn't make it to the stadium by Kol Yisrael, the radio network. They still are, but since 1968, on the day the country celebrated its 20th anniversary, television was added to the excitement.

191

A Jewish family *above* assembles for the Passover meal.

Outside the city walls, in West Jerusalem, stands the Montefiore windmill *right,* once a source of employment, but now serving as a museum.

Israeli televison broadcasts are still in black and white, and the schedule is more or less equally divided with programs in Hebrew and Arabic. They broadcast movies and puppet shows, just like TV stations everywhere. And Israelis get just as caught up as people anywhere else in game shows, police dramas and cowboy adventures imported from America and from Europe. A healthy part of the programming is "educational," which was the only kind of programming there was when TV was first introduced.

A great many Israelis have color TV sets even though there's no color broadcasting there. To make the sets work, they install elaborate antennae on their roofs to pick up English-language color programs from Jordan. They still get game shows and potboilers and the news is slanted a bit differently, but it's a wonderful status symbol to have all that hardware on the roof.

On radio, the news programs are most popular, but classical music is a very close second. Younger people often prefer the pop station, Reshet Gimmel, because it broadcasts some rock music but even they include

"light classical" in their programming.

American tourists, and a very large number of people in Israel and in the Arab countries listen to the English language "peace talk" programs and the American-style disc jockeys on Abie Nathan's Voice of Peace, a radio station that operates 24 hours a day from a ship in the Mediterranean.

Abie Nathan has been talking about peace and working in unorthodox ways to bring it about since he ran for the legislature back in 1966. Using his California Bar and Restaurant in Tel Aviv as a forum, he made a solemn promise that if he were elected he would personally take a message of peace to Egypt's President Nasser.

He lost the election, but decided to keep his promise anyway. He rented a 1927-vintage biplane and painted the word "Peace" on it in English, Hebrew and Arabic. Then, with a petition for Nasser in his pocket, he took of for Cairo. He got as far as Port Said, where the Egyptian authorities told him he'd better turn around and go home. "Can't do that," said Nathan, "my batteries are low and I only have enough gas to get me to Cairo." They gave him new batteries and filled up his gas tank, and to make sure he flew the right way once they let him take off again, they also gave him a jet fighter escort to the border.

He's been an Israeli hero ever since.

The desert shall rejoice and blossom as a rose.
– Isaiah 35:1

Rabbi Nelson Glueck, an American, is another bona fide Israeli here, but what he did for the country had little to do with the tensions between Jews and Arabs. Dr. Glueck is an archaeologist who spent some 40 years in the Negev proving that it was possible for human beings to live there and to thrive. Other experts

195

and investigating committees always came up with the same answer that it wasn't a fit place for man nor beast. But Glueck reasoned that if their forefathers had lived there, modern Jews could, too, and he set out to prove it by uncovering the remains of more than 1,500 ancient settlements.

Among them was a Red Sea port that turns out to have been the center of King Solomon's copper industry. The knowledge made a modern copper industry and the building of a seaport at Eilat a practical idea.

Eilat is a thriving tourist center, too, which is all the more interesting in light of dozens of reports issued over the years that the deserts that meet at this point are completely out of the question for human habitation.

Europeans with a hankering to see what a tropical ocean looks like go to Eilat because it's the closest one they have. The result is that the place is usually crawling with people breathing through snorkels and paddling along on flippers.

The Gulf of Eilat is an arm of the Red Sea, but not the same one where the waters were divided to allow the children of Israel to walk across without getting their feet wet. But modern Israelis can do something similar here thanks to an incredible undersea observatory called Coral World.

It's the brainchild of Morris Kahn, the publisher of the Israeli Yellow Pages, the classified telephone directory. He was on a vacation at Eilat, but burst an eardrum on a deep dive to rescue his son who had run into trouble underwater. He found it frustrating to know there was so much to see down there, but impossible because of his injury. When he went back home, he decided to do something about it.

He had a huge glass diving bell built in Haifa and then trucked it down across the desert to Eilat where it was launched and sunk on the reef more than 100 yards from shore. The anchorage was covered with live coral to attract more sealife and a glass tower was attached to the top to give access to a boardwalk 21 feet above. The view from inside is one that's usually reserved for people hardy enough for scuba diving. There are more than 200 kinds of tropical fish out there, each more exotic than the last.

Seekers of the exotic can find just about everything at Eilat from a resort run by Club Mediterranee to a seaside restaurant called Nelson's Village, where diners

As might be expected, education plays a very important part in the life of modern Israel. *Center left* is part of the Hebrew University in Jerusalem, and *top and bottom left* the Ben-Gurion University of the Negev at Beersheba.

Like a gigantic tree-stump, on a
hillside west of Jerusalem stands
the John F. Kennedy Memorial *below.*

eat at wooden tables on the beach from metal bowls
with their fingers. Nelson never got around to buying
knives and forks for his restaurant. He never had
electricity installed, either. And you can't call for a
reservation; there's no telephone.

Not far outside the city is the impressive mountain
called Jebel Mussa, the place tourist guidebooks often
identify as Mount Sinai, the place where Moses
received the Ten Commandments. The Greek
Orthodox monks who live in the old Saint Catherine's
Monastery at its base are convinced it's the place where
Moses found the Burning Bush. They live there in
isolation, preferring not to get into the scholarly debate
that rages over what may or may not have happened at
the top of their 7,500-foot mountain.

After the Six Day War tourists descended on the
place and completely changed the lives of the black-
robed monks, whose only contact with the outside
world up until then was a tribe of Bedouins who looked
after them. And that contact wasn't exactly eye-to-eye.
The Bedouins are descendants of 400 slaves who were
imported from Romania by the Emperor Justinian,
who established the monastery in the sixth century.
They earned their keep by lowering food and other
supplies in baskets from the top of the walls. Eventually
they intermarried with local Bedouins and were
converted to Islam, even though they worked for the
Greek Orthodox Church. They assembled flocks of
sheep and goats and planted small gardens to
supplement their needs. But those were the only
changes in their existence for more than 1,400 years
until the Israelis started coming after 1967.

197

Today many of them have traded their tents for stone houses and their camels for noisy pickup trucks. They've discovered transistor radios, too, and none of them ever seems to go anywhere without one. They go further from home than ever before, too. Hundreds of them work in Eilat and Sharm el-Sheik, most of them representing the first in the history of their families ever to work for money.

But if their lives have changed, it's nothing compared to what's happened to the monks of Saint Catherine's. A few years ago, when Passover and both the Roman and Greek Easter celebrations fell within a week of each other, one of the monks said it had been "our busiest fortnight in a thousand years." He was probably right. More than 3,000 people paid 40 cents each to walk through the monastery's gates during those two weeks. More than 25,000 went there during that single year. The average before 1967 was less than 100 a month.

But if it made the monastic life a little hectic, most of the visitors agreed the tour was well worth the 40 cents. The monastery contains more than 2,000 icons and precious manuscripts in the oldest library in the world. Only the Vatican Library in Rome has a more important collection. It has a mosaic ceiling that's a real treasure, too. But the thing most visitors come away whispering among themselves about is the Room of the Skulls.

There are 15 monks who live in the monastery on a permanent basis and each of them expects to die there. Over the centuries it became a problem finding enough room to bury all of them in the small amount of space allotted for a cemetery. The only way one can be buried there is to dig up the bones of one of his predecessors. The bones are carefully stacked in a special room. There is no way of telling if any souvenir hunters have walked away with any of them, but the monks have now added iron bars to the library's windows so visitors won't pick up any other interesting mementoes.

The Southern Sinai is one of the last great natural areas in the world that hasn't yet been spoiled. The mountains are spectacular walls of treeless rock, the canyons virtually inaccessible and the plains nearly empty. It's an almost mystical place cut off from civilization. But it's changing fast.

Though there aren't many trees in the Sinai mountains, except around every oasis, there are lush gardens, many of which are going untended these days, now that Bedouin farmers are driving into town for better jobs. They're watered by pools formed by melting snow and trapped behind stone walls built to keep the livestock out. The mountains themselves are a reddish-colored granite that change in color as the sun gets higher in the sky, running from soft pink to gold to lavender and scarlet. The shadows of the wind-shaped stone columns add to the drama and the colors of the little gardens and their stone walls punctuate it. From the tops of the mountains, the view includes the Gulf of Suez and the mountains of Egypt on one side, and the Gulf of Eilat and Saudi Arabia on the other. To the north lies Israel and the Negev, another spectacular sight. No wonder the stone steps that lead to the top of Jebel Mussa are called "the gateway to heaven."

Under the terms of a peace treaty with Egypt, Israel is systematically pulling its border back from the entire Sinai Peninsula, and by now a lot of it is officially Egyptian. The treaty also allows for open borders, and traffic between the two countries has reached almost epidemic proportions. During the years of Israeli control, new roads were built and new tourist facilities added. They put in a new airfield near the old monastery, and the Egyptians have announced even grander plans to make the Sinai a prime tourist attraction. Since the attraction is basically unspoiled wilderness and unbelievable solitude, the plans might just backfire. Take away the natural beauty and what's left is sandstorms and hot sun. But the rocks have endured both for thousands of years and no number of modern hotels and snack stands can take away the beauty of the stars at night. They're so big and bright you almost feel you could reach out and touch one.

Since travel restrictions have been reduced between Israel and Egypt, more than three-quarters of the people in both countries have said they are making plans to take advantage of the opportunity. Tourists from other countries say the same thing. Unless they're pressed for time or are going to Israel on business, almost no one from the United States goes to one these days without going to the other. And the idea has increased enthusiasm for going to Israel in the first place. No wonder so many new facilities are being added!

Israeli forces moved out of the Sinai at the beginning of 1980, moving the border back to a line that runs from El Arish on the Mediterranean south to Ras Mohammad at the tip of the peninsula. Eventually, the border will be moved again to the line that existed before the 1967 war.

The peace treaty also allowed direct telephone and postal connections between Egypt and Israel as well as scheduled air traffic. But Israelis going to Egypt usually prefer to fly to Athens and go back across in a cruise ship. Foreign tourists, on the other hand, often prefer the adventure of driving the 300 miles from Tel Aviv to Cairo, but the drive is far from easy along desert roads that sometimes disappear under sand dunes. The

welcome on the other side is warm, though, even if not as warm as the one that was waiting for the first Israeli who made the trip. Egyptian officials at the border ceremoniously handed her a bottle of Coca-Cola. After a long hot drive across the desert, it was probably a lot more welcome than you think.

Traffic across the border wasn't really anything new to a whole subculture of Bedouins who have been doing it for years, even while fighting was going on. They're people who supplement their income by smuggling.

In preparation for the day when the border was going to be moved, some of them added a new wrinkle to an old game. They buried goods under the sands of the Israeli Sinai then sat back to wait for the border to move and dug the stuff up in Egypt. And it wasn't small-time stuff, either. Their favorite thing to smuggle in that way was Mercedes-Benzes. They didn't turn their noses up at Cadillacs or Volvos either because there's a big market for luxury cars in Cairo, but there's also a big customs duty on the ones that are brought in legitimately.

These same businessmen used to smuggle bombs from Egypt into Israel to be used by terrorists, but most of them have given that up as too dangerous. That's not to say they've given up smuggling, though. They regularly slip across the border carrying cigarettes and coffee, transistor radios and television sets, even gasoline and auto parts for resale to Arabs living in Israel. And they don't go back empty-handed. They take back food that's cheaper in Israeli stores and, of course, an occasional automobile or two.

They also take back hashish, which is hard to sell in Israel, and is therefore relatively cheap. It gets a much higher price in Egypt so it's popular among smugglers.

I am a stranger and a sojourner with you . . .
Genesis 23:4

Though most of the smugglers travel the old routes across the desert, a great many of them go by water in fishing boats between El Arish and the Gaza Strip. It's also the traditional route for gasoline smugglers who buy the fuel at low prices in Egypt and move it up the coast for resale at much higher prices in Israel. A fishing boat isn't an oil tanker, though, so it isn't a high-profit operation. But it's better than going north empty when they're headed for Gaza to pick up more hashish.

The Gaza Strip is home to about 400,000 Palestinian Arabs, many of whom have been living in congested camps since 1948, when they were driven from their homes during the War of Independence. Many more who were born in the camps have never known any other home, but look longingly out from behind Gaza's citrus orchards and dream about towns they've never seen and never will because they don't exist any more. To most people they've become an annoying statistic, to many an ominous threat. Few people can even agree on why they're in Gaza in the first place.

According to the party line in the Arab countries, the Palestinians were systematically driven from their homes by ruthless Israeli soldiers who quickly destroyed those homes so they'd never come back. The official story in Israel is that their own leaders told them to go and promised them that they would return victoriously behind the Arab League who would drive Israel into the sea in a very short time.

There may be a little truth along with a little exaggeration in both stories. But unfortunately, the past is what determines the future. The Palestinian view of the past prompts militants among them to say that with their own state they can remove Zionism from the earth and establish a truly democratic state in Israel. The Israelis interpret that as meaning they can remove Israel from the earth, and add that they have never attacked an Arab population, but have a lot of experience defending themselves from Arabs.

Meanwhile, the situation in Gaza is tense, which is especially ironic because its very name has given the world a word that means the same thing as soft, airy and loose. It comes from a silk fabric they made there called gauze.

The strip of land that runs for 30 miles along the Mediterranean coast from the Sinai to the city of Gaza itself is a lush area with orange and lemon trees stretching about four miles back from the sea. It was where the Philistines took the mighty Samson for a haircut, and where he surprised them by pulling their temple down around their heads. Even then it was a very old city and a convenient stopping-off point for Egyptian traders on their way to Syria. In the years since, it has been a Greek city, a Roman city, a European city under the Crusaders, a Turkish city, a British city; finally, after the first two days of the Six Day War, it became an Israeli-occupied city, a fact of life that was reconfirmed after the Yom Kippur War. Negotiations have been going on almost ever since to change its status again, but it doesn't look like the Israeli Government plans to move out of Gaza any time soon.

In the meantime, Palestinians from Gaza go across the border every morning to work in Israel. It makes their life easier, even reduces some of the strain that comes from living in an occupied territory. But the strains are there and the tension is never easy.

Seen from David Ben-Gurion's tomb in the Negev Desert, the bleak landscape *left* is relieved only by the signs of vegetation on the floor of the valley.

A camel *above* seeks the sparse shade of an almost defoliated tree in the Negev, and two young members of a Bedouin family trek with their animals and belongings near the shores of the Red Sea *overleaf*.

At least the Arabs in Gaza live behind what is more or less an easy border to understand from the standpoint of geography. Arabs who live in the territory called the West Bank, the other disputed area occupied by Israel after the 1967 war, aren't behind a simple border at all. Any reasonable person hearing there was a place with a name like that would naturally assume it referred to the bank of a river extending back a mile or two to the west. Even chronic flooders like the Nile or the Mississippi can't claim much more than that as their banks. But in this case, the "bank" extends as much as 35 miles from the Jordan River toward the Mediterranean in some places. And in some of those places, it gets to within 10 miles of the sea. If that's not strange enough, it crosses hills and mountains before it ceases to be the West Bank of Jordan and becomes "Old Israel." And it's more than just the bank of a river. Several miles of territory at the southern end extend west from the shore of the Dead Sea.

From north to south, the West Bank is about 80 miles long. At the top, the mountains are as much as 3,000 feet high; at the bottom, a desert fills a hole almost 700 feet below sea level. People who believe what labels tell them will be further confused by the fact that the western edge of the West Bank doesn't even match the path of the river or the shore of the sea. It meanders north from the river bank and bulges away from it to form what seems to be the start of a big oval, but as the border heads south, it curves back toward the river again to form a neck with Jerusalem at its

205

head. Then it bulges back west again to form a second oval with Hebron at the center.

It's confusing, but almost anyone in Israel could draw a map of it blindfolded. And visitors to Israel find out right away why everyone there takes West Bank political discussions so seriously. To get from Ben Gurion Airport in Tel Aviv down to Jerusalem, it's necessary to go through the Occupied West Bank. It's that close to home for most Israelis.

Since the area was captured in 1967, more than 20,000 Jews from Israel have made it their home. It's probably the most controversial settlement program in the area since the first Russian refugees arrived in Palestine in 1882. Many of the Jewish settlers see their work as a way of finding roots in a Biblical land. Others, quite simply, see settlement as an effective way of blocking the emergence of a Palestinian Arab State in the territory, and that's the only side of the issue the Arabs choose to look at.

The settlers there are about equally divided among Sabras and new immigrants, mostly from Europe, but including a few from the United States. In either case, the life they find on the West Bank is a whole lot tougher than the life they left behind. They began moving in almost before the smoke of the '67 war had blown away. At first they built new towns on the sites of older Jewish settlements that had been destroyed in other times and other wars. Other settlements on the Golan Heights or deep in the Jordan Valley were a long way from any territory any Arab would have once considered important. To the Israelis they are important as outposts to guard against a surprise attack, of course, and they represented an opportunity for pioneering again. A great many people who have migrated from Europe and the United States in the last decade went to Israel with a strong desire to help build a new country with their own hands. Life in the big coastal population centers isn't exactly what they had in mind, and the new West Bank settlements were just what the doctor ordered. Naturally, people with that kind of dream tend to be young and almost all the settlers are couples under 35 with young children. People with that kind of idealism are usually educated, too, and almost none of the West Bank pioneers hasn't

From the Coral World Underwater Observatory *these pages* excursion boats and glass-bottomed boats set out to view the beautiful and colorful underwater life of this area.

Eilat *right and overleaf,* on the gulf of
the same name, is both a busy port, which
is the terminal for the oil pipeline to
Ashkelon, and a prosperous vacation resort.

had at least some college education.

If those 100-odd little towns were in the United States, advertising agencies would be breaking their necks trying to reach them. They're what the research people like to call "up-scale." Of course, for all their qualities that spell affluence in other countries, many of these people don't live affluent lives at all. They gave up most of the trappings of the good life by colonizing those towns in the first place. They live their lives behind barbed wire fences in communities that began life as a collection of tents and converted boxes. When they do build real houses, they're usually concrete boxes that don't look much better than the old wooden ones they started out with. You can tell which of the communities has dreams of becoming a great city because the concrete boxes are two stories high instead of one. A few towns are home to new farmers, but most of the settlers are commuters who drive to the city each day to earn a living. On the way they often have to dodge rocks thrown at their cars by Arab children.

While they're at work, and in just about every case both husbands and wives go to work each day, their homes and children are watched over by armed guards, both soldiers and community volunteers. When they're at home, the guards still stand watch, but army regulations require that every house must have at least one automatic rifle and more than one person who knows how to use it.

Some of the communities in the West Bank don't have barbed wire fences around them, though they all have armed guards. They were settled by ultra-militant young people who say the whole idea behind the creation of Israel was to eliminate ghettos from the Jewish existence. They say every fence creates a new ghetto and they doggedly refuse to build them.

There are others who say that the existence of the West Bank settlements adds to the wall between Jews and Arabs; especially the newer ones established close to existing Arab towns and cities. Though there are many people who sincerely believe that Arabs and Jews can live side by side in peace, there are many, many others who say it's impossible. In general, the Arabs see the new settlements as symbols that Israel wants territory they think they own. It isn't easy to tell them otherwise when many of the settlements are built on land that was confiscated after the war and often in places that puts a strain on water supply that was adequate before the new towns were built. Israel counters the argument by saying that they never build on cultivated farmland nor on privately-owned land. The new settlements, they say, have been built on ground that was formerly the property of the Jordanian

Government and is therefor the property of the Israeli Government today.

And so it continues. Though organized terrorist raids on Israeli settlements in the West Bank are extremely rare, tension shows itself in stone-throwing incidents, even shootings, and neither side has a record of never having provoked one or the other.

Possibly the hottest of all the West Bank hot spots is Hebron, after the Wailing Wall the holiest of all the Jewish Holy Places in Israel. It's the place where Abraham first pitched his tents in the Promised Land and where he buried his wife, Sarah. It's also the last resting place of Isaac and Jacob and their wives. And there's a legend many believe that says Hebron is where Adam and Eve went when they were expelled from the Garden of Eden and where their remains are today. Hebron is also where David became a king and where he ruled for several years before moving up to Jerusalem. And it's where Herod built a fortress probably even more impressive than Masada, possibly using stones from Solomon's Temple.

If Hebron is important to the Jews, it's also considered holy to the Moslems who live there. Both Arabs and Jews revere the memory of Abraham who is buried in the Machpelah Cave under a mountain that's topped by a mosque. In the old days, Jews and Arabs worshipped side by side there. But back in the 1920s the Arabs massacred all the Jews living in Hebron and decreed that no Jew could climb any higher than the seventh step on the stairway leading up to the mosque. Yet in a way the mosque symbolizes a kind of brotherhood between Jews and Moslems. Both believe they are descended from Abraham. His wife Sarah, convinced that she was barren, told Abraham to "go unto my maid; it may be that I may obtain children by her." The maid, an Egyptian girl named Hagar, gave birth to a son, Ishmael. Later when Sarah herself gave birth to Isaac, she had the servant girl and her son banished into the desert. The children of Ishmael worship at his father's tomb today. But so do the children of Isaac, and that can be a problem.

The problem has been solved, or at least cooled a bit, by a very complicated schedule. The shrine is reserved exclusively for Moslems five times a day and for Jews three times a day. On Friday, a Moslem holy day, Jews can't go into the mosque until late in the afternoon. On Saturday, the Jewish Sabbath, the Moslems are kept out all morning. The rules are strictly enforced by Israeli guards with automatic rifles.

The guards also wear combat boots and that annoys the Moslems no end. In the days when non-Moslems were kept below the seventh step, the entire interior of the mosque was covered with thick rugs, and no one

ever went inside without first taking off their shoes. Now the rugs have been rolled back from much of the floor, and during the designated time for Jews, no one takes their shoes off. Not even combat boots.

The Jews on the other hand say it was a synagogue before it was a mosque, and even though the walls inside are decorated with intricate Islamic calligraphy, they point out that much of the grillwork, which is beautifully wrought, was designed by Jewish artisans. No one bothers to mention that the Gothic arches are all that remains of Christian churches that also graced the spot in centuries gone by.

The biggest of the Jewish West Bank settlements is a suburb of Hebron called Qiryat Arba. It was founded in 1968 as the first Jewish settlement since the 1929 pogrom. The original settlement was in Hebron itself and was started by a small group who checked in at an Arab hotel and never bothered to check out. They said they were Swiss tourists, and undoubtedly every time anyone in the hotel tried speaking to them in German they pretended to be French-speaking and vice versa. Finally, the Israeli Government spoke to them in Hebrew and quietly persuaded them to move out. They moved into an Israeli military base outside town, and they're still there. The community has grown to more than 600 families, and with the infusion of more than $50 million from the government, they've managed to build an attractive town with paved streets, apartment houses and elaborate landscaping, all set down behind a high fence with watchtowers at the corners.

The most modern of the West Bank cities is Nablus, which is not to call it a new city by any means. Nablus is where Abraham built an altar after God promised the land to his descendants and where Joshua brought the Israelites together. It was a huge city and a sacred place in the fourth century B.C. It was where Jezebel played, where Romans held their bacchanals and where Crusaders dreamed of home and gave it a new name. Naples.

The mountain that towers over the town, Mount Gerizim, is sacred to the Samaritans, a small Jewish sect which became outcasts when Ahab married Jezebel. After the Babylonian exile, they were forbidden to join in the work of rebuilding the Temple. Their response was to say "so what?" and to declare Mount Gerizim more holy than Jerusalem. It was here, and not Mount Moriah, that Abraham went through the motions of preparing his son, Isaac, for sacrifice, they said.

There aren't many of them left these days, but Samaritans who still live in Nablus and at Holon gather on the mountain each year at Passover to mark the event in exactly the same manner as their earliest ancestors. They even ritually slaughter the Pascal lamb for the Passover Feast.

Of all the controversial expansion into the West Bank, none excites as much passion on both sides as East Jerusalem. Before 1967 it was called "the Arab sector," but as soon as the war was over, the city's boundaries were extended into the countryside and work began on huge apartment house developments in a semi-circle around the eastern side of the city. The old Jewish quarter was rebuilt around the Biblical sites, too, and today the entire area is home to some 35,000 Jews who say they've come home to stay. Work continues and the neighborhoods are still growing, in spite of criticism from other countries in the world who feel that the occupied territories ought to be the subject of peace negotiations.

But even the most liberal Israelis don't want to see the city divided again, even if other West Bank settlements need to be given up. The debate continues. Other countries, including the United States, meanwhile refuse to recognize Jerusalem as the captial of Israel, and maintain their embassies at Tel Aviv. But in spite of it, Jerusalem, all of it, is an Israeli city and just about everybody in the country seems determined to keep it that way in spite of what the rest of the world says or does.

And as if to show the rest of the world they mean what they say, one of the more elegant apartment houses north of Jerusalem was built in the shell of a partially-completed summer palace Jordan's King Hussein had been building for himself when the war that won the territory began.

There's controversy over settlement north of the West Bank, too, in a place called the Golan Heights. The first kibbutz there was born in the minds of some people who lived not far away in a settlement in the mountains near the Lebanon border. During the '67 war, families there watched the terrible and costly battle that finally ended with Israeli control of the Heights. They decided right then and there that the only way Israel could keep control of the hills was to establish settlements.

A few days after the fighting stopped a group of men from those families went up to the Golan Heights as volunteer cowboys. Thousands of head of Arab cattle had been scattered in the fighting and help was needed to round them up. Within four months they also rounded up their families and moved into a camp of concrete houses that had been home to the families of officers in the Syrian Army. They called their new kibbutz Merom Golan.

The government at the time was less than

In desert lands throughout the world nature, during the course of countless centuries, has carved, using water and wind, incredible shapes out of combinations of hard and soft stone, such as these formations in the Negev.

enthusiastic about the idea of settling the Golan Heights, so they had to find a way to support themselves without much outside help. Their answer to that problem was to make Merom Golan a tourist center. They knew that people would flock there from all parts of Israel curious for a peek at the new territory and by the time the first of them arrived, the Kibbutzniks were ready for them.

They converted one of the Syrian army buildings into a hotel. It wasn't a fancy place, but good enough to fetch $2.50 a night for each of the cots inside. Next door they built a cafeteria. It wasn't fancy, either, but it was the only one in town and just about the only one anywhere on the Golan Heights. Their real gold mine, though, was their gas station. Not only did the tourists need gas and oil, but the shell craters in the roads did

so much damage to their cars, most of them needed repairs as well.

They did a brisk business for five years and in their spare time they planted crops and tended cattle. At the end of the five years their community had grown from less than 50 to more than 200 persons and they had enough money accumulated to think about building more permanent homes.

The army helped them find a spot in the shadow of an old volcano that reason told them would serve as protection against any future shelling from Syria. Reason went out the window when the Yom Kippur War broke out with an artillery barrage and a fighter bomber attack. But kibbutz survived even though, like all the other Golan settlements, they were forced to evacuate their women and children. Four of the men of Merom Golan were killed during the fighting, and when life started up again for the others, post-war shelling from Syria made it impossible to work the fields. Just as bad was the fact that Israeli troops commandeered some of their homes and proved to be less than careful about things they found there.

Added to all that, uncertainty over the future of their hills made life in Merom Golan jittery at best. Finally the politicians agreed to a cease-fire line that put the kibbutz just east of the border and they were able to keep their community and their fields. But even the smallest of their children could lob one of those great, heavy Golan apples over into Syria without hardly trying.

Many couples with small children went back to safer territory during those months, so once the treaty gave them a sort of grip on the future, the kibbutz advertised for new settlers and formed an alliance with other kibbutzim to get more government help.

The settlement has grown a great deal since then and they have neighbors now, too. There are close to 30 settlements in the Golan Heights and the farms that surround them are lush. The soil is rich, black volcanic dirt that wasn't farmed much in the years before the Israelis came along with their plows. Merom Golan has invested well over $12 million, much of it government money they lobbied hard to get, to make it a pleasant place to live. Its buildings are largely undistinguished affairs that aren't much more than concrete boxes with

flat roofs. But they are functional. An artillery shell can score a direct hit on any of them and not do much more than crack the stucco. If it cracked the plaster inside, though, there probably wouldn't be anybody inside to notice. During any alert just about everybody would be underground in the reinforced shelters that are equipped for a very long siege.

The houses are arranged in a semi-circle for more protection, almost like the old wagon trains in the American West. In the center the highest building in town, a two story concrete box, houses the communal dining hall, a general store, a library and a laundry. If the life sounds Spartan, it is. But they also have an Olympic-size pool, their houses have lawns and flower gardens and their children never have to walk more than a few yards to a well-equipped playground.

They finance it all with a multi-million dollar agricultural enterprise that includes a respectable herd of beef cattle and an automated turkey farm. They grow wheat and potatoes, apples and tomatoes, even flowers are a cash crop. And even though they themselves live in concrete houses, they operate two stone quarries and some of their members operate a successful cabinet-making business.

Except for the fact that each of the men stands guard duty twice a week and the women never go beyond the barbed wire without a rifle over their shoulder, life in Merom Golan isn't much different from life on any kibbutz in Israel. But there is one big difference. This one's on the border. Less than 5 per cent of Israel's population lives on kibbutzim or even plan to. Among those who plan to, only a small percentage are willing to take the gamble of moving into a place like the Golan Heights.

Most Israelis seem to prefer living nearer the sea where the air is healthier.

The place where most of them live is the place Dr. Weitzmann stood ankle deep in the sand and listened to the unbelievable story that a great Jewish city would stand there one day and its name would be Tel Aviv – hill of spring.

It's a huge city today, of course, part of an almost continuous city that runs for miles along the coast.

It's fashionable to say it doesn't have a real history, and in terms of other cities in Israel that's possibly true. Yet the people who began building it in 1909 were probably wringing their hands about all that change and growth when Shaham was a boy. If history means tradition, Tel Aviv has little to offer. But if history is a record of change, it's got the richest history of any place anywhere near. And the history of Tel Aviv is the history of Israel itself.

Rock formations *right* assume fortress-like proportions in the Negev Desert where, with imagination and irrigation, crops are able to thrive as well as the desert cactus *overleaf*.

Avdat *above* was the first of the Nabatean towns to be restored.

*Then I came to them of the captivity at Tel-a-bib . . .
and remained there astonished among them seven days.*
Ezekiel 3:15

Back in 1909, about a third of the Jewish population in Palestine lived in Jaffa. It was perfectly natural. Most of them had arrived from Europe by ship and Jaffa was the main seaport most of them went to. As a busy port, it offered jobs for many of them, and most were more at home in cities anyway. They earned fair livings in banks and shipping companies, many opened small shops and competed with the Arabs. But the Arab majority was a problem. The Jews had come to find the Promised Land, but they were still outsiders in a crowded, dirty little Arab city. So some of them decided to move to the suburbs. The only problem was that the few suburbs there were, also happened to be dirty little Arab towns.

222

A group of 60 families got together and decided to make one for themselves. They pooled their money and bought a tract of 32 acres on a sand dune just across the railroad tracks near the road to Nablus. One fine spring day all of them trekked out into the desert to begin their Great Work with ceremonies that included a speech by their leader, Meir Dizengoff, who enthusiastically predicted that their sand dune would grow to a community of 25,000 within their lifetime. Those who snickered at the idea probably didn't live to see the population come to just within the million mark less than 70 years later.

Some suburb!

Also included in the ceremonies that day was the dedication of the town's main street, which they called Herzl Street in honor of the founder of Zionism. After a photographer snapped formal pictures that look for all the world like a wedding at the O.K. Corral, they took off their jackets and rolled up their sleeves. Before work could actually begin, they drew lots for the best building sites on their dream street. But that was settled quickly and just as the sun reached the highest point in the sky they began clearing sand. It was slow work. There was no shortage of shovels, but among the 60 families there was only one wheelbarrow.

It took them a while, but they finally built their houses. As work progressed, their old neighbors from Jaffa dropped by to have a look and to do a little kibitzing. What they saw impressed them and it wasn't long before it was necessary to add another street. They

was very much at home in Tel Aviv, and it was a source of pride to everyone in town for the next 50 years. By 1960, the town had acquired a planning board that ruled it ought to be torn down so that Herzl Street could be extended and the tallest building in the Middle East built on the spot. The Shalom Tower that graces the spot today is 37 floors high. It's worth the small fee they charge to go up to the observatory at the top for a look at how those 32 acres of suburb have grown.

If the original settlers didn't have a plan in today's sense, they did have a few rules that town planners would applaud today. They wanted the place to be quiet and secluded, so one of the rules said there was to be no traffic within their "city limits." The men of the community all commuted into Jaffa each day, and many made the trip back and forth on foot. Those who preferred to ride did it in horse-drawn carriages they called droshkies.

On their time off they tended gardens around their homes and made general improvements as time and finances allowed. The women had to go into Jaffa for shopping at first, but it wasn't too long before their trip was shortened when shops and stalls crept into the area near the railroad. Their idealistic husbands were determined to keep commercial development at arm's length, though, so they were resigned to the fact that they would always have to go out of town for supplies.

On the Sabbath they made it clear that no one was to go out or in by running a heavy chain across the foot of Herzl Street, but that was a gesture that was more symbolic than threatening. They were proud of their garden village and eager to show anyone willing to look what they had been able to accomplish with their own hands.

And plenty were willing. Within the first five years, more than 3,000 souls had been so impressed by what they saw they decided to stay. Naturally that meant more streets had to be built and the town fathers had to retract their rules against commercialism, and a marketplace grew in the center of town, much to the relief of the women.

When World War I broke out everyone in town was ordered out by the Turkish Governor. The mini diaspora relocated them all over Palestine, but it didn't last long. Less than six months after they were uprooted, the British took control of Jaffa and let them all go home again. And with the Turks out of the way, more immigrants came along with them. It was a boom town.

It was also time to think about making Tel Aviv independent of Jaffa. They did it in 1921 and

called it Rothschild Boulevard, probably thinking it wouldn't hurt a bit to honor a man as wealthy as the Baron.

It grew like that without any plan except for the one to build a grand high school, both to bring in paying students from abroad and to educate their own children without foreign influences. They called it the Herzlia Gymnasium, and it was grand all right. They built it themselves on their own designs, which they had agreed should be along the lines of the buildings on Temple Mount. The problem was either that most of them hadn't made the trip to Jerusalem or didn't carry back clear memories of what they saw there. In any case, the Herzlia Gymnasium would have been much more at home in Istanbul than Jerusalem. But it

immediately elected the city's founder, Meir Dizengoff, as their first Mayor. It was a lifetime job, as it turned out. He held the job until he died 15 years later.

By the time it became an independent city, Tel Aviv already had a population of 15,000. People were arriving from Europe in bigger numbers than ever but they weren't stopping in Jaffa any longer. They went a little further to Tel Aviv, but most of them, apparently, didn't want to go any further than that. Most of the people who arrived in those early years came from Germany and they brought strange ideas with them. They didn't think that children had enough respect for their parents. They thought cab drivers and store-keepers were rude and they thought the atmosphere of the town was much too lighthearted for anyone else in the rest of the world to take it seriously.

The reaction of the "natives" was that Germans don't have a sense of humor anyway and they probably never would understand. So they just went on in their lighthearted way and ignored the criticism. It wasn't too long before the Germans discovered their own sense of humor and learned to enjoy their new life. But along the way some of their old ideas stuck and life seemed to be getting better for everybody. There were troubles from outside, to be sure, but they felt a certain sense of security in their town and took Arab harassment in their stride. Not only that, they turned it to their advantage. The idea of becoming an independent city had come along when the Arabs and Jaffa began staging anti-Jewish riots. When the Arabs went on strike in the '30s, it gave them a reason to turn Tel Aviv into an independent seaport. And through a long succession of wars and riots, even including a period during British rule when everybody in town was placed under house arrest for four days, the building has never stopped.

It gives the city a sense of vitality few other cities in the world ever feel. Nobody ever seems to stop working and the amazing thing is that they all seem to enjoy it.

Tel Aviv's greatest appeal in the early days was that it was the first all-Jewish city in modern times. At just about the same time Israel became the first all-Jewish State in modern times, Tel Aviv experienced a sudden burst of growth that brought the Arab city of Jaffa into its limits. The suburb had swallowed up the city. The annexation took place after the British moved all the Arabs out and resettled them in Arab territory. But even though the all-Jewish city had taken in Arab neighborhoods, they were all empty.

In the process, they also acquired a history as long and rich as any city in the country. Jaffa is one of the oldest seaports in the world, for centuries the gateway by sea to Jerusalem. Like the other port cities in the Middle East it's been under the control of dozens of different superpowers from Egyptians to Phoenicians to Crusaders.

It's the place, they say, where Jonah shoved off on his unusually eventful ocean trip. It's also the place where Perseus rescued his future wife Andromeda, an Ethiopian princess who had been chained to rocks in the harbor to make a tasty feast for a sea monster. If you're the sort given to buying things like the Brooklyn Bridge, it isn't hard to find an antiques dealer in Jaffa who might have some of Andromeda's chain lying around in a back room. If you press him, he might also have a trinket or two left over from the treasure King Solomon found washed up on the beach at Jaffa.

The inevitable archaeological digs have uncovered pieces of a fortress built 33 centuries ago. They've found a statue of Aphrodite and some coins left lying around by soldiers in the pay of Alexander the Great. There's a tower at the harbor entrance that was built by Crusaders. And the Turks, as they often do, left behind a very solid jail. The Russian Orthodox Church operates a monastery in Jaffa on the site of a tomb they say was the place Saint Peter raised a man from the dead.

Who says the city doesn't have a history?

After the British drove the Arabs out of Jaffa, officials in Tel Aviv weren't too sure what to do with it. It was a filthy place with a lot of unpleasant memories. The towers of its mosque had been a snipers' nest, its buildings hiding places for Arabs who had been much less than friendly. Besides, they were told, the very idea behind the creation of Tel Aviv was to get away from Jaffa. Added to that, the city had enough problems trying to untangle the mess that was created by allowing it to grow too fast.

Their first reaction was to take a few bulldozers down to Jaffa and start from scratch. The controversy over that idea suddenly made preservationists out of people who until then had been almost barbaric in the rush to tear down old buildings to build bigger, newer ones. The result of their "Save Old Jaffa" campaign is a restoration that's the pride of all Israel. The work is still going on and someday, they say, the beaches and the buildings along them will rival the French Riviera.

Meanwhile, Old Jaffa is an artist colony and the nightclub capital of Israel. A few thousand Arabs still live there, but the population of the quarter is mostly Jews who came after the creation of the State. The result is an international atmosphere in the setting of a casbah. You can get an expensive French meal there or nibble Middle Eastern pastry in an open-air cafe all the while listening to the sounds of a dozen different

Much of the Negev Desert was fertile, it is believed, in Biblical times and today, using modern technology, attempts are being made all over this part of Israel to restore its fertility — as here at the Yod Vata Kibbutz.

languages.

It's appropriate that the first step for most tourists going into the Old City is the Flea Market, where you can haggle over the price of anything from an Oriental rug to a frying pan. They sell jewelry and hand-me-down furniture, old clothes and so-called "antiques." But they never, ever sell them at the first price quoted. Never, that is, unless the customer is foolish enough to pay without bargaining for a lower price.

There are more than 100 art galleries in Tel Aviv and most of them are in the Old City. Their owners drive a much harder bargain than the stall-tenders in the Flea Market because Israelis are good customers for original art. In Jaffa, tourists add to the demand, making it a sellers market. But if there are no bargains, there are good values and looking for them is an adventure in itself.

The night clubs of Jaffa suit every taste imaginable, from topless dancers to smoky jazz to traditional Israeli folk dancing. There are discos too, of course. And lots of those little bars with straw furniture and palm trees where customers can let their hair down over a pina colada or two. Other places are decorated in trendy art deco or stylish stained glass. If it all sounds very European or American, there's a good reason for it. Most of the tourists come from Europe and America, of course, and it's good business to make them feel at home. But more important is an Israeli preoccupation with Western styles. Though they still pride themselves on being independent, they'd rather be that way in a polyester shirt and designer blue jeans.

All the action in Tel Aviv isn't in the Old City. In fact, a lot of people go into Jaffa just to slow down the pace. In the shadow of the Israel National Opera, which is housed in a building that was the Knesset when Tel Aviv was the capital of the country, there are dozens of open air Greek restaurants each equipped with amplifiers playing native music. A little inland the music gets a little quieter and the food a lot faster thanks to the likes of Mr. Wimpy and his competitors who serve up hamburgers and hot dogs, ice cream and pizza. Anyone who survives that gauntlet is rewarded a block or two further north with a quiet neighborhood of charming cafes.

The neighborhood is more attractive to strollers these days than it once was now that traffic goes under it rather than through it. The new square on top of the highway, Dizengoff Circle, is the heart of Tel Aviv's most fashionable shopping area. In the evening it's the place young people gather to meet other young people and to show off the fashionable things they bought that day.

There are two universities in Tel Aviv; Tel Aviv University with almost 13,000 students, and Bar Ilan University with about 7,000, so there are plenty of young people to meet there.

Many of the evening strollers on Dizengoff Circle have more on their mind than seeing and being-seen. They're the lucky ones with tickets to a concert at the nearby Mann Auditorium. It's one of the most acoustically-perfect buildings in the world, and the performances there are almost always perfect, too. There are 3,000 seats in the auditorium and all of them are always filled for every concert. But as an accomodation to tourists, there are 85 seats on the stage behind the musicians that are sold through the Tourist Office as well as in hotels. They also sell returned tickets that way, but there are precious few of those.

After the concert some may wander up to the Tel Aviv Marina for a refreshing sea breeze or an evening of disco dancing. Some of the people already there may be on their way home from an outdoor band concert. Or they may already be home. The Marina accepts sailing vessels only, but many of them are up to 60 feet long and include very comfortable living accommodations. Since the Suez Canal was reopened, Tel Aviv has become an important port of call for international yachtsmen.

It's almost impossible to be bored in Tel Aviv. The city has six resident theater companies, three concert halls and almost 20 movie theaters. It has great sailing, eight beaches and a pool in just about every hotel. It's shy on parks, but there are plenty of sidewalk cafes and other quiet spots to sit and relax. It has coffee houses and restaurants of every description and in every price range. And like every other modern city, the trend is to attract attention with cute names. There's a Chinese restaurant named Jacky Onassis, an Italian place called Me and Me and the real "in" place is a Chinese institution called Mandy's Singing Bamboo. Mandy also has an American restaurant called Mandy's Drugstore and another place dedicated to the glorification of chic called Mandy's Candy Store. Colonel Sanders is there, too, of course, but his Kentucky Fried Chicken is strictly Kosher.

Israelis like good restaurants and there are plenty of them to choose from. They're discriminating enough to avoid the bad ones, so unless a restaurant caters just to tourists it has to be good to stay in business. The country hasn't been in existence long enough to have developed a unique native cuisine, but as a melting pot of different nationalities, it has a lot of variety to offer from Russian to Indonesian.

Most of it is Kosher, to be sure, but the term doesn't have anything to do with cooking or seasoning. The rules cover how animals may be slaughtered; they forbid the combining of meat and dairy products and prohibit eating meat that comes from certain kinds of animals. But how what may be eaten is cooked is mainly up to the cook, and there are plenty of good ones in the kitchens of restaurants all over the country.

The trick, of course, just like anywhere else, it to eat where the natives do. In Israel, the first impression a visitor gets is that the natives eat in the street, in theaters, in buses and taxis and that all they eat is seeds.

They eat sunflower seeds and pumpkin seeds, watermelon seeds and pistachios. It's impossible to go almost anywhere without hearing the constant cracking of shells. According to a philosophical Tel Aviv bus driver it's symbolic of the pace of the country. They can't wait for plants to grow, he theorizes, so they skip a step by eating the seeds.

The "can't wait" mentality seems to be reflected in Israeli breakfasts, too. They make English breakfasts look like light snacks. It's a tradition that was born down on the farm. Farmers and kibbutzniks need to stoke up early in the morning for the long work day and the whole country follows their lead. The day often begins with an array of different cheeses and vegetables served in much the same way as a fine Italian antipasto. It's followed by a fish course sometimes and that's usually followed by yogurt or the curdled milk they call leben. Bread and fruit, especially those marvelous oranges, possibly picked that same morning, top it all off. It's hard to imagine doing a day's work after eating all that food. It's even harder to imagine taking a lunch break.

But they do both. The main meal of the day usually comes in the early afternoon with the evening dinner hour reserved for something light. Probably so they'll

Near Jericho a tractor lays irrigation sprinkler pipes *above right* where this land will one day bear a harvest of crops or fruit *above*.

The Yod Vata Kibbutz *above left* supports dairy herds as well as agricultural produce.

The sun sets *overleaf* over the Negev's capital, Beersheba.

be hungry enough to tackle breakfast the next morning.

Between all those meals and besides all those seeds there are plenty of quick snacks available and eating all day seems to be a national passion. Maybe a little felafel is what it takes to ease the hunger pangs. It's a light snack made of fried chick peas served with salad greens and pickles covered with a hot sauce, and a sauce made from sesame seeds served inside a piece of Arab pita bread. . . . Well, *they* think it's light. Those who think it's too light prefer schwarma, another Arab sandwich that's very much like felafel, but substitutes meat for the chick peas.

Fast food is available everywhere along almost every street. Snackers can find pizza without searching too far. Or if it's a hot day, a slice of watermelon (for a bonus, it's got seeds!). If it's cool, some roasted chestnuts are nice or maybe a potato pancake. About the only thing that's hard to find is bagels and lox.

The feast goes on all the time in the city streets, but it's not just an urban pleasure. If there's anything an Israeli likes better than a snack on the run, it's a picnic. Some of the supermarkets even have whole sections specializing in the special gear to make a day in the country tempting. And the picnics come in all shapes, sizes and budgets. The spread might include fine wine, delicate pâtés or just fruit juice and pastrami sandwiches. Either way, there are picnickers everywhere. And what's more fun than that?

Almost any picnic or any other meal in Israel is likely to include cheese and pickles. No self-respecting Israeli would go through a day without a little of each. And the bread that completes the meal could be any of a dozen different kinds, all of them the best of their kind.

Fresh vegetables and tropical fruits are exported all over the world from Israel, but there's enough left over to make that, if anything, the traditional food of the country. There's fish in abundance, too. What's missing is meat. Most of the meat on Israeli tables is imported, and most of it isn't too good. In spite of the dietary laws, pork is sold almost everywhere and frequently appears on restaurant menus as white steak. Order veal and you'll probably get turkey, but you

Animated discussion in colorful
surroundings *right* at Beersheba
market where Bedouin also bring
their sheep *overleaf*.

probably won't be able to tell the difference.

The best part is dessert, whether it's a fancy Viennese cake or a honey-dipped piece of Middle Eastern baklava. The favorite flavor is chocolate and Israeli ingenuity knows no bounds when it comes to finding new things to flavor with it.

In Tel Aviv, shopping for food is an adventure in itself if it's done in the Carmel market. It's a typical Middle Eastern marketplace, but with a foreign accent. There are some established stores there but most of the businessmen operate from stalls that go home with them at night or they simply pile their produce on the ground and hope they don't have to take any of it home. It's a noisy place with hucksters calling out for attention in a dozen different languages. It has a memorable smell, too, especially at the end of a long hot day. It's a meat market, a produce market, a place to buy fresh fish. It's also a place to buy fresh flowers, something as important as food in any Israeli house. You might buy an umbrella or a pair of shoes at the Carmel market, but the real bargains in merchandise like that is in the Polish market. They sell calculators and watches, used clothing and luggage to pack it in at amazingly low prices.

The marketplaces are noisy places, so is most of Tel Aviv. But there is a quiet time. On Friday nights, people who spend the other nights strolling, generally visit each other in their homes and the streets are comparatively quiet. Orthodox men gather at the Great Synagogue to pray, and traffic is diverted away from it to make their way easier. They walk home, of course, and according to tradition, the angels walk with them.

On Saturday morning they walk back to the synagogue while the rest of the city sleeps late. People are just beginning to stir when they are walking the streets after the services with their prayer shawls neatly packed into little velvet bags. The routine is the same every Sabbath for the Orthodox faithful, and it's a very civilized routine at that. The men walk around for about an hour, then go home for a light lunch that's followed by an afternoon nap.

Meanwhile, less religious families get their extra sleep on Saturday morning, usually emerging about noon-time for an afternoon on the beach, complete with a picnic of course, a bike ride, a soccer game or just an aimless stroll. Some of them stay home and sip tea on their apartment balcony. Others go out into the countryside to see where Tel Aviv's city limits have expanded to since the last time they ventured out of town. Whatever they do, they do it in a relaxed way. And why not? That's what the Sabbath is for.

By late afternoon, just before the sun sinks into the sea with a spectacular combination of colors, the Orthodox families wake up from their naps and go out to their favorite cafe for a little socializing, a cup of tea and a piece of cake, chocolate probably.

After sundown the city comes back to life again with a pace that won't slow down again until next Friday night. As if to ease into it gently, thousands line up to go to the movies, and that's as much a tradition among Israeli city-dwellers as sleeping late on Saturday morning.

The Sabbath is also a good day for museum-going and one of the best in Israel is Beth Hatefutsoth, the Museum of the Diaspora, on the campus of Tel Aviv University. It was created to counter a Sabra attitude that amounted to total indifference about the experiences of their ancestors in exile.

The museum traces the experiences of 2,500 years of Jewish life, but it very carefully concentrates on showing that those experiences weren't all persecution and suffering and passive acquiescence. There isn't an artifact anywhere in the four-story building. The history is told on film, through computers, in elaborate slide shows. It's probably the most sophisticated museum anywhere in the world.

Just inside the door, flashing lights and soft music pull you naturally past models of a Roman arch and a fiberglass representation of the Wailing Wall to the stairway that leads up to the permanent exhibit. In some places corridors in front of small dioramas are purposely made narrow to give the feeling of closeness of the atmosphere of 13th-century Spain or the Poland of 200 years ago. More recent experiences are conveyed on film in tiny theaters that have continuous showings of animated cartoons, of actual film made years ago or movies made from old photographs.

There are about two dozen closed circuit television units to give other parts of the story as well as film strip presentations and multi-projector slide shows. The centerpiece of the museum exhibit area is a huge metal sculpture called the Scrolls of Fire. It's a memorial to all Jews who have died for their faith, and it's the museum's only reference to the Nazis.

The exhibits are built around themes rather than time periods. There are seven of them, including family life and culture, and the most popular is the Chronosphere, a planetarium-like room that gives a panoramic audio-visual show on the history of the migration of all the Jewish people.

Just as popular is a computer that's been programmed with information on 3,000 Jewish communities and with biographies of famous Jews. Anyone who has an idea where his family came from can ask the machine about the place in either English or Hebrew and get a fast answer in the form of a

printout, also in either English or Hebrew.

Beth Hatefutsoth is a walk through history without and dusty relics or sentimentality. It's an incredible trip, a beautiful experience. The only thing wrong is that you can't experience it all in one trip.

. . . Yea, they may forget, yet will I not forget thee.
Isaiah 49:15

There are a dozen or more museums and art exhibits to bring a little culture to a quiet Sabbath afternoon. They include Bet Haganah, devoted to the history of Israel's fighting forces and Bet Ben-Gurion, the former home of the country's first Prime Minister. The Helena Rubinstein Pavilion features traveling art exhibits, and the Tel Aviv Museum is proud of its permanent collection of paintings and sculpture by Israeli and international artists. The Museum Haaretz is a collection of about a dozen different museums with artifacts from archaeological digs and including one devoted to the history of money.

But when visitors from out of the country come to

At the bottom of Eyn Avdat Canyon *left,*
bathers *below* enjoy the surprisingly
cool and refreshing water.

call on a Tel Aviv family, the museum they make a point of showing them is Yad Vashem in Jerusalem.

People who run organized tours in Israel usually make it a point never to route their non-Jewish clients through Yad Vashem early in the day. The experience, they say, is so overwhelming that they can't concentrate on anything for the rest of the day. Their Jewish tourists, on the other hand, have had some advance preparation for it and so are able to bounce back in a half hour or so and can get on with the rest of their tour.

Yad Vashem is a memorial to the Holocaust and its six million victims.

There are three buildings on top of the Mount of Remembrance. They are reached by a road lined with trees planted in memory of non-Jews who risked their

lives to save Jews from death. The first of the three buildings in the almost-silent park is an archive containing the records of families, many of which no longer exist, as well as documents and statistics to serve researchers. The middle building almost defies you to enter. It's massive, stark and cold like a fortification. Inside, the huge boulders that make up the outer walls create the texture of the inside. The room isn't much more than the four walls. Its focal point is a single flame burning in the center of the floor. Around it, tiles set in the floor spell out the names of 21 death camps, and under it a vault contains the ashes of some of the victims. There are no lecturers, no cassette tape recorders to tell you what you're seeing. What you see is what there is. There isn't much, but there is enough

to touch your soul.

The exhibition in the third building traces the history of the Nazis, beginning where the terror began in the Germany of the '30s, and ending with the liberations of 1945. The story is told through the posters of the day, through photographs of the round-ups and the trains going to the death camps. They show newspaper stories and display copies of the edicts that made it all "legal." Pictures recreate the ovens, the stacks of bodies, the looks of terror. But most poignant of all is probably the least pretentious of all: plaques on the walls with the names of countries followed by numbers. The numbers refer to the people who died in those countries. They add up to six million.

I saw, and behold, a tree in the midst of the earth, and the height thereof was great.

Daniel 4:10

American visitors usually also make it a point to stop at the Kennedy Memorial outside Jerusalem, not far from the American-designed Hadassah Medical Center, the largest hospital in the Middle East. The memorial to the American President is another marvel

A few miles from Jericho the Dead Sea glitters in the sun. Normal sea level is indicated on a board *above left,* 1,290 feet above the level of the Dead Sea, which contains a ten-times higher concentration of salt than ocean water! To float in, or, rather, on its waters *above* is a quite unique experience.

of simplicity, containing nothing more than an eternal flame and a bust of John F. Kennedy. Its modern design claims to represent the stump of a felled tree and each of the 50 concrete elements that form it contains the seal of one of the 50 American States. The view from the hilltop is not much different now than it was back when John the Baptist was born not far away. But it's changing fast.

The Kennedy Memorial stands in the midst of a new forest that gets bigger almost in direct proportion to the number of tourists who visit there. Instead of buying JFK T-shirts or picture postcards, many buy seedlings to add to the forest. They can either donate the money to have the trees planted or they can have the added pleasure of turning the earth and planting the foot-high seedlings themselves. In the process, the place becomes more memorable to them, and their memory lives in the form of a beautiful tree.

Planting trees is an idea older than modern Israel itself. Back at the turn of the century, the Jewish National Fund began raising money especially for the greening of the new country. By the time the State was created, they had planted 5,280,000 of them. Less than a dozen years later they had planted almost 50 million. And they haven't stopped yet.

It would be an important program in any country, but in Israel the trees are almost as important as human life. During each of the wars a lot of trees were destroyed and each was counted to be added to the casualty statistics. They add beauty to barren areas, of course, but they also help to raise the underground water table, provide windbreaks for both settlements and farms and they help stop soil erosion. A thick tangle of trees can also stop a tank if it's strategically placed. But the best thing they do is give shade from the hot sun. And there are a great many places in Israel where that is nature's greatest gift.

The gifts of trees have come from Jews all over the world, often in the form of forests or groves and usually given as living memorials. But Israelis themselves give money as well as time and labor to make their country greener. Arbor Day is a holiday everybody takes very seriously. Even the Bedouins in the Negev have gotten in on the fun, something their ancestors would have considered unthinkable. They seem to like the idea of growing their own peaches and apricots or being able to send one of the kids out to pick a pomegranate.

The seed-eating Israelis probably like pistachios best, but they also plant figs and olives as well as acacia, cedar and pine. Oddly, one of the most popular new trees introduced into this desert country, by the Jewish Johnny Appleseeds, is the Australian eucalyptus, one of the thirstiest trees on earth.

Obviously, not many grow in the Negev, but up north in the Galilee the tree is perfect for lowering the water level in the swampy valleys. The first groves of them were planted by the pioneers who founded the first kibbutz at Degania. By now they have a botanical garden there, as well as a museum exhibiting the animal life native to Israel. There are some 2,250 varieties of plant life in Israel, including trees like the eucalyptus that were introduced there by the pioneers.

The native wildflowers that start blooming in January and stay colorful right through the summer include anemones and iris, cyclamen and lilies. In fact, the native iris was the inspiration for the Islamic design that was picked up by France's Crusader King as his own emblem, which he called a fleur-de-lis.

In ages gone by, elephants and lions roared through the northern hills of Israel. Today there are some leopards and polecats, antelopes and ibex, as well as

The modern sculpture *above* is on the roadside by the Dead Sea, near Masada.

snakes and lizards and all kinds of turtles. But most spectacular of all, there are about 400 different kinds of birds.

The Galilee is on the migratory route between Southern Asia and Northern Europe, and almost all the birds making the journey make it a point to stop over for a while to be admired by Israeli bird-watchers. They watch kingfishers and grebes, pelicans, plovers and cormorants. In the higher spots eagles, vultures and osprey watch back. And out on the water, fishermen hoping to catch Saint Peter's fish in the Sea of Galilee or bluefish in the Mediterranean are treated to the grace of gulls and the antics of shore birds.

. . . A land of brooks of water, of fountains and depths that spring out of valleys and hills.

Deuteronomy 8:7

The place where nature is at her very best in Israel is where modern Israel began. The Galilee.

The Jezreel Valley was a mess, but promising, when the first pioneers arrived there in the last years of the 19th century. It has kept the promise. It's a peaceful,

The remarkable fortress at Masada has been subjected to considerable successful archaeological excavation and is a popular venue for many thousands of tourists and students *these pages*.

Stalactites and stalagmites *overleaf* in Sorek Cave, Absalom's Reserve, were discovered during routine quarrying operations in the Beit Shemesh district. They are now cared for by the Nature Reserve Authority.

lush place with carpets of wildflowers leading up to cool, green olive groves and pine forests. The mountains around it rise up about 2,000 feet from the seacoast and drop another thousand feet more on the other side to the Sea of Galilee. Melting snow from high peaks like Mount Hermon and Mount Merion further north creates fast-running streams and brooks. Deep, cool springs create even more. It's a beautiful, peaceful place and symbolically, it's a place where Arabs and Jews live contentedly side-by-side.

The Galilee seems almost unchanged since Biblical times. Women in veils carry water from wells in jugs perched on their heads. Men plow the fields with hand-made plows pulled by oxen and they carry their produce to market by camel or donkey. Their children share play space with little black goats and they play games, the rules of which are more than three centuries old.

But the Biblical time of the Galilee is the New

247

Children of the Samaritan sect are pictured *above* before a sacrificial ceremony at Nablus, on the West Bank.

The Arabs *facing page* live in Awarta, also on the West Bank, and some of the older members of the community, like the two women *top,* still carry the marks of ritual tattooing. It must have been people very much like these who "watched their flocks" in the "Field of the Shepherds", where the church *overleaf* now stands, in Bethlehem.

Testament, not the Old, and tourists with guides often find themselves being turned over to Arab guides when they get here because, as Christians, they know more of what happened here.

The city of Nazareth, sitting just above the plain in the Lower Galilee, is sacred to Christians as the place where Jesus spent his boyhood and early manhood. It is the place, according to Saint Luke, where the Angel Gabriel told Mary that she would bring forth a son, who would be the Son of God.

Today it is a town of more than 30,000, mostly Christian, with a new Jewish quarter, Nazareth Heights. They have running water (the well in the center of town known as "Mary's Well" is equipped these days with a faucet!) and electricity in the old quarters; many people even have television sets, but the pace of life in Nazareth is as slow as it ever was. The marketplace is a relic from other times, in spite of some modern touches here and there.

All the Christian denominations are represented in Nazareth, but even in this place sacred to them all, they can't stop arguing among themselves over what it all means. The new Basilica of the Annunciation, built with the financial help of the Israeli Government, is one of the most impressive Christian buildings in all Israel and was placed on the site of old Byzantine and Crusader churches that were supposed to have been on the spot where the Angel appeared to Mary. Near it is a Franciscan monastery that backs up the claim. Yet less than a half-mile away, the Greek Orthodox Church of Saint Gabriel says the Angel Gabriel appeared there. Significantly, Mary's Well is between the two churches.

The American Southern Baptist Convention has a temple not far away as does the Anglican Church. And on a hillside across town the Salesian Fathers of Saint John Bosco have built a small, Italian-looking church called the Church of the Infant Jesus. Their compound includes an orphanage and a school and the church offers the best view in town, from a long balcony on one side.

Though neither the Baptists, the Anglicans, nor the Salesians claim to have built on a spot where something important happened, the Franciscans have a church on the site of Joseph's workshop and a cave they say was the home of Joseph and Mary. They offer as proof of their claim a slab of rock that looks like a table and pits on the floor that probably served someone as storage for food and wine. A block away the Greek Catholics have built a church they call a synagogue because they say it's on the site of the synagogue where Jesus spoke.

All of it is guesswork, of course. The New Testament is quite silent about the early life of Christ. That could be the result of an old prejudice. To be a Nazarene in ancient Galilee was to be a second-class citizen. According to Saint John, when Philip asked Nathanael to go with him to meet Jesus, Nathanael replied "Can there be any good thing come out of Nazareth?"

Even the Nazarenes didn't want to have anything to do with Him once He announced in the synagogue that "the Spirit of the Lord is upon me." They dragged Him out of town and threatened to throw Him off the highest hill unless He stayed away from them. He never went far away.

It was just a few miles from Nazareth that Jesus performed his first miracle by turning six pots of water into wine at a wedding feast in Cana. Exactly where it happened in Cana depends on whether you listen to the Roman Catholics or the Greek Catholics. The Greeks have an edge by claiming to have two of the original waterpots. On the other hand, some people say Cana itself was miles away in another direction when Jesus was a young man.

People find it hard to agree what the area was like in those days, too. Because the Bible is relatively silent

In Bethlehem *below*, a mainly Christian Arab town, Christian pilgrims venerate the reputed site of the birth of their Saviour.

In Bethlehem *below*, a mainly Christian Arab town, Christian pilgrims venerate the reputed site of the birth of their Saviour.

about old Nazareth, it was once fashionable for scholars to conclude that there wasn't much to be said about it and it must have been an obscure little town. But its location suggests it was probably a fairly lively town. It was convenient to the road to Jerusalem, which was always busy in those days, and not far from the trade route that connected Egypt and Lebanon. And the East-West route from Acre to the interior ran past it, too. Added to that, the beautiful countryside and the climate made it a place no one would hurry past. It may have been small, but it almost certainly wasn't dull.

When Jesus left Nazareth, He didn't travel far. Most of His life was spent near the Sea of Galilee, which is Lake Kinneret to modern Israelis and was known as

Lake Tiberias to some of their ancestors. No matter what name they know it by, everyone who sees it calls it beautiful. The water is a brilliant shade of blue and the hills around it are every color imaginable, usually changing as the sun moves across the sky.

As a lake it's rather large, as a sea it's tiny. At its widest point, it's six miles across and from north to south a voyage on its sometimes stormy waters is only 13 miles. Looking down on it from a rich green hillside it's simple to visualize what it was like 2,000 years ago when Jesus walked along the shore and recruited two men to follow him. The first disciples were Galilee fishermen who went out in boats that probably looked exactly like the ones out there today. In fact, about the only thing that's different about the shoreline today is

the pumping stations that start Galilee water on its way to all parts of the country. It's Israel's major reservoir.

Jesus lived for some time at Capernaum on the lake's North shore. The Franciscans operate a monastery at the edge of the water there but its great attraction is not its claim to be on a spot where Jesus taught, but that its grounds contain the ruins of a great synagogue that was built two centuries after He died. Sites holy to Christians are mainly outside the town in places like Tabgha where a church marks the spot where Jesus fed a multitude of followers with five loaves and two fishes. The story of the miracle is told in an incredibly· beautiful mosaic created in the fourth century as the floor of another church on the same spot.

The Mount of Beatitudes rises above it in the background crowned by a charming Italian church. And south of it is Migdal, the birthplace of Mary Magdalene. South of Migdal is easily the most popular city in the whole area, Tiberias.

There isn't a resort city in the world quite like Tiberias. The water is bluer, the hills greener, the air milder than any place that invites comparison. Modern hotels on palm tree lined streets overlook a charming old city with open-air restaurants on the lake shore that serve fish for lunch that were swimming in the nearby water at breakfast time.

The city was built in the first century by Herod Antipas, the son of Herod the Great. When the Romans destroyed the Temple at Jerusalem it became the spiritual center of Jewish life. By the second

The entrance to the Church of the Nativity *above left* has been reduced in size twice through the years. It was originally a wide, Byzantine doorway which was closed, leaving the typical Crusader entrance which was, in turn, partially blocked by the Turks, allowing only the present, small opening.

Above is one of the sets of "Christmas Bells", of which there are several above the roof of the Church.

Contrasting with the general simplicity of the Basilica of the Church of the Nativity is the ornate Greek altar *overleaf*.

century it had become the home of the Patriarch and the seat of the Sanhedrin. The Jerusalem Talmud and the Mishnah were finished in Tiberias during those years. The work went on under Roman occupation, and when the Roman emperor was converted to Christianity, both religions lived side-by-side here. Then the Arabs conquered it in the name of Islam and mosques sprouted up among the churches and synagogues. Tiberias is just too beautiful to give up just because of competing religious ideas.

It's been destroyed three times by earthquakes, the most recent in 1837, but in spite of them no one ever thought of moving. In fact, when Jews began returning to Palestine in the 1880s there was a sizeable Jewish community waiting for them in Tiberias.

They had been there since the 16th century when Jews were expelled from Spain. Among the victims of the purge was a Spanish noblewoman who had connections with Sultan Suleiman the Magnificent. They asked for, and were granted, the right to migrate to Palestine and the city they chose was this wonderful

On the walls of the Mount of Temptation, where Jesus is said to have fasted, hangs the Monastery of Karantel *right*.

place on the lake shore.

Many choose to go there because of the therapeutic hot springs close by. The hot water from the springs has been curing rheumatism since before anybody knew what caused the aches and pains. The Romans built spectacular baths there and when the Arabs came they made the facilities even more sumptuous. The buildings now there were built in the 1950s, and by encasing the springs, the output has been dramatically increased. The facilities are constantly being expanded and what's available now would have amazed the Romans. The spa usually amazes Europeans, too, who grew up believing theirs the best in the world.

. . . He found them ten times better than all the magicians and astrologers that were in his realm.

Daniel 1:20

Close by is the site of a spring that scholars of the Cabbala thought had magic waters. By drinking it, they said, all the mysteries of creation would become crystal clear. Unfortunately, the spring has long since been covered by the lake so the mysteries are still cloudy.

The Cabbalist search for truth took place in another of the Jewish holy cities a little further north in the Galilee. Safad has hardly changed at all since the 16th century when scholars went there to study the Torah for hidden mysteries. The little houses on the terraced hillside, the cobblestone streets and the people themselves all conspire to give the feeling that the mysteries are still well hidden but that they are surely hidden here.

In their search for wisdom, the Cabbalists re-arranged the words of the Bible into forms based on numerology, geometry and what they believed were magic formulas. They thought that the five books of Moses held the key to the real meaning of life and by shuffling the words, even the letters, around they would be purified spiritually.

The idea was first revealed in a book called the Zohar, "The Book of Splendor," written by a Spanish mystic. It especially inspired Rabbi Isaac Luria who settled in Safad in the 16th century. His teachings, often transmitted to his followers while he was in a trance describing "visions," were sent around the world thanks to the fact that Safad was the home of a printing press, the only one in the entire Western part of Asia.

People in the European ghettos were especially excited about the ideas. Luria, known to them as The Ari, had said he learned the things he knew directly from the prophet Elijah who he claimed had also told him that he would be the one to proclaim the coming of the Messiah.

To say that things were tough for Jews in Europe at that time would be a misleading understatement. Pogroms were in full swing everywhere, and the whole world seemed in the grip of the Black Death. Islam was on the march in the East, and Jerusalem had fallen again. Whole cities were being destroyed by fires or washed out by floods. They were tough times for everybody and it was exactly the right time for a little magic.

Jews believed that all the catastrophes were signs that the arrival of the Messiah was just around the corner. Following the writings of the Cabbalists and the rantings of mystics who spread the word, they became stoic about the way the world was falling apart around them. Many sold their possessions and sat back to wait for the better day they knew was at hand. One of the mystics even computed a date which he said would be the day the Messiah would lead them all home to Jerusalem. Hundreds followed him and when the day came and went and there was no Messiah, they didn't blame the mystic, but claimed Judaism itself had let them down and as a group converted to Christianity.

Of course many of the mystics claimed to be the Messiah. One of them led his followers to Turkey in a Jewish crusade, determined to drive the Turks out of the Holy Land. He even attracted the attention of Samuel Pepys who noted in his diary that London Jews had set up a lottery pool, betting not on his success, but how quickly success would come.

He in turn was denounced by another Messiah who turned him over to the Sultan. The Sultan gave him a simple choice: choose Islam or death. The next day he was put in charge of converting other Jews who might happen to pass through.

Eventually the Eastern European rabbis began to excommunicate the various Messiahs who came along, and made rules expressly forbidding young people to read the writings of the Cabbalists. As a result, the Cabbalists gradually died out and were replaced in the lives of the more zealous by the Hassidic teachings of Jews from Poland.

The original Zohar, the book that started it all, was written by an obscure mystic, but the man who got the credit for it was Rabbi Simon Ben Yochai, who moved to Safad because the air there was pure and the environment perfect for serious contemplation. His tomb is on Mount Meron, the highest mountain in Israel, which is not far outside the city. Every year in the spring, thousands take part in a pilgrimage to the mountain, carrying the Torah from the old synagogue in Safad.

It's a wonderful place to visit any time of the year. Thousands of acres of forest surround hiking trails leading to the top of the mountain where the view is among the most spectacular in the country.

There are several old synagogues on the side of the mountain as well as the graves of many of the great scholars who settled here over the years. The influence of the scholars of Safad on Judaism as it is today is greater than that of any group since the destruction of the Temple.

The city that influenced them is as charming as it is inspiring. During the Crusades the hillside above it was the site of the biggest castle in the Middle East. It was almost completely destroyed by an earthquake in the 19th century, and some of the stones were carried down to rebuild the town. But amazingly, the heavy outer walls of the fortress are still standing in spite of the earthquakes that have shaken it over the years. The Moslems were luckier. It took years, but they finally conquered the castle and took its inhabitants as slaves.

After the War of Independence, during which the Jewish Quarter was cut off for several months, the Arab sections filled up with Jewish immigrants, many of whom were artists. Since then they've used their artistry to bring new life to Safad. But at the same time they've lovingly preserved the old in the section now known as the Artists' Quarter.

They've painted the walls in light colors and added brightness by planting flowers and shrubs. They've restored the stonework and accented the arches. And, of course, they sell their paintings and sculpture, their leatherwork and ceramics from workrooms that overlook the Sea of Galilee, framed by beautiful hills and mountains off in the distance.

Safad is a tiny town that can be seen in a few hours, but almost nobody has ever tried. It's a place that invites you to linger and relax. To be enchanted.

One of the things that makes people want to stay longer is the municipal swimming pool. It's not an ordinary pool, you see. The water comes from an old spring that the Arabs have always believed has magic powers. The special magic is that it can make beautiful women even more beautiful. They believed it fervently enough to pay double for a bride if it could be proven she was a native of Safad. The story isn't hard to believe after even a short stroll through the streets of the town. It's a magical place.

The magic of the Jezreel Valley is more easily explained. At the end of the last century, when settlement began there, the Arabs called it the "Gateway to Hell." To them it probably was. They were desert people and water in the Jezreel was a curse

The various valleys and oases of Israel support a wide variety of flora, as at Wadi Far'a *overleaf,* near Nablus.

instead of a blessing. It had backed up and created marshes and swamps. Anyone who lived there was almost guaranteed to come down with malaria. The Arabs had all they could do to keep from laughing out loud when the Jewish National Fund announced in 1921 that they had bought the valley and were going to develop it as a new home for Jews from Poland.

. . . Beautify the place of my sanctuary; and I will make the place of my feet glorious.

Isaiah 60:13

It wasn't long before they stopped laughing. But making the valley bloom again wasn't easy and the whole world watched as they cut drainage ditches and built their little settlements. Everyone cheered them on, but almost no one believed the valley could ever be as lush and beautiful as it is today. That could be because they weren't reading the lessons of the past. The Plain of Esdaelon, as it was once known, has been home to man since the Stone Age and possibly no other valley in the world has been the scene of so many battles for control of it.

It separates the North and Central parts of the country and was once the easiest route from the sea to the Jordan River and the desert country beyond. It was known as the Via Maris, the Road to the Sea, and it connected the empires of Egypt and Assyria.

The Israelites, goaded by Deborah the Prophetess, fought the Canaanites here. Gideon led them into battle against the Midianites and beat an army of 10,000 with a guerilla action in the valley that would make the IDF proud today. Of course, the Israelites didn't always win. The Philistines brought King Saul to his knees on these plains and the Egyptians picked this spot to kill the young King Josiah.

The Romans fought here and so did the Crusaders. Napoleon went inland across the valley on his ill-fated attempt to establish his influence in the East. Lord Allenby defeated the Turks here, and in 1948 the Jews took a stand in the valley that kept the Arab armies from pushing them into the sea.

Almost all the battles have centered around Mount Tabor, a conical mountain that's a commanding presence in all parts of the valley. The New Testament refers to it as a "high mountain apart" in Matthew's story of the Transfiguration of Jesus. The spot where Peter said ". . . Lord, it is good for us to be here" is marked by a 20th-century Franciscan church built on the foundations of an old Byzantine structure. At one time, the only way to get to the top was by steps cut into the rock. It was a long, hot climb but the view from the top was rewarding enough to make it worthwhile. Today the trip is allegedly easier thanks to a narrow road that twists and turns its way to the top. It still isn't all that easy.

At the base of the mountain is Ein Dor, the place King Saul went to talk over his future with a witch. It was one of the last conversations he had.

His three sons died with him in the battle that took place the next day, and the victorious Philistines displayed their bodies on a wall at nearby Beit She'an where they were eventually burned. It was also the place where, centuries later, Jesus healed the leper.

Like so many other tels in Israel, the one at Beit She'an covered no less than 18 different cities, each built on top of the other. They were excavated by an American expedition that took the best of the artifacts home with them after they were finished.

Israeli archaeologists uncovered a Roman amphitheater there and then set about to restore it. It's one of the most remarkable restorations in all Israel, looking very much as though it has just been built and not at all like it has been covered with mud and rocks for all those centuries.

The valley is rich in old artifacts. One of the best-

Jesus spent His childhood in Nazareth *overleaf* and became the once and for all sacrifice for the Christian faith, a sacrifice that is fittingly commemorated in the Church of the Transfiguration on Mount Tabor *above and right,* as in Christian churches throughout the world.

preserved mosaics in the country is a sixth-century synagogue floor uncovered accidentally by workers digging a drainage ditch at a spot not far from Mount Gilboa. There are stone slabs carved by Egyptians in the same area as well as the remains of one of the ten Greek cities in the general area of the Galilee that the Greeks called the Decapolis.

Both Damascus, the capital of Syria, and Jordan's capital, Amman, which was known to the Greeks as Philadelphia, were part of the federation formed in a mutual defense pact against the tribes of Israel. One of the most interesting of the ten, at least to archaeologists who are uncovering it today, is the city of Hippos on the hill above the kibbutz at Ein Gev. They call the place Susita today, but either in Greek or Hebrew, the word for horse is the only one that suits because of the shape of the rock formation. The diggers have much pleasanter working conditions here than down in the Negev. The climate is only one of the reasons. Every year at Passover, and again in the fall, this kibbutz, on the eastern shore of the Sea of Galilee, is host to a Festival of Music and Folklore that attracts musicians, singers and dancers from all over the world. The Festivals attract huge crowds, too. It was a small affair when it first began, but it wasn't long before the Ein Gev kibbutzniks were forced to build a special concert hall big enough to hold 3,000 people. But the Esco Music Center isn't the only attraction. When they expanded their music facilities, they also expanded

267

The Miracle at Cana, where Jesus turned the water into wine, is simplistically treated in the Franciscan church *right* at Kfar Kana.

their restaurant, which is one of the best in all Israel, serving fresh fish in a setting right at the water's edge.

We have found water...

Genesis 26:32

The Sea of Galilee is both fed and drained by the Jordan River. It begins in the high mountains of the North dominated by Mount Hermon in Israel's Northeast corner. The water comes from melting snow, of course, but before it melts it provides fun and adventure for the Israel Ski Club, an institution that's been growing by leaps and bounds since the winter of 1967, when soldiers fighting there in the Six Day War discovered that ski conditions on the mountain are perfect from December to April. They've since added a chair lift, equipment rental facilities and, of course, the required cafes and restaurants to give the right ending to a day on the slopes.

Even in summer it's worth a trip to the top of Mount Hermon. Much of the view from there is down the Hula Valley, another former swamp that's now a lush green belt five miles wide and 25 miles long, extending down toward the Sea of Galilee. The river is a rushing, bubbling thing at this point as it begins its downhill run to the Dead Sea. Watching it rush by, it's easy to understand why the ancients named it "Yarden" from their word "yored," meaning "to descend." The name Jordan literally means "Down-Rusher."

The upper valley is more than just a beautiful place. Since the earliest days of Jewish settlement, it's been recognized as a strategic defense point because it sticks up like a sore thumb between Syria and Lebanon. When the British set up the lines of their Mandate, the Hula Valley was called Jewish territory and during the years of British rule the Jews did all they could to make sure it stayed theirs by establishing some two-dozen settlements.

When the line was originally drawn there were endless discussions about why this neck of land ought to be included in Palestine. Some said the Mandate would be more secure if the borders in the North were a bit shorter. But the argument in favor of extending the territory was stronger. Without the Hula Valley, said the British, their Mandate would be over a desert country that would only get drier without the water flowing down from the mountains. Fortunately they won their point and the first step after that was to get

Antonio Barluzzi's Basilica of the Transfiguration is shown *top left; center* the Cave of the Seventy Elders, and *bottom left* the cave's interior.

271

The beautiful and blooming land of the Galilee *these pages* is very closely associated with the years of Christ's ministry.

rid of some of that water. Like the other valleys, the Hula was home to millions of malaria-carrying mosquitoes. Much of the land was covered with marshes that had been there for more than 2,000 years. There was a lake in the center that needed draining, too, making the job a little bit bigger than other similar reclamation projects.

Draining the lake came first. It had been formed when a volcano dammed up the river at the bottom end. By cutting away the rock, and then cutting deep canals to drain the marshes into the lake, it didn't take long to make most of the water disappear, leaving behind a rich farm area with the added bonus of peat bogs that were valuable to less fortunate areas in need of soil reclamation. They freed about 19,000 acres for farming, but more important they freed millions of gallons of water that would eventually find its way to the southern deserts through an elaborate system of canals, pipelines and tunnels stretching more than 150 miles across the map of Israel.

The valley is dominated by the Golan Heights, which made working and living there a little tricky until the Israelis finally moved the Syrians out in 1973. Looking down from the Heights today, it seems all the more remarkable that the Hula Valley settlements were ever built, let alone survived since the first, Rosh Pina, was founded in 1882.

. . . And the children of Israel were in the cities.

Ezra 3:1

It's hard to imagine fighting of any kind in the hills and valleys of the Galilee, it's such a beautiful, peaceful

Grapefruit in hoppers, cattle grazing in fields of wild flowers, flowing rivers and lemon trees are typical of the fertile agricultural landscape of the Galilee *these pages*.

spot. It's also difficult to conceive such a rural place so near to the coastal strip that runs from Gaza to Haifa and beyond. It's like one big city back there; crowded, noisy, bustling and, to a lot of the people who live in it, beautiful as only a lively city can be.

The distance from Tel Aviv to Haifa is about 70 miles and almost all of it is thickly populated. Of course, like the corridor between Boston and Washington on the East Coast of the United States, that's not to say there are no breathing spaces or greenbelts. One of the best of them is the Sharon Valley, once just about the narrowest point in Israel before the West Bank was captured. It's a place of orange groves and fields of gladiolus being grown for export to Europe. There are still some sand dunes left, but not many, and their days are numbered as the region makes room for more and more settlers who are more and more willing to move there now that the country's Eastern border is so much further away.

The main road through the Sharon Valley skirts Tel Aviv and goes south to Lod, where the big International Airport makes itself heard. The other end of the road is in Haifa. A generation ago immigrants went south on the road from the seaport, now they use it to go north from the airport. But it's a fascinating trip in either direction.

Lod, the city Saint Peter visited when it was called Lydda, is the place where Saint George, the patron saint of England, was born and is buried. It would be interesting to know the dragon killer's reaction to the fire-breathing dragons we call jumbo jets.

Though Lod is one of the first towns tourists see when they get to Israel, their first impression may be a little surprising. It has an Arab presence that's stronger than many Israeli towns. Once a week Arabs from all over the area set up shop in the marketplace and have a wonderful time bargaining with tourists and local people over things they may well have picked up the day before at the busy, full-time Arab market not far away in Ramle.

The rest of the week, the Lod specialty is Arab food which is one reason why people from Tel Aviv don't mind the trip to the airport to meet visiting relatives. They know they'll be able to add a great meal to the day's adventure.

They find adventure in Ramle, too. It was the only town in Palestine actually established by Arabs. Back in the eighth century, the Great Caliph Suleiman founded a city there that was the Arab capital for 300 years. The Crusaders drove the Moslems out and destroyed their city, except for the mosque. The Arabs came back again in the 14th century and added a white tower to it. It's said that Napoleon went to the top of

the tower to have a look around when he passed by on his way from Egypt. When he compared the trip overland to Jerusalem with the water route to Acre, he opted for Acre and pushed on to the north. That was his first mistake.

The grottos under the mosque are as famous in Israel as Capri's Blue Grotto is in Italy. A boat ride through the three underground vaults is an incredible experience of beautiful stonework and crystal clear water with just a hint of danger in the seat of a bobbing gondola.

Both Ramle and Lod were strategic to the Arab armies during the War of Independence. Their locations helped them cut off Jerusalem and made a good starting point for an attack on Tel Aviv. Before they got around to doing that, however, an Israeli commando unit led by Moshe Dayan rushed into Lod with a caravan of jeeps and drove full-speed down the main street, spraying everything in sight with machine guns. If John Wayne had suggested a scene like that in one of his movies, the director probably would have patted him on the head and suggested he take a few days off. But it really happened, and the Arabs evacuated both towns rather quickly after it did.

After the war was over, the towns filled up with Jewish immigrants. Eventually some of the Arabs came back, too, and many of them went into the restaurant business. And that makes these two little towns very exciting on Friday and Saturday nights.

Some of the people who crowd the streets of Ramle and Lod are on their evenings off work in the winery that produces some of the wine that helps them forget their troubles. Some others spend their work-days in Israel's original brewery. Both the wine cellars and the brewery are at nearby Rishon-le-Zion, the original pioneer settlement. When the Russian immigrants first went there, they had to carry water on camelback to irrigate their farms and they had to plead with the Turks for permission to build a synagogue. The permission was granted, as long as they didn't make what they were doing too obvious to the local population. They complied by disguising their house of worship as a warehouse.

As if being the first settlement wasn't good enough for them, the pioneers were also proud of the fact that Israel's national anthem was written, composed and first played there. It pleases their children to tell you that Rishon was the site of the country's first kindergarten and elementary school. It pleases everyone in town that the first orchestra established in Jewish Palestine was founded for their entertainment.

Though their town is seven years younger, there's a special pride in the streets of Rehovot, too. It's the

A tree *left* forces its way through a rocky outcrop in the Golan Heights.

place Dr. Chaim Weizmann chose to live when he went to Palestine to work and to eventually become Israel's first president. The Weizmann Institute, which he established, is one of the great scientific research centers in the world, with work going on in every field from organic chemistry to nuclear physics. It's in the heart of farm country that produces almonds and grapes, oranges and lemons. The Hebrew University of Jerusalem operates an agricultural research station here, and not far away the government operates a cyclotron for atomic research.

The grounds of the Weizmann Institute are covered with lush lawns and gardens and the modern buildings have been designed to provide a peaceful environment for the scientists working there.

The feeling of peace extends out from the town, too. It's so peaceful that travelers often miss the biggest kibbutz in Israel, which is nestled among the orange groves not far away. Givat Brenner is its name, and its unusual claim to fame is that it was originally established by immigrants from Italy.

There are orange groves everywhere along the coast and they help to take the edge off the sameness of the buildings from one town to the other. Almost all the buildings are made of concrete and have an air about them that suggests they had to be built in a big hurry on a tight budget. The impression is probably accurate on both counts. From the very beginning, Israelis haven't had a lot of time or money, and similarity in architecture is one of the prices they've had to pay. It's probably one of the reasons why they're all so interested in digging up the remains of older, more interesting styles.

It's not such a problem in places like Jerusalem or Acre or Safad where the older styles still exist. But a flair for style is something that's rare in cities and towns built in modern times.

A wonderful exception is the resort city of Natanya, about half-way between Tel Aviv and Haifa. It was originally intended to be the centerpiece of a citrus industry when it was established in 1928 largely with funds provided by the American philanthropist Nathan Strauss, whose name inspired that of the city.

The citrus industry in Natanya has long since been overtaken by another important Israeli export: diamonds. The industry is centered at Ramat Gan in the Tel Aviv area, but a great many of the cutters and polishers prefer the atmosphere of Natanya.

Diamonds are mined in 20 different countries in the world and 15 of them are in Africa. The Republic of South Africa alone produces half the diamonds in the world and Israel's close relations with South Africa as well as with the other nearby diamond producers keeps the supply steady, which makes Israel the world's biggest producer of small polished stones and the second biggest, after Belgium, of all cut diamonds.

Jews who migrated to Israel from Belgium started the industry on a small scale back in the 1930s. It was what they had done in the old country and they were thinking more in terms of making a living than starting an industry. But they hadn't planned on World War II.

When the war hit Holland and Belgium it put them out of the diamond business for the duration and put the spotlight on the little factories in Palestine. By the time the war was over, more than 4,000 were working in those factories and almost all the rough stones in the world were passing through them.

When the war ended, the Europeans were back in business and the big mining syndicates went back to them. Israel's own war turned a lot of diamond cutters into soldiers and by the late '40s it was beginning to look as though the country would never have a diamond industry after all. But Israelis are improvisers and their ingenuity saved the day again. The bigger countries were concentrating their efforts on bigger stones, so, as a small country, the Israeli producers decided to concentrate on smaller ones. The experts call them "kleine brillianten," stones of less than a carat. Nobody else in the world wanted to be bothered with them, but there was a market for them and before long Israel had that market cornered. About one out of three diamonds sold anywhere in the world these days was first sold by an Israeli factory that had turned it from a rough piece of stone into something beautiful.

And that's something beautiful for the Israeli economy. Only tourists and citrus exports are bigger revenue producers.

Many of the diamond cutters in Natanya encourage tourists to visit them and leave some money behind by offering diamonds at a discount. And these days, the industry has expanded well beyond producing only small stones, so it's usually a worthwhile trip.

Everything in Natanya seems to cost less. For all its beauty, and the fact that it operates as a year-round seashore resort, it doesn't put on airs. The town itself sits on top of a bluff overlooking the sea. At the edge of it, a beautifully-landscaped promenade catches the breeze and leads the way to stairways that go down to no less than eight beaches, any one of which could be called the best in the country. They're separated by breakwaters that form little bays. The town above is filled with little rooming houses, low-cost hotels and restaurants of every description. The streets are usually filled with strollers who smile a lot. They've got a lot to smile about!

During the years of the British Mandate, Natanya was a hotbed of smuggling. The human kind. It was an important spot for quietly getting "illegal" refugees into the country. But the bigger ships used Haifa as their port of call. The reason why it was perfect for them was that the first thing the British did when they arrived was to dredge the harbor. What they had in mind was not to make it easier for shiploads of refugees, but to make Haifa what it has become 40 years later, one of the best seaports in the entire Mediterranean.

It's also one of the most beautiful port cities anywhere in the world.

The setting is Mount Carmel, an indescribably beautiful mountain with lush pine forests and scrubbed white houses marching down to sandy beaches and a bright blue sea. It's the third-largest city in Israel today. But back in 1898 when Theodor Herzl steamed into the harbor on his first visit to the Holy Land, it was a tiny suburb of Acre, which was a tiny city itself. Even then it was a captivating place, and he wrote of it as the "City of Tomorrow." Immigrants who followed came to know it as "the point of first joy," because in pre-airplane days Haifa was usually the first place they saw. If it was a joyful experience, it must also have been a pleasantly surprising one. In just about everyone's mind, Palestine was a land of desert and swamps. But this place was neither. Herzl burst into tears of joy when he first saw it. He surely wasn't the last to do that.

In other cities in Israel, litter and less-than-attractive housing are almost taken for granted. But among the new cities and towns, Haifa is a wonderful exception. The first settlers came from Germany and they brought along some no-nonsense ideas about cleanliness and orderliness. Their legacy is a solid, well-run, spotless city with plenty of parks and gardens and a general feeling of civic pride that makes everyone in town eager to keep it that way.

Haifa's atmosphere is even more incredible considering that it's a major industrial city as well as a busy seaport. It has shipyards and oil refineries and factories of every description. But, oddly, in Haifa's case all that activity complements the picture by making it look like a place where life is solid and rewarding in every sense of both words.

Haifa is really three cities. The main business district is on the lowest level along the shore. The town itself runs across the middle of the mountain in an area called Hadar HaCarmel, meaning the Beauty of the Carmel. And the most affluent part of town, naturally, is at the top of the mountain. It takes ten minutes to go from the bottom to the top in the only subway in the country, the Carmelit.

It's worth a trip to the top for the view, of course, but the summit of Mount Carmel is also a popular spot

The old city wall of Tiberias leans somewhat precariously at the water's edge *left,* and *below* is shown the tomb of Rabbi Meir Baal Haness.

for people looking for a complete rest at one of the convalescent homes there. Mount Carmel has been known for generations as a magic mountain, and it's a favorite place for the older generation to get a new lease of life.

There's a feeling of affluence in the neighborhoods on the top of Mount Carmel. There are elegant houses and even more elegant hotels, one of which has a restaurant built around the view. It's a favorite place to watch the sun set, a very dramatic experience in this part of the world, and to watch the lights of the city come on one by one. The ships in the harbor add an even more festive touch. After dinner, most people take the long way home by way of Panorama Road, one of the most aptly-named streets in the world.

The business district on Mount Carmel, the Merkaz, is surrounded by landscaped parks and private homes with yards bursting with flowers, almost as if keeping up with the Joneses in Haifa is only a matter of keeping ahead of weeds and insects.

It's all the legacy of the late Mayor of Haifa, Abba Hushi. He was a tough task-master who usually started his workday haranguing the street cleaners and ended it with a white glove inspection of their work. But for all his fanaticism about "the city beautiful," he managed to inspire his constituents not only into compliance, but into re-electing him every time he ran.

His theory was that city people needed beauty around them. "If people walk among flowers and trees," he said, "they smile. Flowers can shape the character of people."

He even got kids into the act. If he was planning a park for children, he asked them what they'd like to see in it. It was the same with schools and even institutions for adults. He thought that since the city would be theirs some day, they ought to have a hand in what it would look like.

One of the most beautiful institutions in the city is one he had very little to do with, yet he was certainly happy to have it there. It's the Bahai Temple, high on the slope of the mountain.

The Bahai religion is strong in the belief that religion's purpose ought to be to bring people together and not keep them apart. It's a revolutionary idea even in the 1980s. The idea began in Iran in the mid-19th century in the mind of a Mizra Ali Mohammed, who called himself "El Bab," which means the gateway. He chose the name to symbolize that he was the channel for man's communication with God. He chose the name "Bahai" for his religion because it means "glory."

Millions of people all over the world today still believe his ideas were glorious. But his contemporaries thought otherwise. The religion was outlawed and he was put to death. His followers went underground and many eventually found their way to Mount Carmel where they built a spectacular, domed building and surrounded it with peaceful Persian gardens. Later, they had El Bab's body moved to the spot, which had become the world center for their religion.

If Haifa is like three cities in one, there's a fourth part, too, that would be the pride of any other. It's called Technion, the Institute of Technology. When it was originally established, it was one of the schools the experts said had to do its teaching in German because there weren't enough words in the Hebrew language to cover technical subjects. Naturally, Hebrew won the day, and today it's used to teach aerodynamics and nuclear physics, in the midst of a 750-acre pine forest, to more than 8,500 students. Another 5,000 study humanities and social sciences at Haifa University not far away.

Haifa is one of the few cities in Israel where some of the shops don't shut down for a long break in the middle of the day, and it's also one of the few places where public transportation doesn't stop on the Sabbath. During the days of the British Mandate, the authorities turned over responsibility for personal matters such as marriage and divorce to the Chief

Rabbinate. Their authority extended to other matters like observance of the Sabbath, and they ruled that although public utilities could continue operating, public transportation should not. It was no big problem to the less orthodox because there were Arab-run buses in most places anyway. But when the State of Israel was established the Arabs went out of business although the rule didn't change. It caused inconvenience in many places, particularly in Haifa where the trip from the top of the mountain to the bottom and back was tiring, to say the least. They appealed and won the right to keep their buses and the subway running every day, in spite of the Sabbath ban. Interestingly, the argument that won the appeal was the need of the people to get to the beach.

Orthodox Jews among the city's boosters will say, as well as believe, that the buses run on Saturday to accommodate Haifa's big Arab population, which does happen to be among the biggest in the country, and swells dramatically during the work week when thousands of Arabs commute from small villages to work in the factories there.

When Israel was a child, then I loved him . . .
Hosea 11:1

They may all disagree about a lot of things, but Arabs and Jews and Bahais, Moslems and Christians all agree about one thing in Haifa: the air is cleaner and healthier, life is more rewarding and stimulating, the food is better, the people friendlier and the transportation system works better. You name it, and they'll tell you it's better in Haifa than anywhere else in Israel, the Middle East, even the world if you care to listen long enough.

Call it self-deception if you like, but in Israel it's called local pride and it's practically an epidemic all over the country.

If someone from Jerusalem says the air is fresh there, someone from Haifa will say the air blew down from Mount Carmel. Another from Tel Aviv will swear it picked up a bracing hint of excitement on the way. Though they seem to be given to a lot of exaggeration that sometimes threatens to bore visitors to death, regional chauvinism has a positive side as well. When people from the same community meet for the first time away from home, in the military, on business, or just relaxing, they become instant friends. It may be true they form a team that makes them more formidable at the game, but that only adds to the fun.

Cities like Jerusalem that have football teams add

The Sea of Galilee is firmly fixed in the minds of many people as the place where Jesus' Miracle of the Loaves and Fishes, featured in the mosaic floor *above,* took place.

Perhaps not so well-known is the Sanctuary of the Primacy, or Mensa Christi – the Table of Christ – *right,* just by the water's edge, where Simon Peter was appointed to the office of the Primacy with the words: "Feed my sheep".

another dimension. And it's deadly serious. Fans of Beitar Jerusalem take their team so seriously it affects everyone around them. The butchers and greengrocers of the Mahane Yehuda market are very tough to bargain with for a whole week after the team loses. But if you catch them on the day after a victory it's possible to save a lot of money and get a smile in the bargain. One of them once told a radio interviewer that he didn't shed a tear when his father died, but when Beitar Jerusalem lost a crucial game he cried like a baby.

The pride shows itself in other ways, too. People from cities are convinced they've got the secret of the good life locked up, but kibbutzniks are just as sure they do. When they get together the kibbutz-raised Sabras talk pridefully about how much they contribute to the national community even though they are in the minority. Any kibbutznik will quickly turn any conversation around to the fact that a very high percentage of their young people don't wait to be asked but volunteer for military duty. City people counter by saying it's because they can't wait to get out of the kibbutz. But that doesn't stop the argument because kibbutzniks will always keep it going by pointing out that most of the members of the elite units as well as most of the jet pilots are kibbutz-raised. Their cousins from the city say that's because they become career soldiers so they don't have to go back to the kibbutz. And so it goes, far into the night usually.

Yitzhak Oked, a reporter for the Jerusalem Post,

Fishing boats *left* at rest
in the harbor at Tiberias.

calls it the "Masterlock Syndrome," and he finds it helpful to him in his work.

"Israel is a country of many cultures, of different backgrounds," he says, "and we are always looking for persons who have things in common with us. If, for instance, two Israelis are suddenly brought together for reserve duty and they don't know each other beforehand, there is a greater chance of forming some sort of accord if they suddenly discover that they were both born in Poland or that they live in the same city or possibly went to the same school.

"The more things you have in common with other Israelis, the greater your chance of opening doors with them.

"I was born in Venezuela, so anyone from the Latin American continent, no matter whether it is Argentina or Mexico or Brazil, is close to me. I went to school for seven years in the United States, so I have a common key with Americans, too. My parents came from Besarabia, so both the Romanians and the Russians feel a kinship with me. My wife's parents came from Poland, so I have allies among the Poles.

"When I go to interview somebody, I immediately try to find the right key that will open doors to me. The same holds true for businessmen in just about every field you can think of in Israel."

*A feast is made for laughter, and wine maketh merry:
but money answereth all things.*

Ecclesiastes 10:19

No matter where they live or where they came from, just about everybody in Israel agrees they have one thing in common; they lead a "pressure cooker" life.

In the first six months of 1980, the cost of living in Israel went up 48.9 percent, and it was already high at the beginning of the year. In 1979, it increased 111.4 per cent over the previous year. To keep up with it, just about everyone leads a life on the run. People lucky enough to find a second job usually have one and those who don't spend all their free time looking for one.

Most of them give up a month each year for military duty, which adds to the burden. In most families, both husbands and wives work, and occasionally both work at two jobs, which puts a bit of a strain on family life. Everybody in the country has a single goal in common: to "finish the month."

Early in 1980, Israel's currency was changed from the pound to the shekel. It was a move in line with the governments's emphasis on Biblical tradition and their announcement of the change pointed with pride to the fact that the Old Testament mentions shekels

287

An almost timeless scene as the day's catch is landed from the Sea of Galilee *these pages*.

A little way inland from the Sea of Galilee
rises the Mount of Beatitudes, where Jesus is
said to have preached the Sermon on the Mount,
on the top of which stands the lovely Church
of the Beatitudes *these pages.*

five times. Originally it was a weight measure of about half an ounce, but by the time Abraham paid 400 shekels for his wife's burial site in Hebron, it was the name for a silver coin.

If life is a pressure cooker in Israel, it isn't all running and worrying. It's an experience everybody shares, and making it to the end of the week still solvent is another point of pride. It's a reason to have a celebration, too. That usually takes place every Friday night just about everywhere in the country. The traditional Friday evening get-together is an Israeli custom that solves several problems for the couples who keep it going. Most important, it gives them an opportunity to socialize with the maximum number of friends in the minimum amount of time. Most people can sleep late on Saturday, so Friday is a perfect night to socialize.

By custom, no one ever shows up much before ten in the evening. The Friday evening meal is a family affair and it's usually followed by a short nap, which is part of the depressurizing ritual that allows everyone to arrive with their minds sharp enough to keep up with arguments and ahead of the needling that's sure to be an important part of the evening.

It's a movable feast, with each of the couples in the circle of friends taking turns at being host. The menu includes the inevitable seeds: pistachios, sunflower seeds and nuts. Sometimes, but not always, liquor is served, the favorite being American bourbon. Toward the end of the evening coffee and cake, chocolate of course, are usually served along with oranges and other fresh fruit in winter, and melons or ice cream in summer. It's carefully timed not to be served so late as to spill over into the Sabbath.

Towards the northern tip of Israel, in Upper Galilee, stands Rosh Pina *left,* the first of the Jewish settlements of the Galilee, founded in 1879.

The menu almost never varies, but the conversation does. The Israeli grapevine has its roots firmly planted in these Friday evening get-togethers and all the current rumors are repeated and embellished for transmittal the following week in stores, factories and offices all over Israel.

To the tune of cracking nuts, the government and its ministers are taken apart and the country's problems are solved in theory. While the women discreetly take their sweet brandy out of earshot, the men exchange off-color jokes which they'll trade for new ones during the work week ahead. They also pass along jokes about the government, which is, after all, the most interesting and sometimes funniest topic of conversation any Friday night.

They argue a lot in those Friday evening discussions. Everybody is an expert, of course, on the topics they discuss, which range from economic to military to political to just plain gossip. The events of the preceding week provide the springboard and everyone makes it a point to keep up with everything that's going on, and by Friday everyone has a pre-formed "expert" opinion. It's real-life theater with plenty of gesturing and grimacing as everyone in the room lets off a little steam. By the time the coffee is served, they're all a little more relaxed, usually sure they've won the argument, and ready to take on the world again for another week.

Friday evening is a traditional time for family groups to get together, too. It's a perfect time to celebrate a cousin's birthday, a nephew's Bar Mitzvah, a sister's wedding anniversary. Since many family groups are large and resources often small, the Israeli talent for improvisation shows itself on those occasions almost more than any other.

For big family occasions, it's often necessary to hire a hall or a synagogue, which can get expensive. And to leave an uncle or cousin off the guest list can almost amount to an international incident. Israelis are masters at solving the first problem and avoiding the second.

One family from Jerusalem invited a long list of relatives to a special party miles away on the top of Mount Sinai and, just to make sure the turnout would be small, scheduled it so all the guests could watch the sun come up. Many others plan parties at Masada, presumably to share in the pride and tradition of the place, but of course, they get a lot of turndowns.

A favorite trick for celebrating Bar Mitzvahs is to invite family and friends to the Western Wall. It's perfect for the boy, nobody can deny that. It's even better for his parents if they schedule the event on a weekday morning and their guests all live far away

Girl recruits in the Israeli army receive
instruction in all manner of weaponry,
including heavy armor *below and right*.

from Jerusalem. That way, anybody who accepts the invitation has to give up a day of work and use up expensive gasoline to make the trip. They usually make up for not showing up by sending a gift.

And he made in Jerusalem engines, invented by cunning men.

II Chronicles 26:15

It isn't known for sure whether the Israeli talent for improvisation is an inherited skill or an acquired one. Those on the side of inheritance point out that David couldn't have killed Goliath if he hadn't been an improviser. Others say the ancient Israelites were forced to learn to improvise when Moses tried to answer God's question about where he wanted to lead his people. According to their story, Moses' stuttering answer of "Ca-Ca-Ca-Ca . . ." made God think he was trying to say Canaan and that's where he sent them. Actually, they say, he was trying to say "Canada," and the children of Israel have had to improvise ever since!

Many hold a view that combines both heredity and learning. They say that Jews in exile during the Diaspora were forced to live by their wits and it eventually became part of their character.

Whatever the reason, creativity is part of the Israeli soul. It's second nature to most people who get through life by improvising, often without even realizing it. If it's a learned skill, there are few better schools than the Israel Defense Force, and everybody

in the country gets a chance to learn there.

By the time a young person gets a job – high school, the youth organization, the IDF and the university have all provided valuable lessons and the skills are used almost from the first day to get a better office or a telephone or even a private secretary.

Occasionally, the improviser even uses the talent to help the employer.

In one case, a pair of metal workers invented a new lock to make their neighborhood more secure and made enough money to move to a better neighborhood where they started their own company. Workers in a citrus processing plant discovered that the peels could be used to make a natural sweetener and started another whole new industry. Reprocessed waste from the Dead Sea Works brings $15 million a year into the

Israeli economy because someone created a way to process it.

A lot of the time improvisation improves on improvisation, which is a problem for foreign businessmen who sell licenses for their ideas to Israeli industry only to find that a worker has figured out how to make the idea work better and the company doesn't need the original any more. It happened to one of the world's leading authorities on mushroom-growing who took his knowledge to Israel to see if mushroom farming would be practical there. He's still scratching his head over the experience.

"I've set up mushroom farms all over the world," he said later, "especially in the Far East and Africa. Whenever I arrive at one of these farms for a visit, I find the staff dressed in white smocks and armed with

Life in the Israeli army differs little for male or female recruits *these pages*.

A well, a reminder of the days of the
caravan route, still stands in one of
the old squares in Acre *left and below.*

clipboards and pens to write down every word I say. I
listen to their problems and tell them how to solve
them. They always answer with a curt, nearly military,
'yes, sir!' and write down all my instructions which they
carry out to the letter. None of them ever questions nor
argues about what I say.

"The Israelis, on the other hand, astonish me.
When we made our venture in Israel, it was something
entirely new for them. So you can understand that
when I went back to Europe I was astonished not to be
receiving any feedback from them, no word on how they
were coming along. It was disturbing because I knew
that growing mushrooms is a very delicate matter that
requires a great deal of experience.

"When I arrived on my first visit to Israel after the
plant was working, not one of the Israelis was wearing a
white smock. There were no clipboards, no pens and
no problems. To say there were no problems is an

understatement. They had gone through a terrible running-in period with a large number of set-backs.

"They gave me a thousand and one excuses for their failures. They explained that they had tried improvising to save their mushrooms. When I tried to explain to them where they had gone wrong and how they could have saved themselves a lot of trouble, they didn't answer with a curt 'Yes sir!' They didn't admit they had done a thing wrong and nobody was writing down my instructions. Instead they started arguing with me. Yes, me, the greatest authority in the world on growing mushrooms! And they were not only novices in the business, but their first attempt had failed!

"What is outstanding about these improvising Israelis is that they don't know how to take 'no' for an answer. They will continue battering their heads against the wall with one improvisation after another. And then, lo and behold, after a while, they have come up with their own better way of raising mushrooms!"

Some Israelis say their jails are full of people who are too good at improvising. Not long ago, two partners in the heating oil business devised a double action pump for their delivery trucks that allowed the oil to flow back into the truck after it had passed through the meter of homeowners' tanks. Not all of it, mind you, but enough to add substantially to their profits without making customers too suspicious. Unfortunately, their customers were also good at improvising and now the oil tycoons have a nice warm place to sleep every night in jail cells.

It extends to matters of the heart, too. A married man, who also happened to be an officer in the reserves, told his wife that he had to be away in the evening a lot because of pressing military business. Israelis never question matters of "military business" even when they come between husbands and wives. But in this case it was more funny business than military.

One night his commanding officer came looking for him, but the only person at home was the wife, who complained bitterly about all the evenings he was forced to be away.

"He hasn't been with our unit," said the officer, "he must be working for the other side!"

What he was working was both sides of the street, but the divorce that followed was only part of his troubles. He had to go to a lot of trouble to explain himself to the military authorities first.

. But mostly, stories of improvisation in Israel have happier endings than that. Consider the story of Leah and Armin Gottlieb, who left Hungary for Israel about 30 years ago with not much more than a suitcase full of clothes and a lot of talent.

Armin Gottlieb had been a raincoat manufacturer in the Old Country before the war, so the couple decided to go into the apparel business here.

Mrs. Gottlieb sold her wedding ring to buy cotton fabric and they went to work producing a line of baby clothes. But what they knew best was raincoats and it wasn't long before they decided to switch their product line. It was a tough sell in a country of deserts, so when that failed they improvised.

Israel isn't all desert, of course. It has wonderful sunny beaches, too. It's a terrific place to sell bathing suits and that's what Mrs. Gottlieb decided to do. She used the leftover cotton fabric from the baby clothes/raincoat venture to make swimwear, and to Israeli women it was the answer to a maiden's prayer.

They reinvested their profits in a new company they called Gottex Industries. In just a few years, with Leah Gottlieb as designer and her husband as business manager, they had a thriving factory in Tel Aviv and were turning out bathing suits made with imported fabrics that were exported to some 60 countries.

Early in the game, Mrs. Gottlieb decided it didn't look right for her models to appear for buyers wearing nothing but bikini bathing suits, so she began designing matching cover-ups. It was another improvisation, and it changed the outlook of the industry all over the world. For the first time, high fashion hit the swimwear

Basking in the clear, Mediterranean
sunlight lies Acre's Fisherman's
Harbor *right and overleaf.*

business, which was good news for retailers; even better for young men who haunt the world's beaches but don't expect to go near the water.

It wasn't long before the company began producing dresses as well. But at the same time, Mrs. Gottlieb's designs for one-piece maillot bathing suits have made bikinis a relic of the past for women who want to appear on the beach in the height of fashion.

Their Tel Aviv factory makes more than a million bathing suits a year and much of their output goes to the United States, where the company is the biggest foreign manufacturer in the business. The people who work in her factory call her "Lady Gottlieb," a title she's surely earned. By her own choice, some 80 percent of the people who work for her are women. "I like to work with women," she says. But, on a more practical level, she also says she prefers not having to work production schedules around a work force that's forced to take a month off for military duty each year.

O House of Israel, are not my ways equal?
Ezekiel 18:29

Only about a third of Israel's workforce is made up of women and there aren't many signs that opportunities for them will open up any time soon. It's a paradox because women have been active in the Israeli Government since the very first days.

Once there was a rash of attacks on women alone in the streets at night. The problem became severe enough to be taken up in a Cabinet meeting where the concensus was that there ought to be a curfew forbidding women to be on the streets after dark. Golda Meir was a member of that Cabinet.

"But it's the men who are attacking the women," she protested. "If there is to be a curfew, let the men stay at home and not the women!"

The motion for a curfew was dropped altogether.

The laws in Israel are very careful about not making women second-class citizens, but the common view is that they are child-bearers, which is just about as important as anyone can be in a small, growing country. Of course, that creates a special problem for single women.

On the face of it, they have no problem at all. The last time anyone counted, there were 20,900 single people in Israel between the ages of 30 and 34, and of that number, 10,200 were men. The picture gets even better for single women between 25 and 29, where there were 44,000 single men and just 26,500 single women. On paper, it looks like there are plenty of guys to go around. The problem is, the girls don't know where they are.

By the time an Israeli woman is 25, and past the average marrying age of 23, people begin giving her funny looks and asking personal questions. The same pressure doesn't apply to a man in the same predicament since everyone assumes he's just waiting for the right girl to come along and he's giving the matter careful thought.

But it's a family-oriented society. Single girls aren't usually invited to the Friday evening discussion groups, and even if they were, single men aren't either. Matchmaking is a job for the professionals.

Sometimes women go to professional matchmakers or they place ads in the "matrimonial" columns in newspaper classified sections. There are some "singles" clubs in the cities, and they help in a small way. But once a woman has passed the age when her family and friends think she ought to have a husband, she becomes an outcast to them. She's almost an outcast to eligible men, too. "If you're not married yet, there must be something wrong with you," is what they most likely think.

The problem goes even deeper when unmarried women decide to leave their families and go out on their own alone. It's almost impossible to rent an apartment anywhere in Israel, most of them are for sale. The government eases the burden on immigrants who need housing by finding apartments for them and loaning them the money to buy them. But most of the housing has been designed for families, and isn't available for singles. The loans available for married couples can run as high as $30,000. The maximum for a single immigrant is $9,000.

But if things are tough for single Jewish women in Israel, even married Arab women, especially in smaller villages, are light years behind them. The law gives them full equality, but custom often prevents them from getting an education or holding a job. Most of them have never even heard of the Women's Movement and few will ever feel its effects. For all practical purposes, there is no Women's Movement in this part of the world. On the other hand, considering the historical background of women's rights in the Middle East, Israel has made amazing gains without it. Women are actively involved in every part of Israeli life and generally share the same opportunities as men. But it helps a lot if they get married first.

A lot of the single female immigrants in Israel are originally from the United States and many of those who decide to go along with the local custom go back to North America to find husbands, but only on the condition that, like Golda Meir, they go back and pick

up where they left off in Israel.

. . . I opened my doors to the traveler.

– Job 31:32

In many cases, it's his first trip. Though there are some 1 million tourists poking around Israel every year, adding some $750 million to the Israeli economy, it depends on which statistic you read how many American Jews have ever made the trip. Even the most optimistic of the studies says the figure is something under ten percent. In fact, one of the reports, now a few years old, suggests that Christian tourists in Israel outnumber Jewish tourists by as much as ten percent.

Bad news for the single women is that among the Jewish tourists, more than 60 percent are married couples and their children, often very young, who add to the statistics for single tourists. Those same statistics say that more than half of the Christian visitors are single, but it should be noted that a lot of them are priests and nuns.

And, yes, like every other country in the world, a big percentage of Israel's tourism is coming from Germany and their numbers are growing, It presents some problems in some areas where the wounds of World War II are still tender. But a lot of Israelis themselves came from Germany, so the welcome isn't frosty enough to prevent more from coming to convert Deutschmarks into shekels.

European tourists usually take advantage of special charters available from most parts of the Continent that allow them to fly to Tel Aviv and stay there for a week in a four-star hotel for about the same cost as a round-trip ticket on a regular airline. Some Americans have found some advantages in combining a trip to Israel with a trip to London, because the British carriers offering charter flights allow Americans to take advantage of their low rates.

Israeli inflation doesn't affect foreign tourists because, as inflation rises, the rate of exchange follows right along. Some tourists have found another way of making their money go further, too. Anyone who takes Israeli Developement Bonds into the country may redeem them for their full value, plus interest, in local currency even if they haven't matured. In places like New York, it's possible to buy the bonds at a discount for redemption in Israel at full value. The money can't be used for transportation to and from Israel, but it can go a long way within the country.

Many younger tourists don't worry about such things at all. Once they're in Israel they work on a

On the coast *below,* south of Acre, at Rosh Ha' Nikra – the Ladder of Tyre – the waves sometimes rush and roar through rock caverns and passages such as those *right*.

kibbutz or a farm for their bed and board. More than 15,000 students descend on the country every summer to sample Israeli life. Many kibbutzim welcome them with open arms and put them to work for six hours a day. The only catch is that they have to stay at least a month and they have to be willing to work. The Kibbutz Aliyah Desk in New York helps young people find accommodation but warns:

"Kibbutzim are not places where people roll in and everybody dances the hora with you. These are established societies with cliques and groups and some don't talk to each other."

The volunteers are housed in special barracks and don't live with families, but they find out just about all there is to know about the life families lead there.

At one time, the number of kibbutz volunteers who were American Jews were outnumbered more than two to one by Scandinavian Christians. But the government has begun discouraging non-Jews from volunteering, on the ground that the basic idea of the programs is to allow young people to sample Israeli life and in the process decide, hopefully, to become Israeli citizens. Another less-mentioned reason is the attraction of all those blond, blue-eyed Scandinavians to Sabra youngsters who sometimes wind up marrying them.

Christians are still welcome, of course. Anyone

The caves at Rosh Ha' Nikra *below and left* can provide an awesome spectacle but can also be places of chilling beauty.

willing to work is never turned away. But no one is going to any trouble and expense to recruit them.

Young people who volunteer for work on an archaeological site work even harder and often have to pay a few dollars a day for room and board, but the work pays off in college credit as well as satisfaction for many of them, so it all seems worthwhile.

All seven of Israel's universities offer summer programs in English for foreign students who learn everything from Bible history to spoken Arabic. But students looking for the Israeli experience in those programs find they're forced to discover it on their own. Israeli students rarely sign up for summer courses, so everyone on campus between June and September, except for the faculty of course, usually turns out to be a foreigner.

Many tourists in Israel these days also try to make side trips to other countries in the area, especially Egypt. In spite of reassurances to the contrary, though, it helps not to be Jewish in all of them except Egypt.

... For thou art a stranger and also an exile.
II Samuel 15:19

On the other hand, most Israelis would ask, "why bother?" There's enough to see and do in Israel without going to all that trouble. If it's Arabs you want to see, there are plenty of them in Israel after all, and there's so much more to marvel at. History has been restored, a new civilization has been built and the Holy Land has come a long way from the days when Mark

309

Twain couldn't wait to get out of there, and Herman Melville described it as an accumulation of rubbish so bad that even a ragpicker would pass it by.

They hope you'll like what it's become so much that you'll want to come back to stay.

In the first ten years after Statehood just about everyone who came, came to stay. They arrived by ship back in those days from Naples or Marseilles, most with nothing more than the clothes on their backs. During the crossing, Jewish Agency "selection boards" helped each of them get ready for their new experience including the tough decision about just where they ought to go after the ship docked at Haifa.

After the decisions had been made the ship's radio sent word to other Agency workers on shore who worked out the details of ground transportation. Then, before they were loaded into trucks and buses, they were given money and enough food to last for ten days. If they had small children, the food package also

Pictured *previous page*, in its lovely Persian garden setting, is the Bahai Shrine, its golden dome dominating the city, much as does the Dome of the Rock in Jerusalem.

contained a good supply of candy. The last detail before they were on their way was to sign a contract for a house or an apartment as well as a receipt for the basic furniture: beds and some blankets, some chairs and a table, a stove, a bucket and a broom. Everything would be paid for in time, but each new immigrant was reassured that nothing was expected of them until they began earning a living.

In those days just about everybody was encouraged to settle in the Galilee or at Beersheba; the former to strike a more comfortable balance with the large number of Arabs there, the latter to help spread the population of the country more evenly. Either way it was a culture shock. Many had never seen dark-skinned people before. Others missed the houses and towns they had left and wondered if they had done the right thing. They had a new language to learn and a new way of life. One man, the father of two small children, who arrived on the country's tenth anniversary, summed it up for all of them:

"I am happy here," he said. "I expected very little, and I certainly didn't hope for this little flat. They need building plasterers, I've heard, and tile layers. I can work until I make up my mind what to do next. I feel liberated. You sense the freedom here on every side. This is my patria. I will do any work. My children will be free."

Times have changed since then, but attitudes like that haven't. The huge, early immigration waves have quieted somewhat, but still they come, still looking for the same dream.

Ironically, today's immigrants are mainly coming from the same place the original immigrants came from, the Soviet Union.

Mount Carmel affords an ideal viewpoint overlooking Haifa *below left,* and by night *overleaf,* which boasts a great deal of modern technology, such as the solar reflector powering the water purification plant *below,* as well as such architectural treasures as the Bahai Temple, presiding over the main street leading down to the harbor *below right.*

In the early 1970s pressure was brought on the Soviets to "free Russian Jewry." The campaign, part humanitarian and part a move to give a boost to lagging Israeli immigration, succeeded is freeing more than 240,000 Jews in less than 10 years.

The peak month in all those years was October, 1979, when just under 5,000 Soviet Jews secured exit visas for Israel, but in the first three months of 1980 the average dropped to less than 1,000 a month. One of the reasons is that the visa offices in the Ukraine, which is where most of the immigrants come from, have become stricter than they once were. No applicant without a written invitation from a close relative in Israel is even allowed to apply. In the office in Kiev, that relative must be a parent or a child. In Odessa, officials frankly admit that the reason is that the Jewish exodus has been taking away too many of the well-educated

from the cities, a brain-drain that can't be tolerated. "If Israel can use these people," they say, "so can we. If we let the Jews go to the West, they'll be so rich in 20 years they'll come back and take over."

Not very likely. Not many want to leave once they've migrated to Israel.

One of the ones who was lucky enough to make it is Larissa Vilenskaia, an engineer and parapsychologist who arrived from Moscow in the fall of 1979 and now lives in Hvar Saba, near Tel Aviv. Parapsychology is a profession highly prized in the Soviet Union, so the Russians weren't too happy to see Larissa go. But she was deliriously happy. Not long after becoming an Israeli, she went on a tour to encourage free world support to help others who were still waiting to get out of Russia. In the process, she's had the experience of going home to Israel twice. She describes those

Grasses and yellow field poppies
right blow in the breeze in a meadow
near Caesarea.

For 600 years Caesarea *above* was the capital of the Roman province of Judea and much of the area has now been excavated and is being restored.

experiences best herself with entries in her diary written during her first months in her new home:

"I have arrived here only a month ago, but it seems to me as if I have lived here for a long time, and that I have always known this small and comfortable village in the suburbs of Tel Aviv.

"This place where we have gathered is the place where we are going to stay for the first few months. When I started to learn Hebrew, I discovered that Hvar Saba means "the village of the little girls." It used to be a small village but now it has developed into a beautiful town with lots of parklands. Tel Aviv-Hvar Saba is still a

very young city. It is less than 70 years old, and for a town this does not seem to be a long time.

"All the sufferings are behind me. More than two years of waiting for the permission to leave the country, botherings, questionings, harassment, house arrests, life under constant pressure. Checking out through the Customs at Moscow Airport took more than three hours, with endless inquiries and arbitrary acts on the part of the airport employees. All these things are behind me now. Yes they are over! And I want to forget all these unfortunate and sad times as quickly as possible!

"I am going to recover, but obviously I will still remember some of the restrictions, such as not being able to mention something on the 'phone. But then I realize that I can do that now because I am not in the

Soviet Union any more!

"Up till now it was still strange for me to be able to talk openly about everything in apartments or in rooms or in hotels, and to be able to read any kind of book freely without having to be afraid that someone will tell on me and that my books will be confiscated.

"Two weeks after my arrival I visited the seashore at Herzlia. I was delighted like never before because the seashore here cannot be compared with any of the popular resort places at the Black Sea. Here in this country you can reach any point at the shore within one hour, perhaps one hour and a half from Dimona, but there are only a few Israelis living there.

"I have used the word 'Israeli' and just as on the first days of my arrival here, I have shades of doubt again. Do I have the right to call myself an Israeli? . . . Without anybody disturbing me or threatening to take

away these rights?

"I am sure you will understand me. After I have lived in the Soviet Union, it is difficult for me to feel as a free person immediately.

"There has been one thing which I came to like very much at once, and that is the good will of all the people I have met. If you ask anyone for the location of a street, even in imperfect Hebrew language, it has never happened that somebody just pointed in one direction or another, then walked away without saying a word, as happens frequently in Moscow. Here everybody stops, explains and tries to be assured that you understood the explanation. If somebody does not know the answer, he will ask someone else for you or he will go with you to the spot even if it takes 10 or 15 minutes.

"But these things are all natural for them. Sometimes you get into a funny situation when you have difficulties in explaining something in Hebrew and it usually turns out that the person you have been talking to speaks Russian fluently or sometimes English.

"I like to speak Hebrew and I don't even mind struggling in order to get experience. It is even more pleasant for me to listen to Israeli songs and to sing them myself.

"Recently I took part in the Jewish holiday Rosh ha-Shanah for the first time here in Israel. It was heartwarming to see Jewish people from different countries all over the world gathered together in our Absorption Center. They were all singing together: 'hene ma tov uma naim sevet alim gam ealiad' . . . 'how good and how pleasant it is sitting together·with our friends.'

"It was so pleasing to sing together with my new friends and I was remembering how we celebrated this event in the Soviet Union. We had to go outside the city of Moscow and while we were singing our songs we were being closely watched by policemen and by agents of the State. We sang these same songs in many farewell parties saying good-bye to our friends who had got the long-awaited permission to leave the country. Some people left, but others had to remain there waiting for a long time for the permission. Some people who were friends of mine had to wait for two, five, even ten years to leave.

"When I was in Moscow waiting for permission to leave, some American tourists brought me picture postcards from Israel. Just like my friends, I had no idea how much time was still left before I could actually go there. I could see the lovely stones of the Wailing Wall and the wonderful architecture and the lush greenery and I would say to my friends, 'The next year we are in Jerusalem!' but I was almost crying. 'But

when? When can we be there?'

"And here I am. Finally the time has arrived! I can go out and touch the sacred stones of the great wall which has seen thousands of years of tears.

"When I first arrived in Jerusalem and asked where I should go to get to the Old City, the answer was 'It is too far, you should go by bus and not on foot.' People just didn't understand why I did not want to go by bus. Why? It is the first time I am here, and I want to see everything! It would have been strange to me to have a look at the streets from the window of a bus! It was wonderful to see the mixture of old history and our modern time; to see all the things I had been dreaming of for such a long, long time.

"Everything seemed to be so simple and soon I was going through the Jaffa Gate into the Old City. Then I went to the Wailing Wall. I cannot express the feelings I had at that time.

"I met some women there who were strangers to me and we all embraced each other and we cried and we laughed. Nobody was at all interested in what language the others spoke or where we came from. What was important was that we were here at last where we knew we belonged. We wonderfully understood each other without having to say a word.

"Tel Aviv is not as great a city as Jerusalem is, but here you see a wonderful mixture of the East and the West. The Central Bus Terminal and the nearby marketplace – with the merchants who praise their goods – this is the East. The streets of Allenby and Dizengoff with all the cafes and shops – this is the West. But if you walk in one of the nearby streets,

Tel Aviv *previous page and these pages* is the
largest city in Israel. It is a fast-growing, modern
city and resort *overleaf,* that now includes within
its boundaries the ancient port of Jaffa.

everything is quiet and silent as if you were not in a city
at all.

"In many districts of the city, particularly the
religious district, many of the buildings are only two or
three stories high. I wondered why that was so in such a
small country where the land is so valuable and higher
buildings would make better use of it. The answer is
simple, and beautiful, too. It is not possible for the very
religious to use elevators on the Sabbath Day, therefor
the buildings have been built for the convenience of
everybody.

"I love walking on the silent back streets of Tel Aviv
and of Hvar Saba rather than on the main streets that
are so full of shops and colored lights. In the small and
quiet streets nobody disturbs me while I am looking
and while I remember the past and think of the future.
Enough for me to get away from the endless
conversations about inflation, difficulties and this and
that . . .

"Yes, we have difficulties, and we do not fail to
confess them. But we have our own land and this is
what is most important to all of us.

"A lot of people can ask me: 'OK, you are very
happy to be living in Israel. But what about all the
difficulties? Isn't it very hot there?'

"I answer, yes, it is very hot in Israel. But where are
the flowers so beautiful in the spring and the sky so
blue in the summer. And, oh! The palm trees, the
apricot trees and the mandarin trees!

"Have you ever seen a mandarin tree? Its yellow-
orange fruit is tucked away among bright green leaves.
If not, you cannot imagine how wonderful it is!

"Words are not enough to express my feelings
about Israel. Only a writer would be able to speak about
this place. When words are not enough to express my
thoughts, then I send picture postcards to my friends
who are still in Russia. I send them to those who keep
on repeating in camps and in exile in Siberia: 'The next
year, I am in Jerusalem.'

"I send them, but I do not know if these cards will
ever reach my friends and that they will receive them.

"Over the past few months I happened to be not
only in Tel Aviv and Jerusalem, but I also saw London
and Birmingham, Liverpool and New York, the giant
skyscrapers of America and the comfortable houses of
old England. But when I returned to Israel I knew I was
coming home. As a matter of fact, nobody was waiting
here for me, and what is more I had not been able to

get a flat either. Nevertheless, I felt that I had come home.

"There will be a time when I will be able to see even more countries and cities. I like to travel and to see new places and meet different people. But there is only one place where I want to return from each trip to be 'at home,' and that place is Israel."

Another new immigrant from Russia said:

"When I was in the Soviet Union, I was always called a Jew. I wanted very much to be accepted into Russian society and to be known as a Russian, but nothing I did ever helped. Everyone just laughed at me and said, 'You were born a Jew and you will die a Jew!' Then I came to Israel. All I wanted when I got here was to forget that I had ever been a Russian and to be called an Israeli. But here I am now called by everyone a Russian!"

It isn't easy to be a newcomer in any country, as a lot of Americans can testify. But "greenhorns" in Israel usually assimilate into the society a lot faster than they would in other countries.

No matter where they come from, immigrants get a warm welcome and plenty of help in getting established. Every Israeli knows that a growing population is the only real security they have. And nearly half of them were immigrants themselves once.

We will dwell with you and we will become one people.

Genesis 34:16

There's a strange mystique about going "home" to Israel, fulfilling a dream that had been kept alive for centuries by people who treasured little packets of soil from the Holy Land that would be buried with them if they were unfortunate enough to die in an alien land.

After the doors were opened following World War II, David Ben-Gurion explained why the new immigrants were so very important to the new country. His words are as true today:

"It is most misleading to regard immigration as just a geographical transfer of individuals. Getting an entry permit and transportation are not the end of it.

". . . Immigration has real value only if it can take root in the nascent economy and play its own part in settlement, and the rate and pace of settlement in turn determine how large immigration shall be.

". . . It is useless to survey only the country as the British 'experts' did. We must also take into account Jewish capacity and potential. Twenty-six years ago, what expert could have forseen how varied in their intense production the new agricultural villages of Jezreel and the Jordan Valley would become, if he had only seen the waste-land and knew not all the pioneer passion that came to fertilize it? The key to immigration is the people, not the land, not the lifeless crust of earth but the dynamics and creation of farmer and factory hand."

Of course, the "lifeless crust of earth" is as precious as life itself to the Israeli people and nothing gives them more pride than bringing life to it. Even the fact that the government owns the land they work and turns it over to them in 49-year leases is part of the pride. The earth is not for sale, they'll tell you, because it's far too valuable to establish a price on it.

Their love of the land is obvious in what they've done with it. As Golda Mier said:

"Every mountain, every valley in our country, tells of our belonging, of our being here. This is where we were for thousands of years. This is where we belong. The years of dispersion form one of the most tragic chapters in history. Massacres, hate, humiliation – that was our lot.

"And did the desert in Israel bloom as long as we were in exile? Did trees cover the Judean hills? Were

Tel Aviv has all the ingredients for an ideal resort – excellent beaches *left* and a marina for pleasure craft *below*. Some idea of the size of the modern city may be gained from the night photograph *overleaf*.

marshes drained? No – rocks, desert, malaria, trachoma – this is what our country was like before we came back."

The pioneers have now passed the torch to their children, the Sabras, who make up a little more than 51 percent of the population. Though the name comes from the tough-skinned sweet prickly pear, there's a word in Arabic: "sabre," that comes close to describing them, too. In English it means "patience."

Almost all of them agree that whatever their differences, Sabras, pioneers and recent immigrants all have something important in common: they want to live. Only people who have gone to war time and again to preserve their country and who have broken away from an old life that made them outcasts everywhere they went can be so positive about survival. It gives a special kind of determination and, most important, patience.

They are secure enough about the future to argue about it, and secure enough about the present to be fatalistic about it. They look for peace with their neighbors and they look for a better standard of living for themselves. If not today, tomorrow will do because everyone is absolutely sure of one important thing, that they will be here tomorrow just as surely as they are here today.

They've developed a style for themselves that's less Jewish than it is Israeli. They walk upright and proud, grim but not unsmiling. They move quickly through life greeting each other with slaps on the back instead of handshakes. They are their own people, full of confidence and enthusiasm. They have no debt to the past, only to the future. And you can see it in their eyes; the future is theirs and they're not letting go.

The streets of Tel Aviv *above and right,* were crowded with people on the occasion of the 1980 Independence Day celebrations.

To the Jews of the Diaspora the greatest thing that could happen to their children was to become an intellectual. To these people the ideal is heroism and courage, to live a life free from humiliation. And the best part is that they've succeeded without throwing away intellectualism.

One of the most famous of all the Sabras, Moshe Dayan, is a perfect example of a native Israeli who combines all those qualities. A brilliant military strategist and politician, he's also an accomplished writer and archaeologist. His own view of the past and the Bible as a history of his country as well as an idea of how he views the present was the subject of an interview in The New York Times not long ago. His interest in archaeology prompted him to say his interest went beyond the Bible:

". . . It's with whoever else lived in the country," he said. "That was a difference between myself and the other Israelis – for instance Golda Mier or David Ben-Gurion. We'd go somewhere mentioned in the Bible, like where gazelles took shelter above the Red Sea. It doesn't matter to me who's living there now. So Arabs are there, so what? Or a Jewish settlement. But when Golda or Ben-Gurion saw a Jewish settlement, it was a fulfillment of their dreams. If Arabs were there – well, it wasn't meaningful for them.

"The country itself – Jordan, Mount Carmel or Gaza – as part of the historical Biblical life, didn't mean much for them. For me, if I see people living in tents, it might be Bedouins, surely not Israelis. But it could also be like one of our Patriarchs, like Abraham or Isaac.

". . . What I really like is to remove the lid of the land. In the first three of four yards, you discover the way it was four or five thousand years ago. Even at that time it was not Jewish everywhere. Always there were Canaanites here with others. Nor do I need to find a Jewish dwelling. It's enough that I open the door of a house that existed a few thousand years ago – whether it be Canaanite or Jewish or Philistine.

"For years my life was spent building my country. In those years I think I met more Arabs than Jews. It was a limited field. You had to fight, to build. My world was planting trees and having children, fighting wars, building our bridges. My interest today has gone in two directions – toward knowing my country as it was and toward meeting Jewish people elsewhere, as they are now.

"I used to hate going to some countries, America and others, to meet the Jewish communities. I didn't have the language and I hated their way of life, and how they laid on their Jewishness – everything.

"Now, with age, I say: 'Well, these are the Jewish people we have today, and I really enjoy being with them.' Not that I don't criticize. Many of them have intermarried and many criticize us. But as long as they stay Jewish, and there are still 14 million, I'm extending my field from old Palestine to around the world. So now I finally understand what Ben-Gurion meant when he said, 'I'm Jewish first, before I'm an Israeli'."

Not everyone in Israel agrees with Moshe Dayan any more than everyone in the country agrees with all the official policies of the government. Israel is a democracy and that's one of the things that makes it unique in all the Middle East.

Life isn't easy for the average Israeli. Everyone there agrees on that. But that's a point of pride too. As they used to say in the Old Country:

"You can only get pearls from a sick oyster!"

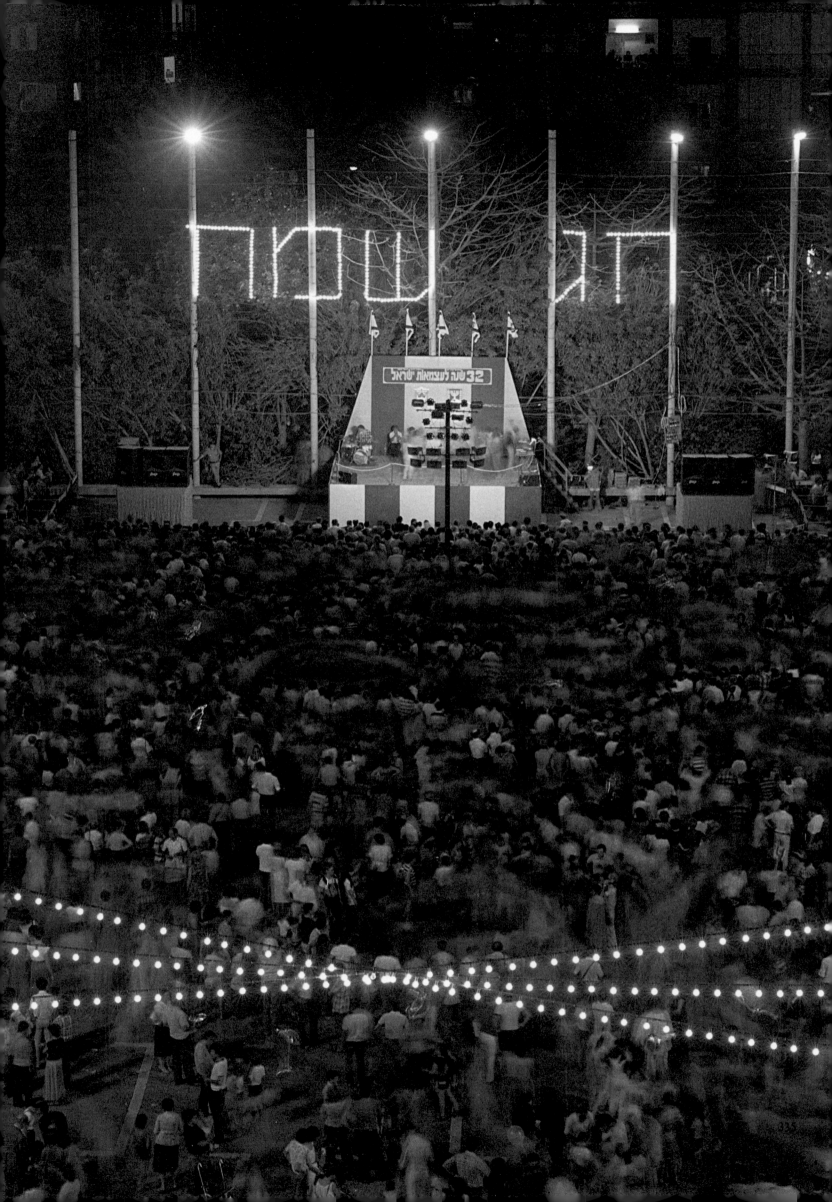

First published 1980 by Colour Library International Ltd.
© 1980 Illustrations and text: Colour Library International Ltd., 163 East 64th St., New York, N.Y. 10021.
Colour separations by FERCROM, Barcelona, Spain.
Display and text filmsetting by Focus Photoset, London, England.
Printed and bound by JISA-RIEUSSET, Barcelona, Spain.
All rights reserved.
ISBN 0-8317 5120-7 Library of Congress Catalogue Card No. 80-13716
Published in the United States of America by Mayflower Books, Inc., New York City.

eusset,S.A-D.L.B. 28104-80